Extranet Design and Implementation

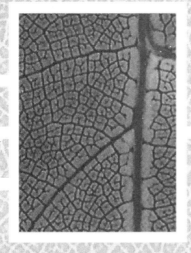

Extranet Design
and Implementation

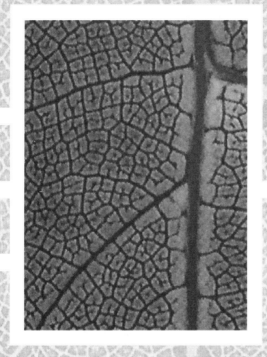

Peter Loshin

San Francisco • Paris • Düsseldorf • Soest

Associate Publisher: Guy Hart-Davis
Acquisitions Manager: Kristine Plachy
Acquisitions & Developmental Editor: Guy Hart-Davis
Editor: June Waldman
Project Editor: Kimberley Askew
Technical Editor: Morgan Stern
Book Designers: Patrick Dintino, Bill Gibson
Graphic Illustrator: Patrick Dintino
Electronic Publishing Specialist: Bill Gibson
Production Coordinator: Michael Tom
Indexer: Ted Laux
Cover Designer: Archer Design
Cover Photograph: The Image Bank

SYBEX, Network Press, and the Network Press logo are trademarks of SYBEX Inc.

TRADEMARKS: SYBEX has attempted throughout this book to distinguish proprietary trademarks from descriptive terms by following the capitalization style used by the manufacturer.

The author and publisher have made their best efforts to prepare this book, and the content is based upon final release software whenever possible. Portions of the manuscript may be based upon pre-release versions supplied by software manufacturer(s). The author and the publisher make no representation or warranties of any kind with regard to the completeness or accuracy of the contents herein and accept no liability of any kind including but not limited to performance, merchantability, fitness for any particular purpose, or any losses or damages of any kind caused or alleged to be caused directly or indirectly from this book.

Library of Congress Card Number: 97-66378
ISBN: 0-7821-2091-1

Manufactured in the United States of America

10 9 8 7 6 5 4 3 2 1

For my son Jacy and my wife Lisa.

Acknowledgments

No book gets published without the help of many hands, and this is no exception. For providing insight about extranets, I would like to thank all those who helped me understand the material in this book. In particular, those affiliated with the various software vendors and their representatives who made sure I had up-to-date information on their extranet offerings. Special thanks to Mark Andreesen of Netscape for first bringing extranets to my attention and to Dick Woodbury of Wing.Net for sharing his extranet expertise.

Thanks also go to the people at SYBEX who made this book possible, starting with Guy Hart-Davis, acquisitions editor, whose enthusiasm from the start helped keep it on track. Thank you also to Kimberley Askew, project editor; Morgan Stern, technical editor; and June Waldman, editor, who, respectively, kept the book on track, technically correct, and comprehensible. Thanks also to Patrick Dintino who managed to turn my chicken scratchings into the clear and clean illustrations you see.

My friends and colleagues at BYTE Magazine provided invaluable assistance simply by offering me such a stimulating and exciting work environment.

Finally, very special thanks to my wife Lisa and my son Jacy for their support and inspiration.

Content at a Glance

Table of Contents

Chapter 8   **Detailed Examples of Extranet Software**   **287**

Chapter 9   **Managing and Administering Extranets**   **307**

Introduction

The ability to take a sturdy old idea, dust it off, put a new name (and perhaps a new coat of paint) on it and start selling it at a premium is the task of the marketer. A prime example is the intranet: research labs, universities, and computer hardware, software, and networking companies have been running organizational internetworks based on the TCP/IP protocols, with more or less access-controlled links to the Internet, since the middle of the 1980s. It took a marketing genius to package TCP/IP client and server software for the organization and create the term "intranet" to refer to organizational internetworking.

The marketing name game is playing out again with the term "extranet." That's what this book is all about.

SPOILER WARNING: If you want to get the full effect of the dramatic tension revolving around this strange new term "extranet," the punchline is coming up in the next paragraph.

Here it is in an over-simplified nutshell: an extranet is simply the result of applying TCP/IP internetworking technologies to provider interoperability across organizational lines. In other words, an extranet is just an intranet, with an Internet connection, that has been jiggered to allow in outsiders in some form or other (they could be random consumers browsing the World Wide Web, or they could be business partners).

Of course, if that were truly all there was to extranets, this book would end after the first chapter with a pointer to a list of good books about TCP/IP (for example, *TCP/IP Clearly Explained*, APP 1997, by the author of this book, and the upcoming *Mastering TCP/IP for NT Server* by Mark Minasi) and books about building intranets. In fact, there is a nice shiny coat of paint on the extranet in the form of a set of extranet-related services, security facilities, and distributed computing interfaces that distinguish the extranet from its predecessors in form and function, and also justify the use of a new term for purposes beyond those of mere marketing.

There is an extra layer of security mechanisms and distributed computing infrastructure that has to be deployed before you get a working extranet. Similarly, there are certain extra constructs required to build networks that can connect people and organizations, securely, without respect to organizational boundaries.

This book explains what exactly an extranet is, how it works, and what it is made of.

- The first four chapters present an introduction to the concepts on which the extranet is based, providing an introduction to extranets, an explanation of what differentiates an extranet from any other type of internetwork, and discussion of the logical and physical architectures upon which extranets are built.

- The next two chapters provide an overview to the most important building blocks of the extranet: security tools and extranet services. These are the mechanisms that must be in place to enable an extranet to provide services across organizational borders.

- The last four chapters address implementation issues, from planning and building the extranet to managing the extranet to planning a path for future development of the extranet.

- The appendices include a brief primer on TCP/IP internetworking; a guide to products, resources, and organizations (with URLs) in support of extranet and extranet functions; and a glossary of important extranet-related terms.

Reading this book will no more bestow the ability to build an extranet from the ground up than successful wrist surgery will bestow the ability to play the piano: but, in both cases, you will be better equipped for the task after the event than before. All readers will come away from this book with a better understanding of what functions extranet technologies will enable organizations and individuals to perform.

Part I: Extranets Inside and Out

The first part of this book provides a basic grounding in the concepts of internetworking in the context of the extranet. The first chapter introduces the concept of technology waves and examines how the extranet wave fits into the evolution of modern computing technology. The second chapter examines more closely the distinguishing features of the extranet, and explains how to differentiate an extranet from other types of internetwork. Chapter 3 provides an overview to distributed computing, and examines how distributed computing is integral to extranet applications. The fourth chapter discusses the components and architecture of actual extranets, as they exist as physical entities.

Chapter 1: Introduction to Extranets

This chapter introduces the concept of extranets, explains the concept of internetworking technology waves, and illustrates how extranets fit into the historical development of extranetworking. This chapter will both define terms and define functions with respect to actual business problems.

Chapter 2: What Makes An Extranet

This chapter discusses the basic extranet elements. This includes conceptual elements (for example, distributed object architectures), security protocols (required for protecting data across public and semi-public networks), security constructs (mostly firewalls and proxy servers), extranet topologies (use of public, semi-public, and private network segments), and extranet backbone structures. Each of these elements will be discussed in greater detail in later chapters.

Chapter 3: The Extranet Object Architecture

The CORBA distributed object architecture, developed over the past few years by a consortium with over 700 corporate members, and the Distributed COM framework, developed by Microsoft, are the two most important attempts to define the structure of the world of internetworking for the foreseeable future. Using an object-oriented approach to building network objects means that people and organizations can interact seamlessly and transparently across operating system, hardware, and organizational boundaries. These architectures define the extranet functionally as well as philosophically, and are increasingly basic to building extranet applications.

Chapter 4: Extranet Infrastructure

An extranet can exist in various different topologies: it can exist directly within the global Internet, overlap with it, or consist of private links between private, organizational intranets. This chapter examines how these different approaches work, what's involved in implementing each type, and what impact the topology will have on performance, function, cost, and security. Also covered are some guidelines for building extranet backbones, including discussion of backbone design, routing and management. The chapter discusses how to approach the task of building a private backbone for an extranet linking two or more organizations' intranets. This chapter includes strategies for small and large extranets, with examples and pointers to design resources, as well as discussions of virtual private networks (VPNs) and how they fit into the extranet topology.

Part II: Extranet Building Blocks

Extranet security and extranet services are the beams and girders that make up the infrastructure of the extranet: without security, interorganizational interactions cannot be achieved safely; without services, interorganizational applications cannot be completed reliably and robustly. Chapter 5 provides an overview to the security mechanisms available to and commonly used by extranet developers, while Chapter Six examines the extranet services commonly used by extranet developers.

Chapter 5: Extranet Security

Extranet security issues differ not so much in kind as in scale from current intranet and Internet security problems. These are multiplied by their complexity, as it may be just as important to maintain accessibility to data as it is to exclude unauthorized uses of data. This chapter discusses firewalls as well as issues like user authentication and Internet security protocols. Security at all network layers, from the link layer to the application layer, is discussed.

Chapter 6: Extranet Services

Network directory services are an integral part of extranetworking: the ability to locate across a network a person, a network resource, a system or a piece of data or program function. Discussed here are services and protocols including X.500, X.509, LDAP, and others. Discussion of certification authorities, what they are and how they work; Kerberos key distribution and digital certificates will also be included, as will discussion of the issues related to Java and ActiveX code authentication.

Chapter 7: Building Extranet Applications

Building on the experience of early extranet implementers, as well as extrapolating from related structures (for example, VANs, or value-added networks, have been widely implemented for EDI), this chapter presents some of the possibilities for extranet applications and examines how they can be implemented using tools already available. It will also present descriptions of actual extranet implementations and tips from extranet builders.

Chapter 8: Detailed Examples of Extranet Software

This chapter contains a listing of some of the software products available and explanations of how they fit into the modern extranet. The list includes three categories of internetworking software: Web application servers, "Webtop" client software, and message queuing.

Chapter 9: Managing and Administering Extranets

Managing and administering an organizational network is already a heavy task; taking control of an inter-organizational network like an extranet may be impossible—which doesn't mean that implementing extranets leads to anarchy. This chapter discusses some of the approaches to extranet network management, configuration and administration tasks, with particular attention to managing virtual private networks.

Chapter 10: Combining the Future and the Past

This chapter summarizes not just the contents of the book, but offers a historical perspective on how extranets will operate in the world as we know it now—or are coming to know it—and how extranets will affect the way we implement internetworking technologies in the coming years, as the next waves in internetworking overtake extranetworking.

Appendices and Glossary

Appendix A provides a starting point for the reader interested in gathering more information about extranets, including contact information for software vendors offering extranet products and pointers to Internet resources for information about extranet-related open standards.

Appendix B offers a lightning introduction to internetworking with TCP/IP as a refresher for the experienced network professional and as a primer for readers who have had less exposure to internetworking. This appendix highlights the use of network reference models, encapsulation, Internet addressing, and the most important Internet applications.

Finally, the glossary provides definitions and acronym expansions of some of the extranet terms that may be unfamiliar.

PART

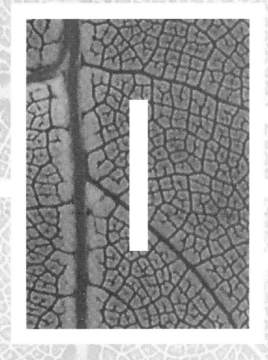

I

EXTRANETS INSIDE AND OUT

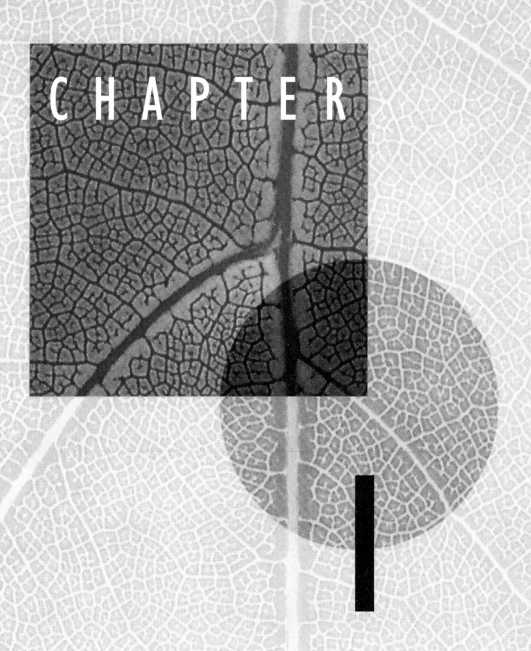

CHAPTER

1

Introduction to Extranets

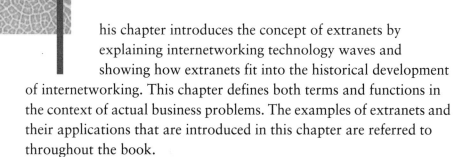

This chapter introduces the concept of extranets by explaining internetworking technology waves and showing how extranets fit into the historical development of internetworking. This chapter defines both terms and functions in the context of actual business problems. The examples of extranets and their applications that are introduced in this chapter are referred to throughout the book.

What Is an Extranet?

In the simplest terms possible, an *extranet* is a type of network that crosses organizational boundaries, giving outsiders access to information and resources stored inside the organization's internal network. For a simple example, an online catalog that displays product information dynamically retrieved from the vendor's own internal product database gives potential customers a direct look at information that is stored on the vendor's internal network. When the product description, price, or availability change, the page display changes too. Explaining how this process works is what this book is all about.

Technology Waves

Tracking the progress of how we integrate a new technology into our daily lives is difficult, especially from a distance of many years. Television, telecommunications, the internal combustion engine, steam power, and air travel are all examples of technologies that have taken decades to change the world. Businesses and individuals had many years to get used to these newfangled technologies, to plan for them, save for them, and to slowly try them out. The leisurely pace suits us— it is manageable, and our lives change slowly. We still speak of "dialing" a phone number, even though rotary-dial telephones are fast becoming collectors' pieces. Likewise, we still speak of "cranking" a car engine, even though we actually use electronically controlled ignitions to start our cars.

The velocity of change has been accelerating over the last half century. As the 1960s turned into the 1970s, about the same time man first stepped on the moon, the dual seeds of today's internetworking revolution were being planted. Research that would ultimately result in the precursors of today's Internet was starting in 1969 and 1970, and the first microprocessors were rolling off assembly lines by 1971. Moore's Law, stipulating the doubling of microprocessing power every 18 months, and an Internet that has been roughly doubling in size annually for almost 20 years have combined to produce a business world with ubiquitous desktop systems capable of computing feats far beyond the abilities of yesterday's million-dollar mainframes. And these desktop systems are all connected (or soon will be connected) through robust open networks.

The rapid growth of technology deployment means that businesses no longer have the luxury of waiting a few years to see how new technologies work out for the early adopters. Early adopters may be only a year—or even just a few months—ahead of the rest of the pack, and waiting two years to implement a new technology may be enough to brand a company as old-fashioned.

New technologies, such as computing, networking, and the Internet, have life cycles. They begin in universities and research labs as ideas, and if the creators can find sponsors, the ideas and concepts eventually find a more concrete expression in projects and experiments. Again, if they succeed at this stage in demonstrating the kernel of a useful product, they may be developed into prototypes and perfected through trial and error. Successful prototypes that find financial backing eventually appear on the market as products, and successful products spawn imitators and competitors. This continuous buildup is like the surging of a wave, building in intensity until it breaks as it meets the shore—the market. Many waves fizzle out with relatively little impact; under certain circumstances they may alter the structure of the beach on which they land—but in all cases, they are followed by more waves.

The parallel developments of the microprocessor and internetworking technologies have generated those special circumstances in which large waves of new technologies wash over us in rapid succession. Businesses and people who understood the implications of the Internet in the early 90s and moved quickly to take business advantage of those implications have benefited. Businesses and people who understood the implications of intranets in the mid-90s and moved to take business advantage of those implications have also benefited. Similarly, at the end of the 90s, businesses and people who understand the implications of extranets and take business advantage of those implications will also benefit.

Understanding a new technology—what it is, how it works, and what it can do for your organization—is a key step to using the technology to achieve your organization's goals and is an absolute prerequisite to deploying that technology. This book will help you achieve the goal of understanding the new technology called an *extranet*.

The terms *internetwork, Internet, internet, intranet,* and *extranet* are all discussed in greater detail throughout this book. However, for the purpose of clarity, I will to refer to any network running TCP/IP as an *internetwork*. Within this framework, *internetwork* includes the Internet, intranets, and extranets.

A Very Brief History of Internetworking

For their first 25 years, the history of internetworking and the history of the Internet were essentially the same. Although a detailed historical account of the origins of the Internet protocols is beyond the scope of this book, a very brief overview will lay the groundwork for the topics at hand.

A very successful data communications network was well in place by the late 60s, with terminals in almost every home and office in North America. Those terminals—also known as telephones—can connect people (or computers) virtually anywhere, as long as the copper, fiber, microwave, or satellite links are in place. At the height of the cold war, the U.S. government decided that telecommunications links, especially those used for command and control of strategic weapons systems, were vulnerable to attack. Telecommunications switches offer enemies attractive targets, with single points of failure that can bring a network to its knees or worse. Figure 1.1 shows how such a single point of failure would sever communications between the eastern and western parts of the United States.

FIGURE 1.1

A switched network with a single point of failure is highly vulnerable to disastrous failure.

In the late 60s the U.S. Department of Defense (DoD) Advanced Research Projects Agency (ARPA) began funding research into ways to protect strategic networks from nuclear attacks that could destroy large parts of the networks. The basic idea, as shown in Figure 1.2, was to create a network of networks, or an *internetwork,* with multiple links between each network. Failure on any given link between any two networks would not necessarily break the rest of the internetwork. If a link fails, data would be intelligently rerouted to its destination over some other link or combination of links.

FIGURE 1.2

With multiple links and no single point of failure, an internetwork can withstand considerable damage without losing connectivity.

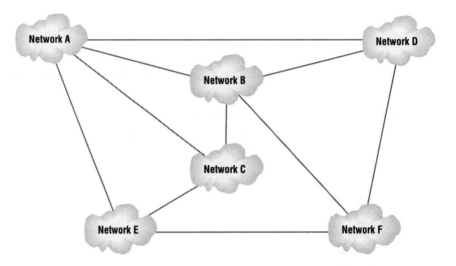

The very interesting saga of how this idea became a reality is best told elsewhere—what interests us here is how this experiment grew into a global infrastructure. The heart of the problem was not so much a technical issue as it was an issue of the big messy world we live in.

Robust internetworking would, of course, be easiest in the best of all possible worlds—where all connected systems are compatible, where all systems are connected with the same type of network medium, and where a central authority manages all the systems connected to the internetwork. Programmers could easily write software for that single platform—software that could deliver data, efficiently and quickly, between any two connected systems, using the centrally administered directory. Broken links and failed networks could be managed elegantly and simply, and performance would always be excellent.

The problem is that such a world is not only impossible to achieve but also destined to experience overwhelming systemic failure in a few years (and probably much sooner). This closed static system would very likely prohibit any significant scalability—any significant increase in the number of systems or networks connected to the internetwork would soon doom it. One possible solution to scalability problems is the introduction of new technologies in the form of hardware, software, or network media capable of handling more traffic—but this avenue is closed, since it would require all systems, networks, and hardware to be updated simultaneously. Any bug, error, or miscalculation would quickly strand all users.

Scalability is the degree to which any networking product used by more than one user at a time is able to handle ever-increasing numbers of concurrent users. Network wiring, network server hardware, and network server software will usually have some implicit limits on the number of concurrent users. The ability of a networking product to gracefully handle increasing loads determines how *scalable* the product is.

The potential number of hardware, software, and local area network combinations on systems that we might like to link together is virtually limitless. Defining the problem in terms of linking disparate computers and running unknown software over unimaginable networks made the research task was more challenging than trying to link similar computers running on uniform networks, but ultimately the rewards were well worth the effort. The result is a technology that allows us to create applications that operate globally without knowing anything about the systems on which they will run, the networks that will carry the data, or the systems and software used to store, process, and deliver the results.

Engineers and programmers needed more than 20 years to develop internetworking into a commercial technology, capable of supporting seamless interoperability within heterogeneous networks. As those technologies are developed into products, they enable the technology consumers to achieve their organizational goals by making information systems work for the organization, rather than against it.

The new internetworking technologies have obviously not developed all at once. They break upon the market sequentially, very much like waves. Each wave brings profound changes in the way people think about working with computers, working with networks, and working with each other. The waves relevant to this discussion are

- The Internet wave

- The intranet wave

- The extranet wave

- The next waves

The Internet Wave

In the late 1980s most large U.S. colleges and universities had begun to offer their staff and students access to e-mail and other Internet applications. For the first time a large population of students had access to a far more powerful tool than was available to most corporate computer users: global e-mail. By the early 90s the U.S. government started to pull out of the business of running the Internet, and corporations started to notice the potential benefits of getting connected.

Awareness of the Internet was reaching a critical mass, but actually getting connected to the Internet and using standard applications like e-mail was still difficult. A few commercial software vendors were selling often inadequate (and usually hard to install and use) TCP/IP implementations, and most major hardware, networking, and operating systems companies were still looking at TCP/IP as competition for their proprietary network solution.

The World Wide Web provided the fuse to ignite that critical mass of potential Internet users. The Web provided a single consistent user interface, giving access to text, graphics, and virtually any other kind of data file, as well as offering an easy-to-use front end for the more esoteric Internet applications like File Transfer Protocol (FTP) and Telnet (terminal emulation). The Web's graphical user interface replaced the UNIX-like command syntax of most then-current Internet applications and made Internet resources accessible to a much wider audience.

The new products and companies doing Internet work washed over the marketplace in a virtual wave, as vendors like Microsoft, IBM, Novell, Apple, DEC, and others adjusted their product strategies to accommodate this new technology, some with more success than others. Despite all the hype about the Internet as a new information resource, the World Wide Web was most useful as a resource for information about the Internet and the World Wide Web during its first few years—if you were interested in other topics, relatively little information was available at first. This situation is not surprising; most of the people connected to the Web at first were involved in building and testing the technologies, and the most logical application was to provide information about the Web on the Web.

The first important Internet application was global e-mail, enabling people to communicate easily and cheaply across any organizational boundary; the Web did not become a significant research resource for several more years, and it continues to be a mixed blessing (see Note).

Unquestionably, the Web now provides a vital and immediate communication medium that carries news, technical information, and commerce. At the same time, it carries gigabytes of paranoid rants and misinformed lecturing, lurid and lewd entertainment material, jokes and pranks, and untold numbers of personal home pages with pictures of the owners' cats. Accessibility for all to the means of publication is a good thing for society, as long as accessibility does not threaten the medium itself.

The companies that were most successful in this wave were companies that made the Internet accessible. Internet service providers quickly moved in to fill the void the U.S. government created when it stopped subsidizing access. Software publishers selling products that helped individuals get connected, like browser programs, did particularly well. Software publishers selling products that helped companies get their message online, like Internet servers, did well, as did companies selling tools for creating, managing, and updating Internet content. Web site publishers able to deliver mass audiences, particularly those providing the important service of Web indexing, also did well through the sales of advertisements. Hardware vendors manufacturing the routers, gateways, and other networking devices necessary to keep the corporate Internet systems up and running also prospered.

The Internet wave was mostly about building an infrastructure for users of the new technology; the creative use of the technology to achieve business goals would have to wait until enough systems were online and enough people knew how to use them. As shown in Figure 1.3, Internet applications are built on a client/server model. The end user uses a piece of client software running on a local system, which connects to another piece of software running on another computer connected to the Internet somewhere else.

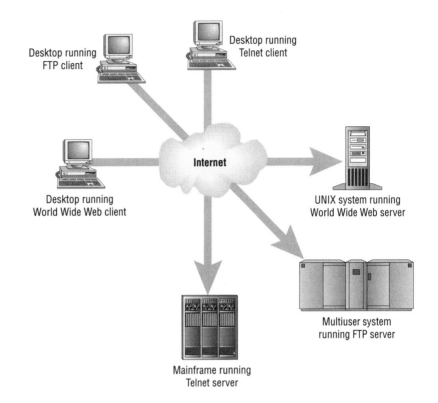

Desktop running
FTP client

Desktop running
Telnet client

Internet

Desktop running
World Wide Web client

UNIX system running
World Wide Web server

Multiuser system
running FTP server

Mainframe running
Telnet server

The key, as well as part of the limitation, to the Internet is an explicit, though virtual, link between the client and the server, which is never far from the end user's consciousness. The idea of using an Internet application like FTP or Telnet always involves the user in the question, What and where is the system to which I am going to be connecting? An explicit interaction between the client software and the user *always* begins each session. The software asks the user, "What system do you want to connect with?" and the user responds with the name or address of the remote system. This interaction is only slightly less explicit with the World Wide Web, where the user can specify a home page (or accept the default home page) and use Web hyperlinks to navigate from system to system.

The Intranet Wave

The idea of building an organizational internetwork is not new. Research labs, universities, and corporations had been doing so for almost as long as the Internet (and its predecessors) had been around. The idea of having a single set of protocols for all networking, running on all computer platforms, is compelling. For example, a single set of protocols can

- Eliminate problems of software compatibility and data accessibility

- Cost less than proprietary commercial solutions offered by hardware and software vendors

- Accommodate growth, mergers, and downsizing easily

However, most corporations tended to avoid even considering alternatives to their proprietary LANs for data communication. The TCP/IP alternative may have been more elegant, robust, and appealing, but the costs of replacing their Novell NetWare, IBM SNA, and Digital DECnet networks did not seem to generate any appreciable benefits in terms of increasing network usability or deploying any significant productivity applications.

The World Wide Web changed the networking picture. Information professionals soon realized that putting the friendly Web front end on their corporate systems would make computing easier not only for the end users but also for the MIS and systems support staffs. A further benefit was the ease with which they could deploy multiplatform support for new systems. Any system capable of running a TCP/IP stack and a Web browser could access corporate resources over any internetwork—the Internet or an intranet.

Intranets are simply smaller versions of the Internet. They operate as self-contained internetworks, as shown in Figure 1.4. The Internet "cloud" is separated from the intranet cloud only by a gateway; network clouds simplify the representation of an internetwork, since they show that some kind of connectivity exists within the cloud, but the exact structure of the cloud is immaterial. An intranet may be linked to the Internet through a plain gateway, but more often a firewall to stem the flow of data in or out of the organizational intranet stands between the two systems.

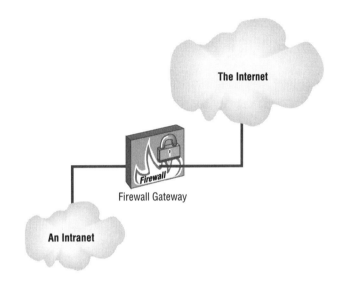

Some of the same companies that benefited from the Internet wave also benefited from the intranet wave, particularly those selling the internal corporate infrastructure components—which turn out to be almost exactly the same components of the Internet infrastructure: browser and server software, routers, and gateways. Internet software and hardware companies soon realized that the market for Internet products was relatively limited in comparison to the market for internal organizational internetworks. The most successful vendors continued to sell their products for use on the Internet but began to concentrate on positioning their products as intranet solutions. Witness the campaigns by Lotus, Microsoft, and Netscape to position their Web servers as corporate resources within intranets rather than as

World Wide Web servers. At the same time, the leading browsers have been expanded from mere World Wide Web clients to include e-mail and network news clients, scheduling and calendaring features, and collaborative computing tools, all to lure in the corporate customer. Likewise, Digital's AltaVista software division developed an outstanding Web site search engine, which, when marketed strictly as a World Wide Web server tool, also had a limited market. However, by expanding its scope as an intranet tool, and even as a desktop search tool, the AltaVista search engine has a considerably wider audience.

The Extranet Wave

The creation of the predecessors to the global Internet through the 1970s and early 1980s solved an important problem at the time: how to allow access to scarce resources from anywhere in the world. Mainframes and supercomputers were the scarce resources, and the applications were terminal emulation and file transfer. After all, a session with a supercomputer will always take place over some sort of terminal, so why not extend that application to make it accessible to anyone with any type of terminal—including a virtual terminal through an Internet connection.

As the 1990s brought ever-more powerful systems to the average desktop, and as supercomputer manufacturers hit hard times, users were interested in access to a different kind of scarce resource. As high-performance computers became increasingly plentiful, the really important commodity became seamless and instant access to timely information.

Information stored on a legacy mainframe system connected to the Internet or to an intranet is accessible to users as long as they are able to run a terminal emulation program on their desktop systems—and as long as they have a valid user ID and password and are able to use the legacy software running the mainframe application. Users needing this information may in fact have access to it, particularly if they are employees with workstations inside the corporate firewall.

Unfortunately, employees working outside the firewall, corporate business partners, or customers are far less likely to have access to this information, even though it may be in the organization's interest to provide at least partial access to some of this information.

The current wave of internetworking technologies creates a level of abstraction that rises above the network and addresses the underlying information. The ability to assemble information and make it available to those who need it (and are authorized to have it) is the basic concept underlying the extranet. Defining applications and data to be independent of any underlying platform means that end users can access the information they need seamlessly, across any intervening networks, and in a manner appropriate to the platform they choose to use.

Figure 1.5 shows how the extranet overlays corporate boundaries and the Internet. Relevant information is pulled or pushed onto the individual desktop from whatever sources are required. Whether the data resides on legacy systems, on a corporate mainframe on the user's intranet, on some other organization's legacy system on a remote intranet, or on public or semipublic servers on the Internet, the extranet desktop aggregates the information and presents it in a useful form to the end user.

The companies that will profit most (and are already profiting) from this wave sell the software components that make extranets happen—in particular, tools for creating distributed-object frameworks for accessing organizational information and the tools for securing private transmission channels that traverse open networks like the Internet. The first group includes makers of Java and other platform-independent software and software development tools; advanced e-mail, Web, and other types of Internet client and server software; middleware for accessing and publishing data from legacy systems; and sophisticated network management and administration tools. The second group includes hardware and software vendors building firewall systems; secure gateways and routers; and tools for encrypting and digitally signing data, applets, and applications to be transmitted across open networks.

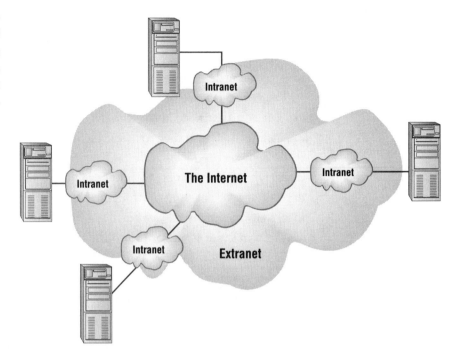

The Next Waves

One way to predict future internetworking waves is simply to look at the technologies and products that academic and industry researchers are working on today. These coming waves will be discussed in more detail in Chapter 9, but a brief mention of the next three obvious waves is in order here.

Ubiquitous High-Speed Internet Access

As of mid-1997, most Internet access is either through a corporate connection (for most organizations) or through a dial-up connection with a modem over POTS (plain old telephone service) lines. Many corporate links run over high-speed, high-bandwidth connections like ISDN, T-1, and T-3 telecommunications links, which support high-bandwidth applications like audio and video, although bottlenecks to

Internet connectivity performance are still common. Dial-up links, on the other hand, are currently limited to a maximum modem transmission rate of 56Kbps, and users of typical modems are limited by modem speeds as low as 28.8Kbps or less. These links tend to be adequate for relatively low-bandwidth applications like e-mail and still-image graphical browsing but tend to be insufficient to support audio, let alone video, transmissions.

Bandwidth is a term that describes the frequency characteristics of a data transmission medium; in practice, the higher the bandwidth of a data transmission medium, the more data can be transmitted over it in a given unit of time. If you imagine the network medium as a pipeline carrying physical bits of information, higher bandwidth pipes would appear much fatter than lower bandwidth pipes, which can carry less traffic. Links using the publicly switched telephone network (PSTN) are generally limited to bandwidth of no greater than 56Kbps (56 kilobits per second); 10BaseT Ethernet can support 10Mbps; gigabit Ethernets can support up to 1Gbps of data.

The bandwidth problem is this: how to get all those many megabytes of interesting audio or video to your desktop when your modem can only handle 28.8Kbps or even 56Kbps? Some solutions are already coming to market, for example devices that allow cable television operators to provide high-speed Internet access service and satellite access that supports high bandwidth for incoming data. These access solutions, however, are still in the early-adopter phase. The entry costs are high, and the market is still highly segmented. Even more daunting is that the industry has yet to establish standards. Therefore, a cable modem that works fine when connected to one cable provider's system may not work when connected to the same provider's system in the next town. Of course, this situation is more of a problem for cable operators, who might like to see standardization to bring down the costs of producing these devices, than it is for consumers, who don't have a choice of cable provider from which to buy Internet service.

Consumers and mobile workforces will soon see standardized high-performance, high-bandwidth Internet service delivery in one or more forms—for example, ubiquitous support for high-speed 56Kbps modems, with much speedier technologies like cable and satellite access becoming more common in the next couple of years. That type of access will make spawn an entire new class of Internet services, starting with audio- and videoconferencing and the delivery of other types of video and audio content.

Market Acceptance of Digital Commerce

Despite a promising start, the market is far from granting general acceptance to digital commerce. Transactions over the Internet are rapidly increasing, scores of companies are offering Internet commerce services, and specifications for secure electronic transactions have been drawn and agreed upon by the major players, including Visa and MasterCard. And yet, it will take some time before buying over the Internet is as widely accepted as buying through a catalog or over the telephone. Two of the most important reasons for the public's slow acceptance of Internet commerce are that too few consumers and too few full-service merchants are connected to the Internet.

Merely transferring a telephone or mail-order operation to the Internet will not lure consumers away from their known and trusted methods of shopping. As merchants add value to draw new customers, however, those customers will find that online shopping may be less expensive and more convenient than traditional trips to the mall.

Merchants who add the most value to the online shopping experience will tend to do best, as will companies selling merchant services and companies manufacturing products that can be delivered digitally.

HomeNet and BodyNet

Microprocessors continue to get faster, smaller, and cheaper. As this trend continues, it makes more sense to embed computers into what used to be very simple devices and to expand the capabilities of existing embedded microprocessors. *HomeNet* and *BodyNet* refer to networks that intelligently link intelligent devices used within the home and worn on the body, respectively.

Special-purpose computers have long been integrated into products as diverse as automobiles, toasters, telephones, and thermostats. Increasingly, people are carrying an array of electronic equipment wherever they go, including pagers, personal digital assistants, cellular phones, digital watches, and even global positioning systems. As all these computers gain new capabilities, the next logical step will be to link them together.

The current upgrade to the Internet Protocol, IPv6, expands the available address space enough to assign a fairly large personal network to each person on Earth with plenty of room to spare for other networking purposes. Extending internetworking technologies to our homes and to our personal lives opens up many interesting possibilities, as well as many risks. These opportunities are discussed at greater length in Chapter 9.

Network Address Space

Any network requires a unique identifier for each network connection—otherwise, it cannot be sure that its devices can send data to the proper destination. The *network address space* is the set of possible, valid, network addresses.

For example, Ethernet network addressing uses a six-byte (48 bits) address, or the potential to have as many as 2^{48} different Ethernet addresses. In fact, part of the Ethernet address is reserved for a vendor code to identify the manufacturer of the Ethernet card, so the Ethernet address space is somewhat limited. The Internet Protocol version 4 address space (discussed in more detail in Appendix B) is limited to 32 bits, or at most about 4 billion different unique addresses. The way these addresses are organized, however, means that in practice far fewer addresses are available in the IP address space.

The Coming Wave: Extranets

Extranets are already being deployed, and some have been in use for years throughout the Internet and within private networks linking groups of business partners. The extranet wave should peak sometime in the next year or so as organizations quickly move to make their information accessible to those who need it, over whatever internetwork they choose for the task.

A Logical Extension of Internetworking Technology

Internetworks enable *seamless interoperability*, which simply means the ability to interoperate across networks, hardware platforms, and software architectures as if the communicating systems are directly connected. Seamless interoperability is closely tied to another function of internetworking, *platform independence*. The ability to connect any two systems seamlessly frees the end user—and the application developer—from dependence on any single platform.

The next logical step in this progression is to create a system in which information resources are *portable*. Separating information from the application with which it was created, and from the system on which it resides, extends the benefit of highly networked systems. With portable resources, the individual can enjoy rapid access to information from various sources, all controlled by the individual rather than by systems managers, application developers, and database administrators. The user can control what information is retrieved—from where, how frequently, and how it is displayed and used.

To illustrate, consider one of the new features found on browsers released during 1997: the ability to drag and drop content resources that are published on a Web site into the end user's desktop. In Microsoft's Internet Explorer 4.0, for example, a software component displays a stock ticker, with data drawn from an online stock quote service. The user can grab the control with the mouse pointer, drop it onto the desktop, and incorporate stock quotes into his or her Windows desktop. The software component includes options for adding and removing stocks from the ticker, as well as for searching for a stock symbol. All the information functions are performed remotely through the content provider, but the user controls how the information is displayed.

Early demos of Netscape's Constellation technology included a similar function, showing how any Web service could be piped through the system and displayed on the desktop. For example, a user could request that news stories about extranets be made available in some form (a pull-down menu, in a ticker, or somewhere on a live section of the desktop) as they came in from a news provider. A compelling example of this technology is a system that links the user's desktop to online package-tracking services, like that pioneered by Federal Express. The software component could take tracking numbers from the mail room over an organizational intranet, periodically check on their status with the delivery company over the Internet, and notify the end user when the package arrives.

An extranet extends the concept of the organizational network beyond the boundaries of the organization. Extranets imply an opening up of the organization's resources to those who need access from outside the firewall. Extranets also legitimize the use of resources external to the organization to support internal business objectives.

Extranet Application Architectures

The boundaries and topology of an extranet will vary from one instance to the next. (Extranet topologies are discussed in greater detail in Chapter 4.) However, an organization that attempts to implement an extranet topology without implementing an appropriate application architecture, will not reap the complete benefits. Access to extranet systems without the proper distributed-object application tools, as described in Chapter 3, limits the portability and utility of extranet resources. The next two sections discuss how extranets might appear as networks, ignoring (for the moment) the issues of application architecture.

External Intranets

On first hearing, the concept of an *external intranet* is clearly an oxymoron. After all, *intra* means "internal," and the word *intranet* originally meant an "internal internetwork." *Intranets* are often defined as organizational TCP/IP internetworks that operate within a single organization, behind the organizational firewall, and deny access to everyone outside the organization. The very idea that an intranet can be external to the sponsoring organization seems as ridiculous as saying that a television station that accepts paid advertisements is "noncommercial" or as illogical as a "private" club that is open to all.

A moment's thought will explain the paradox. Even though an intranet belongs to a single organization, the organization is not necessarily a monolithic entity. Large, modern organizations have any number of different departments, subsidiaries, joint ventures, and business partners. They operate out of huge skyscrapers, suburban office campuses, branch offices, and home offices; and their employees include top-level executives, bonded security officers, managers, professionals, temporary-agency clerks, consultants, and contractors.

Restricting access to an organizational intranet, in the traditional sense of allowing only employees of an organization working at the organization's physical plant, severely limits the intranet's usefulness. A corporate intranet that can be accessed from inside as well as from outside the confines of the corporation becomes much more useful to those who

- Travel on behalf of the organization

- Work from home or the road

- Consult for the organization

- Work from branch or satellite offices

Safely constructing an external intranet, one that permits access from outside the boundaries at which firewalls protect the internal intranet, can substantially increase the usefulness of the intranet. The simple example in Figure 1.6 shows one approach to the external intranet. Users at branch offices can access the corporate headquarters intranet by tunneling encrypted data streams across the Internet, and users at headquarters can access branch-office intranets the same way. In other words, users connected to the headquarters intranet or any branch office intranet have access to the same resources, whereas anyone else is denied access to these systems. Furthermore, while the traffic passes across the Internet, it is encrypted to protect against interception; in addition, it is digitally signed to protect against fraudulent transmissions. The result is sometimes referred to as a *virtual private network* (VPN) because it allows organizations to use public networks (i.e., the Internet) to carry private traffic securely.

Figure 1.7 shows how the users of this extranet view its structure. It is simply a big intranet connecting all the branches of the organization as well as its headquarters. The effect is similar whenever an organization extends the means by which users outside the corporate firewall can access the organizational intranet.

Extended Intranets

Although much of the information floating around inside any given organization is private—for example, personal information about employees, long-range strategic plans, or proprietary product information—most organizations have a sizable volume of information that they must disseminate publicly or semipublicly to their potential customers, existing customers, and trading partners.

FIGURE 1.6

Encrypting data streams allows use of the Internet to create a virtual private network.

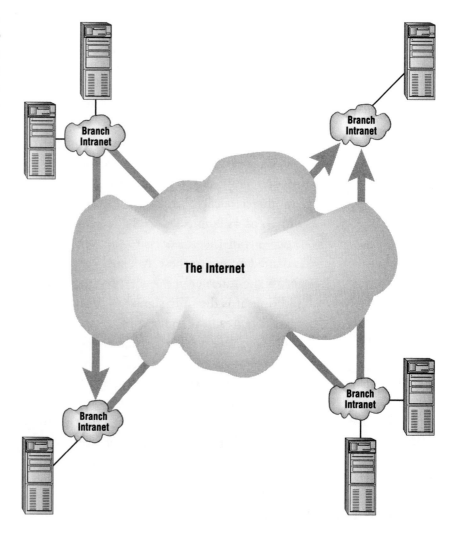

Again, you can use various methods to achieve the goal of extending an intranet to allow access to those outside the organization. These methods are discussed throughout the book. For now, I will outline two extreme examples of extended intranets. The first type, which has already been widely implemented, is usually set up by an organization that maintains a large customer service department to handle incoming customer queries. Federal Express, which built an interface between

FIGURE 1.7

One objective of the extranet is to make access to remote hosts (and data) transparent.

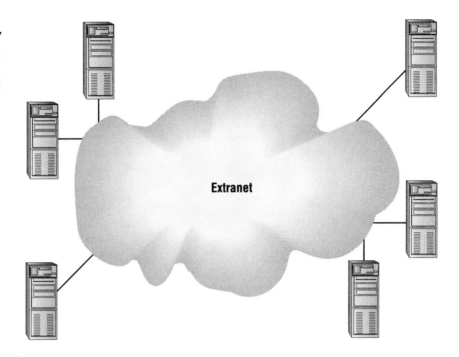

the corporate database of package deliveries and the World Wide Web, is an excellent example of this type of organization. Any customer seeking the status of a package can bypass the human customer service representative and directly enter what amounts to a database query to the Federal Express corporate database through the World Wide Web. A graphic representation of this approach appears in Figure 1.8.

For the purposes of package tracking, virtually anyone connected to the Internet can connect to this organization's extended intranet and access a subset of the data contained in the organization's databases. The rest of the organizational database, which may very well contain proprietary information such as customer lists and billing information, remains inside the corporate intranet.

Some critics dismiss this type of extranet as simply an extension of the function of the Internet and the use of simple tools that give companies a mechanism for publishing information stored in legacy systems. However, as user applications become more sophisticated, this

FIGURE I.8

An organization opening up some data in its corporate intranet can create a type of extranet.

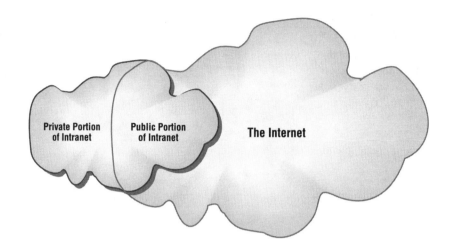

type of service becomes much more interesting. For instance, application software capable of using shipping information retrieved from within an organization's intranet to verify package status through the delivery company's extranet can be valuable to any company whose business depends on shipping goods promptly.

Although this approach is obviously useful for companies with broad customer bases, at the other extreme are companies who do business with a handful of business partners. The larger the amount of money involved in any particular sale, the more likely that a high level of communication between the vendor and the customer is necessary. For example, the Air Force doesn't just call up Ace Aircraft Company, order 200 fighter jets, and give a credit card number—a huge amount of interaction occurs as the buyer and seller agree on specifications and prices for the jets, as the manufacturer designs and builds the planes, and as the finished goods are delivered and serviced.

Figure 1.9 shows how this type of extranet might look for three firms working together on a very large project. All three firms share the same objective of completing the project on time and under budget, which justifies the possible security risks of linking their intranets. This risk can be minimized by each organization taking responsibility for securing its own systems and making shared resources available to the partners. Simply interconnecting the companies' intranets will not be sufficient; the companies also need to create a higher-level data abstraction to which all three can communicate. Otherwise, the astronomical costs of getting all the organizations' computer systems to interoperate could easily exceed any savings.

FIGURE 1.9

Connecting private intranets, with no external connectivity, creates a private extranet.

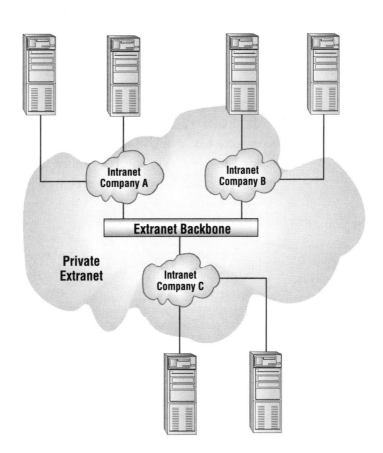

Organizations whose information is extremely valuable, or vulnerable to attack, may consider creating this type of extranet. Electronic Data Interchange (EDI) companies have been running value-added networks (VANs) for some time with a similar architecture, though with much greater focus. Banks, electronic merchants, brokers, and other financial institutions, as well as defense contractors, government units, and law enforcement agencies, might consider this approach.

What Exactly Is an Extranet?

As this discussion makes clear, an extranet, whether it is an extended intranet, an external intranet, or something else, goes beyond conventional internetworking as deployed in the Internet or on organizational intranets. At the moment, we do not have a single, universally accepted definition of exactly what differentiates an extranet from other types of internetworks.

Extranets must provide information in a form that any extranet-connected system can use transparently. This requirement means taking interoperability to a higher level than TCP/IP provides (see the following Note). The degree to which an application can support interactions with other applications varies with its degree of connectivity:

- A system that is not connected to a network at all may support interaction only between applications running on the same system.

- A system connected to a LAN can access services running on other systems connected to the same LAN as long as they are all using the same (or compatible) LAN software.

- A system connected to the Internet can interoperate, through its client software, with any other system connected to the Internet through its counterpart server software.

The extranet usually adds one more layer of abstraction on top of the whole stew, by making *objects*—that is, individual bits of function connected with information—accessible to other authorized objects living anywhere else on the network.

The TCP/IP protocols (described in more detail in Appendix B) provide a set of rules that enable any kind of computer connected to any kind of network to interoperate with any other kind of computer connected to any other kind of network—as long as some level of connectivity exists between the two networks. *Interoperability* means that each system can exchange data and requests for data without having to know anything about the other system or the networks through which they are both connected.

Although the concepts of object-oriented systems are not new, their application to internetworking is. A detailed discussion of objects, Object Request Brokers (ORBs), and distributed objects is beyond the scope of this book, but these elements are integral to any discussion of extranetworking. The next section provides a brief introduction to these concepts, and they are developed in greater detail in Chapter 3.

Extranets and Distributed Objects

Very simply, objects package function with data in a way that allows other objects to use them. This level of *interoperability* goes well beyond the interoperability available to a browser interface to a legacy database. For example, you can use a distributed-object architecture to embed object front-end access to legacy systems into a Web page—making the data living in those systems accessible to any authorized user (person, program, or object). Another feature of some object architectures is that the objects can be self-describing. In addition, the interaction between objects does not necessarily have to be explicitly spelled out ahead of time but can depend on the contents of the interacting objects.

Consequently, client front-end software can navigate through a network searching for objects that meet a user's criteria and present the results in the desired format. In comparison, when using intranets or the Internet, the end user must have the correct client for the remote resource. Even when legacy system resources are available through a GUI or Web browser front end, the information remains stored in a single system; an object architecture enables a single front end to accumulate information from various resources and present it as a unified result.

The success of TCP/IP as an internetworking standard has much to do with its global acceptance as a nonproprietary standard. Without this acceptance, TCP/IP would be just another set of protocols that might have gained limited implementation in certain organizations or industries—and a proprietary solution probably would not have achieved the same degree of success in the market. A similar drive to a single set of standards for distributed objects is occurring now. With so many sets of standards, organizations are unwilling to commit to any for fear of committing to the wrong one. However, as of 1997 the options appear to have been narrowed down to two: Microsoft versus the rest of the world, with Microsoft's solutions increasingly being put forward as another, more attractive (according to Microsoft) set of open standards.

Microsoft's Object Linking and Embedding (OLE), which is built on the Common Object Model (COM) and Distributed Common Object Model (DCOM), is the model that Microsoft (for obvious reasons) would very much like to become the object architecture of choice, as it will encourage the use of Microsoft products. The alternative is being developed by the Object Management Group (OMG), a project in which more than 700 organizations are participating. The result is called the *Common Object Request Broker Architecture* (CORBA), and it has been revised and expanded to provide cross-platform (and cross-object architecture) interoperability with the Internet Inter-ORB Protocol (IIOP).

Many other companies have joined Netscape Communications in backing CORBA as the appropriate architecture for the future of internetworking. Although the so-called browser war, which started between Netscape and Microsoft in 1996, has captured the lion's share of media attention, the battle over extranet object architecture is significantly more vital to these two companies, as well as to anyone interested in the future direction of internetworking.

Both of these architectures are discussed in more detail in Chapter 3. However, although a single, universally supported object architecture is the ideal, it does appear that for now we will have to deal with two: Microsoft's OLE/COM/DCOM and OMG's CORBA/IIOP.

Extending Internetworking Technologies

Extranets are more than merely extended or external intranets. Essentially, extranets provide a superset of the functions provided by standard TCP/IP internetworking. TCP/IP internetworks can be characterized as seamlessly interoperable and platform independent; extranets add resource portability through object architecture. The result is to further the goal of submerging the network into the background while making the information resources on the network even more accessible.

Seamless Interoperability

In TCP/IP internetworks, any connected device running a protocol-compliant client program can use the services of any other connected device running a protocol-compliant server. The only requirement is that both client and server conform to the same protocol. Neither device needs to know anything about the other except for TCP/IP addressing information. The brand of TCP/IP software, hardware platform, or local area network medium is irrelevant. Likewise, neither device needs to have any information about where the other is on the internetwork, what routers lie between the devices, or what route the actual data takes to arrive at its destination.

Seamless interoperability made it possible to create applications like the World Wide Web, which simplify the task of accessing remote (and separated) internetworked resources through a single client. Extranets can extend this seamless interoperability with object architecture. Objects can interact in predefined ways to gather information or to complete transactions; they can also interact in unexpected ways to complete relatively complex tasks. Objects can be published within an extranet for public or private consumption; customers may pay for their use, or publishers may make them available at no cost. In any case the ultimate use to which the objects may be put cannot be predicted or predefined, but is ultimately limited only by the imagination and ingenuity of the user.

Platform Independence

That any computer running TCP/IP can interoperate with any other computer running TCP/IP may not seem so miraculous anymore, particularly if you have forgotten (or never had to deal with) the many competing and totally incompatible computer systems vendors produced in an effort to differentiate their systems and lock corporate customers into their unique architectures. The resulting babel of operating systems (*and* data representation schemes) meant that in the 1980s the desks of some information workers held as many as four CRTs, each with its own special cable: the VT-100 terminal connected to a serial cable, next to an IBM mainframe terminal hooked up to a terminal server, next to an Intel-processor PC on the office LAN, and possibly even a Macintosh connected to an AppleTalk wire for good measure.

A TCP/IP intranet consolidates those monitors and cables, since a single workstation can be used to connect to all resources. Although eliminating extra hardware and cabling is a good thing, the true benefit of internetworking goes well beyond hardware savings. All those separate systems and terminals prevent organizations from making the best use of their information and computing resources. Information that is stored on the mainframe, put into a mainframe file by a mainframe application using the mainframe EBCDIC character set is not accessible to anyone not using the mainframe. Even if there were a simple way for the PC and the mainframe to exchange files, the file format, character set, and application prevent the PC from using the mainframe file for any useful purpose.

TCP/IP protocols eliminate these platform incompatibilities and allow a single workstation to act as a terminal to all remote hosts. The same workstation can also download data transparently from remote hosts, or upload data to those hosts, without having to worry about how the remote host stores its data.

This platform independence supports seamless interoperability in TCP/IP networks. Extranets extend the concept of platform independence to the data itself, not just the representation of the data. Data living within an object is no longer tied to some particular application on some particular host, but can now be distributed to any other connected host, independent of the software, hardware, and network platform.

Solving Real-World Problems

Connectivity for the sake of connectivity is not sufficient reason to allocate the time, money, and resources necessary to upgrade a corporate LAN system to an intranet. The return on investment must be greater than the savings from shared hardware. And, in fact, the potential return from these upgrades is vast and extends to many areas. For example, certain internal documents, such as human resources handbooks, telephone directories, and operating instructions, can be expensive to publish as hard-copy publications. They must also be continually, and expensively, updated. Using the organizational intranet to publish these documents may result in an immediate and significant cost savings, often large enough to justify the cost of the entire exercise.

Less concrete savings, such as productivity gains, often follow these initial savings when an intranet is installed. Using e-mail and workgroup applications to replace paper mail and decades-old work flows can result in incredible increases in productivity as digital communications can expedite processes that were previously bound by lengthy paper delivery times. Formal intranet work-flow systems and tighter integration with legacy systems eventually result in platform-independent legacy system data entry and retrieval.

The speed with which businesses have embraced intranets is no less astonishing than the value those intranets bring. Extranets will likely be embraced at least as quickly as businesses discover that this technology will not only reduce costs but also generate additional revenue.

Extending Intranet Functionality with Extranets

As the concept of the extranet matures, extranets will be more easily differentiated from intranets, but for now, an extranet will look very much like an extended, expanded, or external intranet. Many of the examples of extranets may appear to be nothing more than intranets whose boundaries have been extended or Internet Web sites whose functions have been expanded, but as distributed objects are increasingly deployed to solve business problems, extranets will be more easily identified as an entirely different animal.

An intranet's function, in the broadest terms possible, is to enable information resource sharing within an organization. As the boundary of the intranet is stretched to accommodate the extranet, the borders at which the organization is defined are stretched by the expanded function of the extranet: to enable information resource sharing within the organization and within the groups of parties interacting with the organization. In its simplest form, an extranet simply extends intranet access outside the confines of the organization. Opening an intranet resource to customers, suppliers, or business partners need not require any technological changes in the intranet.

Another important application of the extranet is to replace costly and inefficient dedicated and dial-up connections and to take advantage of the Internet to carry intranet traffic securely and efficiently. Replacing these links with less expensive Internet connections not only saves money but also simplifies matters for end users who no longer need to use different sets of tools for intranet and Internet tasks.

Distributed objects will be one of the distinguishing marks of the mature extranet because they will make possible applications like these:

- Procurement departments will be able to deploy internal catalogs of office products, drawing product descriptions, illustrations, specifications, and pricing from a range of suppliers' databases— dynamically displaying current stock levels, shipping options, and availability, and even replacing primary approved products with secondary suppliers' products depending on availability.

- Engineering firms will be able to submit designs and modifications in minutes or hours instead of days or weeks.

- Manufacturers can automate ordering procedures through suppliers, linking them all through warehouse and workshop inventory systems.

- Individuals will be able to reliably conduct complicated, conditional transactions with Internet merchants. Travelers may be able to specify sets of alternative-yet-dependent itinerary options, for example, booking airline tickets, rental cars, and overnight accommodations in a single step.

Extranets will extend intranet function in two directions:

- Expanding the borders of the intranet

- Expanding the possibilities of what may be done with information resources

Expanding borders means allowing public or semipublic access to an intranet resource through the Internet; it can also mean simply linking one intranet to another intranet or building a private network of intranets. With distributed-object technologies running across extranets, the possible functions explode because applications that were formerly difficult to program become much easier. For example, complicated transactions requiring access to information on legacy databases can be implemented more easily when existing software and existing components can be readily adapted to interface with those databases. Extranets can be deployed without object technologies, but extranet applications will be much easier to create and maintain using objects rather than using more traditional client/server programming techniques.

Building Business Relationships with Extranets

An intranet, by definition, is strictly about and within the organization. If it is connected to the Internet at all, it is guarded by a firewall gateway to keep intruders outside and keep organizational inmates inside. An intranet may cut costs and improve efficiency, but it has no direct effect on an organization's customers, suppliers, or partners. Although intranets do link individuals, groups, and units within the organization, and help foster relationships among those entities, all the relationships remain entirely within the organization.

Extranets, on the other hand, are intended to foster relationships between the organization and its customers, suppliers, and partners. By opening up organizations to other organizations and individuals, extranets add value for their users. This corporate glasnost requires careful implementation to avoid security problems, but new extranet risks are unlikely to overtake the disgruntled or greedy employee as a source of security breach.

Fostering Internet Commerce with Extranets

The most popular type of business relationship is the one between buyer and seller. Any mechanism that encourages or enhances relationships with businesses cannot fail to foster commerce. Extranets, with distributed objects, will certainly propel Internet commerce from a cumbersome novelty to a mainstream market channel. Even though the Secure Electronic Transaction (SET) specification should bring some order to a disorderly world of digital commerce before the end of 1997, it is only the first step to making Internet commerce a viable way to do business.

Although SET offers a mechanism by which credit (and charge and debit) card transactions can be consummated across the Internet, many other steps occur in the process of making a sale. Before the sale is completed, the buyer and seller may need to negotiate pricing, specifications, delivery, and options. After the sale is complete, the buyer and seller must continue their relationship as products are assembled, delivered, and serviced—and payment settlement is completed. Extranets will provide not only the infrastructure upon which buyers and sellers can transact their business but also a framework upon which complex financial transactions can be consummated to the satisfaction of all concerned parties.

Adding Value with Extranets

Just as some businesses are more successful than others at building sales through catalogs, direct mail, telemarketing, or retail outlets, some businesses have been more successful than others at using the Internet to achieve their business goals. Businesses whose Web sites function are little more than brochure servers don't get the full benefit of their connectivity investment. On the other hand, businesses whose Web sites provide customers with enough information about their products to make a buying decision, in an attractive and easy-to-use format, and enable online transactions, are more likely to see a payoff.

However, merely turning a Web site into an order server provides neither competitive advantage to the merchant nor added value to the consumer.

Creating a Web site that simply replicates a more standard buying process, for example, duplicating a catalog purchase experience, offers the buyer no compelling reason to switch. In fact, online catalog shopping is often a less-than-satisfactory experience when bandwidth to download product images is at a premium or when product colors are poorly reproduced on the consumer's monitor. Internet merchants who use the Internet to add value, however, can more easily attract new customers—for example, merchants who not only accept orders 24 hours a day, seven days a week but also process and ship all orders immediately, rather than waiting for the next business day (as some Internet merchants do); merchants who provide a single source for complete specialty product lines; and merchants who offer digital delivery of their software or other digital product.

Extranets will offer even more opportunities for sellers to add value for their customers. One very early example is the Federal Express Internet package-tracking page described in the chapter. As these extranets start deploying with distributed-object technologies, and as the customer's organization integrates desktop information systems with internal shipping systems and with the delivery company's extranet, the process of package tracking will be further streamlined and simplified.

The rest of this book explains how extranets can deliver on this promise, safely, reliably, and economically.

CHAPTER

2

What Makes an Extranet

lthough you should already realize that every extranet is a unique entity, all extranets are built from the same basic components. This chapter introduces the basic elements of the extranet, each of which will be discussed in greater detail in later chapters. These elements include

- Distributed-object architecture

- Extranet topology

- Extranet security facilities

- Extranet services

- Extranet applications

Most of the technologies underlying these components are reasonably well understood and have enjoyed varying levels of real-world testing and market acceptance. Organizations can enjoy true synergy by deploying them in concert as an extranet.

Extranet Components

Technically, any organizational internetwork whose borders extend beyond those of the organization running it can be called an extranet. Using such a broad definition misses the point though, because businesses are increasingly opening their intranets to outsiders.

Whether by offering limited access to legacy data or by providing contractors and consultants with dial-in access to some or all intranet systems, some degree of authorized "leakage" may occur even in a securely managed intranet. Similarly, whenever an organization publishes legacy data through a Web interface, the result might be termed an extranet.

More rigorously, an extranet is defined not only by its use of existing internetworking structures, such as the Internet and intranets, to enable seamless interoperability across platforms but also by its use of a distributed-object architecture to enable real platform (both software and hardware) independence. The fact that distributed-object architectures make extranet applications much easier to implement also suggests that support for such architectures may be strongly recommended, if not explicitly required, for an extranet. In addition, security mechanisms are a necessary component of any extranet because extranet communication can take place over the Internet. Finally, extranet services are extensions of the services required for any internetwork. The following sections consider these components of extranets in detail:

- Distributed-object architecture

- Topology

- Security

- Applications

- Services

Distributed-Object Architecture

The development of LANs was accompanied by the development of new ways to use those networks. Network operating systems quickly became far more than the means of sharing printers. Using software redirection, the network itself could be abstracted out of the development process.

Software and data residing on a LAN server could be accessed as if it were directly connected to a system running a program needing those resources, as shown in Figure 2.1. It was still necessary for these systems to be running the same network operating system, and the software and data had to be stored in a format compatible with the requesting system, but standard interfaces for network redirection removed a significant burden from the backs of networked applications developers.

FIGURE 2.1

Providing standard LAN application interfaces helps simplify the task of LAN application development.

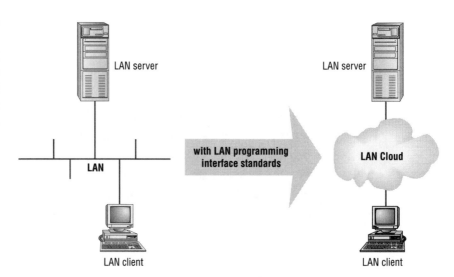

TCP/IP (see Appendix B) internetworking connected those networks and provided a method for simplifying not just local area network communications but also communications between dissimilar systems and between systems connected to dissimilar networks. Again, standard network interfaces and application programming interfaces simplified the task of software developers who were writing applications to be used across internetworks, as shown in Figure 2.2.

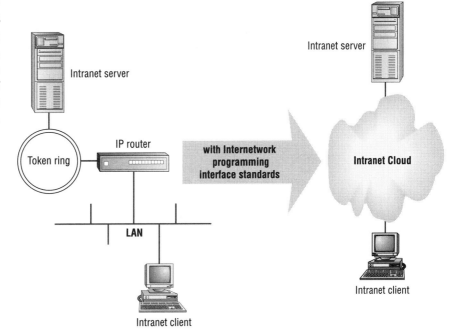

With the added advantage of using a distributed-object architecture
to further simplify the task of the application developer, extranets
build on these technologies. These architectures provide standard interfaces not just for accessing specific network resources but also for the
actual information stored within the network resources. Figure 2.3
demonstrates how the use of standard interfaces at the network, internetwork, and extranetwork levels removes much of the complexity
that surrounds network application development.

Distributed-object architectures such as CORBA and COM/DCOM
have grown out of efforts to improve the way software is created,
rather than directly out of any network-specific issues. The goal of
objects is to encourage the reuse of software (in the same way that
hardware components help manufacturers create new computer
designs from new processors, memory chips, disk drives, and other

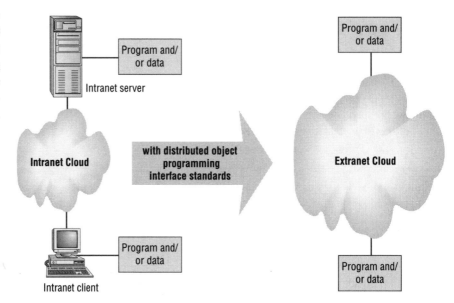

FIGURE 2.3

Providing standard
distributed-object
interfaces helps simplify
the task of distributed-
application development.

components), rather than to require software developers to re-create
all the housekeeping and data-plumbing chores every time they write a
new program. Some estimates suggest that as much as 80 percent of a
program's code deals with tasks having nothing to do with the actual
execution of program logic, as shown in Figure 2.4. This overhead
tends to raise the cost of entry beyond the means of cash-starved start-
ups; distributed objects can help control these costs.

What's So Special about Distributed Objects?

Distributed objects offer the following advantages over more traditional program development models:

- Distributed objects can be combined to interact with any other objects
  and thus create brand-new applications with minimal programming.
  Therefore, programmers can reuse software objects in many applications, rather than custom build software objects for individual
  applications.

- Distributed-object applications can interoperate with other object applications, making them independent of operating systems, hardware, or network platforms.

- Distributed objects can be used from any type of platform that can access the system hosting the object. For example, an object residing on a mainframe can be used, without modification, from a Macintosh, Windows PC, UNIX box, or any other type of platform.

- Distributed objects can work with existing systems (*legacy systems*) because objects can be built to interface with those systems. An object interface to a legacy system extends the usefulness of that system to a wider audience and eliminates the need to rebuild legacy applications to make use of distributed objects.

- Distributed objects are easy to manage. One object can be changed without recompiling the entire application, and updates can be propagated through the object architecture automatically.

FIGURE 2.4

Traditional networked application development requires significant housekeeping and plumbing development as well.

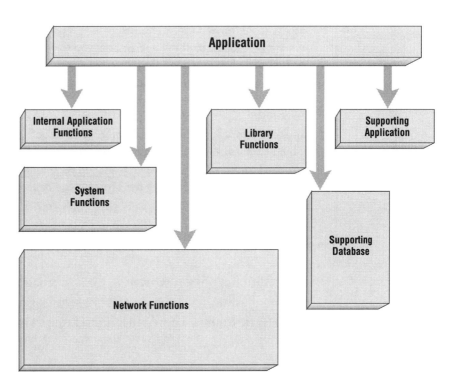

The distributed-object architectures allow software developers to create *objects* (sometimes referred to as *components*)—units of function and data—that can be accessed through standard interfaces. These objects differ from predecessor software technologies like function libraries and objects written for "traditional" object-oriented languages in several important ways. In particular, distributed objects use a standard interface that allows any software component that conforms to the same interface to access them. In contrast, functions that have been incorporated into a library can be accessed by any program written to use that library, but any changes or updates to functions require recompiling, which can limit reusability—especially for libraries shared by more than one application.

The Benefits of Reusing Objects

To illustrate, a login object would be a very useful type of software that could be reused for almost any networked application that needs to limit resource access to authorized users. This object would have a specific function: to submit a login request to the specified host and to return the result (acceptance or failure of password and user ID) to the object that invoked the login object. The client software, which might also be an object, would need to know only that the login object existed and could discover how the login function worked by querying it for its self-description. If the login object is modified to require an account number along with the other information, the client software would discover this change the next time the login object is called—without any need to reprogram the client. The end user would now be prompted for the additional information as if the program had been changed, and all other client programs that used the same login object would also appear to have been modified.

Traditional objects written in C++ or SmallTalk may offer added flexibility, but they impose a cost in terms or additional programming and less flexibility. These objects tend to be distributed as source code, which removes the financial incentive to create truly reusable code, and these objects are still tightly bound to their own language, which limits their reuse by programs written in other languages. And the problem of adding or modifying functions remains—even "small" changes requiring lots of recompiling.

Distributed objects, however, use interface standards that allow them to be used by any program. Upgrading or adding functionality to an object changes nothing in the calling programs, since they operate through a standard interface. Application logic can be contained within the object, so processing need not even happen on the system where the calling program is running. Objects contain data, but don't allow direct access to that data, so security can be more manageable.

Objects operate in a way reminiscent of other types of programming interfaces, like Winsock. The architecture defines a standard way to represent data and then requires developers to write the application software above to convert output to the standard representation, while the network software below is written to accept this standard representation and convert it appropriately for the network medium in use.

One more advantage that distributed objects provide for extranet-working is *scalability*. Companies successfully providing services over the Internet quickly find that success can be dangerous. The basic server technologies available in 1997 can still quickly overtake the capacity of the database and legacy systems to which they are linked. Distributed objects hold the potential for simplified load balancing as well as other technology that allows easy scaling from the hundreds to the hundreds of thousands (and more) simultaneous connections necessary for successful ongoing operations of mass-market applications.

In short, distributed objects are the ideal mechanism for creating an infrastructure that enables transparent and seamless exchange of information. This chapter introduces the important extranet object technologies that are available today; Chapter 3 focuses on how they work.

Extranet Topologies

Every network—even a wireless one—has a *topology* that describes the media over which data is transmitted. (For wireless, that medium is the electromagnetic ether.) Topologies become more important as networks are linked together, but the details tend to depend on which networks are being connected and how the service and reliability requirements are written.

Networking and internetworking topologies are reasonably well understood and well documented. Network topologies are described in terms of

- Cable

- Repeaters

- Bridges

- Servers

- Backplanes

Internetwork topologies submerge some of the finer-grained network topology details while focusing on

- Routers

- Gateways

- Networks

- Subnetworks

- Backbones

Extranets use other types of internetworks—intranets as well as the Internet—as their data transmission media, so extranet topologies are described in those terms. Complete descriptions of extranet topologies, however, may require

- Internetwork routers

- Firewalls

- Gateways

- Various protocols used to create virtual circuits and protocol tunnels across those internetworks

This chapter deals with the basic extranet topologies, while Chapter 4 explains how they work in more detail.

Security Facilities

Computers have long been most intimately entwined with the very lifeblood of business, with accounting, financial, and human resource applications usually among the very first to be automated. As long as those systems were implemented on freestanding mainframes isolated behind locked doors, physical security was sufficient to keep out the bad guys.

Networks, particularly internetworks, pose the single greatest security threat to business computing. Any networked workstation is a potential entry point for intruders and a potential vector for viruses. Even more alarming is the vulnerability of data flowing across networks: system passwords, proprietary corporate information, personal messages, product orders, payment information, and even digital products can all intercepted, falsified, or stolen unless measures are taken to protect them.

The extranet security facilities discussed below and in Chapter 5 address these issues:

- Protecting the communication channel

- Authorizing access to resources

- Authenticating requesting entities

- Assuring data provenance and reliability

WARNING Improperly implemented security mechanisms can lull users into a false sense of security and are far more dangerous than going without any security mechanism at all.

The security mechanisms relevant to extranets sometimes take on new attributes or methods of deployment, but networking professionals will be familiar with most of them.

Extranet security, like intranet security, is provided through the agency of barrier technologies that are intended to deny access to intruders. For example:

- Firewall gateway systems

- Token/password authentication systems

Extranet Applications

Any application requiring interaction across organizational boundaries is a potential extranet application. This definition obviously includes any function relating to commercial transactions—from gathering purchase information to after-sales support functions.

Extranet applications tend to be written as networked applications, meaning they are written as Java applets or ActiveX controls. These applications are more or less portable chunks of function, intended to be run from any network platform. In theory, extranet applications can be written on any platform with any programming environment, which is exactly what happens as interfaces are written to legacy applications.

An application becomes an extranet application based on the function it fulfills. If the application allows an outsider to get a peek at information stored inside an organizational intranet, it is an extranet application. For example, a television network could publish a schedule of available commercial advertising slots for access by advertising agencies, who buy these slots for their clients.

When the application allows a user to access information stored on someone else's intranet, and can integrate that information with information stored on the user's own intranet, that extranet application can become even more useful. It would be advantageous for the ad agency to take the information published by the television agency and combine it with internal scheduling and budget databases to help the media buyer meet client requirements.

Some applications will examine flows of data and notify users or other applications of specific events, for example, investment applications that monitor market tickers and notify investors when particular financial instruments change in price or when other events occur. Other applications may automatically generate orders for products as inventory levels fall or link consumers and sellers of time-sensitive products.

Still other extranet applications can be identified by their complexity. Perhaps the most important category will be the *digital commercial transaction*. These transactions, while ostensibly between only two parties (the buyer and the seller), can easily grow to include quite a few interested parties. The credit card issuing bank, the credit card association, the company providing transaction settlement, and the seller's merchant bank are all eager to join the transaction. And because some or all participants may be using digital certificates, certification authorities will have to take part to certify all the digital signatures.

Paradoxically, while the actual commercial transactions that can occur with extranets are becoming even more complex, they are becoming easier for end users to take advantage of. Extranets will help travelers book the exact combination of accommodations they desire (tickets, hotel, and rental car, for example) in a single step.

The ability to identify areas where customers or users are best served is key to the development of extranet applications. Organizations must decide whether they can improve a service by implementing it within an extranet framework.

One method for ensuring that a piece of data has not been tampered with, and that it originated from the person or entity whose name is on the data, is to use a digital signature. A *digital signature* is a string of data that is generated by the originator of the data using a special key known only to that entity. The recipient can use the originator's public key to certify the data as having arrived unchanged from the originator. A *certification authority* (CA) is a third-party entity, trusted by both the originator and the recipient, that stores public keys and will retrieve them on demand. These concepts are discussed at greater length in Chapter 5.

Extranet Services

Even the smallest networks require certain network services. Internetworks that use named systems, for example, must have a way to translate those names into network addresses. The Domain Name System (DNS) provides this service for the Internet and intranets.

While we describe networks as a means of linking computers and internetworks as a means of linking networks, we can describe extranets as a means of linking information and entities.

Networks link computers, internetworks link networks, and extranets link information and entities.

Within extranets, certain facilities must be offered as standard services, which include the following:

- Identifying entities through directories

- Maintaining trusted publication of public keys for verifying digital signatures

- Managing the distribution of cryptographic keys for access to secured systems and channels

Directory services are necessary to facilitate connections between humans (and other entities) across extranets. The most important standards are the ITU X.500 distributed directory standard and Lightweight Directory Access Protocol (LDAP), which provides easy access to X.500 directories for personal workstation users.

The bulk of data transmitted across the Internet, and most intranets, comes with no guarantees of accuracy or attribution. Unless it is digitally signed, you cannot be sure of the genesis of any information you retrieve over the Internet. With digital signatures, however, you can be sure that you receive information as the sender sent it. Extranets, particularly those facilitating commercial transactions or organizational proprietary information, rely on digital signatures, as well as encryption using public keys. Without public key cryptography, described in greater detail in Chapter 5, extranets are useless. The problem with digital signatures, though, is being able to reliably link a public key with its owner. The ITU X.509 standard provides a mechanism for creating directories of public keys and their owners, and extranets must implement and support this and other certification standards.

Finally, public key encryption is important because it assures users that their data has not been tampered with. However, for secure channels where data streams must be encrypted at the source and decrypted at the destination, public key methods require too much computing power to be effective. Key distribution is therefore an important service within the extranet, and various methods, notably Kerberos (discussed in Chapter 6), are in use.

Distributed-Object Architectures

Organizations have so many good reasons for building applications based on distributed-object architectures that it is hard to understand why they haven't already done so. The answer, of course, is that the organizational and global network infrastructure to support these architectures has only recently been set in place—and the software tools to support these architectures are only now starting to come to market.

Very simply, the driving force behind distributed objects is to stop being dogmatic about where data and business logic live, where processing actually takes place, and how the data and business logic are processed. As long as an object conforms to its architecture's specifications, other conforming objects can interact with it.

Once you've built an object, you can use it anywhere it is appropriate. For example, a catalog merchant who is interested in operating through a Web site must build pages that display her products. A low-tech approach would be to code separate HTML pages for each product or product category, manually entering product descriptions, prices, item number, and so forth. This methodology presents a major problem for catalogs of any size (even for catalogs whose contents rarely change). Every time a change occurs, the merchant must recode the HTML page.

An alternative approach is to use CGI to code an interface to the legacy database on which catalog information is stored. Although this solution is an improvement, it still requires a fair amount of effort to produce the CGI code and to make it work properly with the underlying database—and any substantive changes in the catalog will still require major changes in the Web pages.

With distributed objects, however, the story is different. The merchant simply creates an object that can query the legacy database and return the results; that object can replace most of the CGI code. Distributed objects enable the merchant to produce an online catalog that reflects the exact contents of the legacy database. Here's a summary of the action:

- For the opening page of the catalog, the developer can have the object query the database for a list of all catalog product categories.

- The results (a list of product categories) can then be passed first to the server and then to the Web client browsing the page.

- When the customer clicks on one of the categories, the object would be used again, this time to get product name, price, description, and image for all products in the chosen category.

So far, this procedure is relatively straightforward. With objects, though, ease of development and deployment of applications gets even better. Business logic can be added to objects, which makes them even more versatile. For example, another object might sense the preferred language of the customer and cause all information to be displayed in that language. A third object might determine pricing, checking the legacy database to see if the product is on sale and calculating the sale price.

Another real benefit of objects is that they are easy to use and can be relatively easy to build (or buy). The language in which the object is written is immaterial, as long as the object conforms to its architecture's standards. Finally, objects can be called by any other object, so they become easy-to-use programming tools.

The only question left is which object architecture to choose. As networking professionals used to say in the 1980s, the good thing about standards is that there are so many to choose from—and if you don't like the current selections, a new crop will appear next year. Right now, the object-architecture decision is shaping up as a coin flip between Microsoft's Distributed Common Object Model (DCOM) and the Object Management Group's Common Object Request Broker Architecture (CORBA).

A brief survey of these issues follows; Chapter 3 provides a more detailed introduction to distributed-object architectures.

Introducing Object Architectures

Producing a distributed-object architecture is quite complex, and this book provides only a basic introduction to the topic. However, because distributed objects are probably further from the daily experience of most networking professionals than the other topics in this book, I'm taking the opportunity here to introduce some of the acronyms and concepts that are discussed in greater detail in Chapter 3.

The two dominating forces in distributed objects are Microsoft and the Object Management Group (OMG). Microsoft has been working toward an object architecture through its adoption of OLE (see Note) and the Active-prefixed products, technologies, and standards (ActiveX, Active Desktop, etc.). Microsoft has developed the Common Object Model (COM) as the framework within which OLE operates; Distributed COM (DCOM) is an extension of that model to the distributed network environment.

OLE was originally used as an acronym for the expression *object linking and embedding*. However, the term *OLE* is no longer used as an acronym; it has achieved status as a word in its own right.

The OMG, an industry group with over 700 members, including almost everyone except Microsoft, has defined CORBA as a framework within which objects can interoperate. OpenDoc, usually paired with CORBA, is comparable to Microsoft's OLE. The Components Integration Lab (CI Lab, formed by Apple, IBM, Novell, Oracle, Taligent, SunSoft, WordPerfect, and Xerox) developed OpenDoc as a cross-platform component software architecture.

The two sets of standards are now vying for leadership in the distributed-object world, and the battle pits Microsoft against the rest of the industry. Gateways to facilitate interaction between the two sets of standards will help, but will not be able to provide the level of performance and interoperability that a monolithic implementation can achieve. Over the years, developers have had to choose between platforms: Macintosh versus PC, Windows versus OS/2, Unix versus Windows NT. With distributed objects, for now at least, developers will have another choice to make.

The Portable Desktop

Many knowledgeable workers routinely use three (or more) different computers: office workstations, home computers, and laptop or notebook computers for travel. The problem with this arrangement is synchronizing data and applications across multiple systems. Internetworking can help, but only when servers can remember the state of the desktop when accessed through different clients.

Objects enable end users to have access to the same *virtual desktop* from any system they are using—even a public network computer accessed at the airport. All the necessary documents and tools are stored on some server (or combination of servers) connected to the user's organizational network. Every time the user gets connected to that network, the same desktop appears. The state of the desktop is saved from one session to the next, which eliminates the need to copy files to take them to another computer. The files are always available on the virtual desktop and are accessible every time the desktop is accessed.

Both OpenDoc and OLE seamlessly create documents that contain data from multiple applications. These complex documents can be used to integrate data and applications spanning different systems as well as to allow users to access a single desktop from different platforms. The portability of the individual desktop and the interoperability of shared data/application components across systems are key attributes of extranet implementations.

ORBs and CORBA

The OMG was formed in 1989, well before using distributed objects across internetworks was a mainstream idea. Its goal was to create standards for designing reusable software objects that could interoperate with any other objects conforming to the standards. The underlying idea is that if software, like hardware, can be designed modularly, you can custom build large and reliable applications simply by plugging in the appropriate modules. As long as a hardware component plugs into a standard interface (and works), the way that component was designed or built is irrelevant. The same cannot be said of traditional software development, where each application had to be built from the ground up as a complete entity.

The CORBA specification enables software objects to interoperate with other independent objects through an object request broker (ORB) and standard interfaces. The ORB mediates between objects, acting as middleware to accept requests from objects and forwarding them to other objects—for example, taking requests from clients and forwarding those requests to a server to retrieve information from a legacy database.

By defining a CORBA, the OMG makes it possible for software components that support different vendor's ORBs to interoperate. CORBA defines certain basic services that all ORB environments must support. Because these services are defined as part of the environment, they no longer have to be implemented as part of the application.

CORBA services cover functions that allow objects to interoperate—for example, object naming, object events, transactions between objects, and object security.

The Object Request Broker (ORB)

Hardware manufacturers have a big advantage over software publishers. They don't have to recreate every computer from scratch, including all the infrastructure for moving data from one place to another. Hardware makers know that their hardware must be able to plug into standard interfaces over which they must send and receive data.

The ORB provides a basic interface over which objects can communicate with each other. It is a software version of the hardware bus. If an object submits a request to an ORB that is directed at another object, the ORB makes certain the request will be delivered to the destination object—and the response returned to the requesting object. The two objects might be on the same system, or they might be on different systems connected to the same network or internetwork.

The ORB allows a client object to call a piece of code running on another system (a server object), execute that code on whatever piece of data the calling object requires, and get the result back. The ORB permits this sequence of events to happen with only a minimal amount of coding on the client's system and no additional programming or configuration on the server's system—even if the two systems are running different operating systems and even if the server has no prior knowledge that the client will be calling that code.

The Internet Inter-ORB Protocol

Most of the CORBA (as well as COM) object-architecture specifications grew out of functions occurring either within a single system or across some nonspecific networks. The current version of CORBA (version 2.0) includes the Internet Inter-ORB Protocol (IIOP) that defines how ORBs can communicate using TCP/IP as a communications medium. Using IIOP, different CORBA-compliant ORBs can pass messages to each other.

IIOP supports some of the really interesting capabilities of CORBA, allowing objects to interoperate across TCP/IP networks—and as a result, across virtually any software, hardware, or network boundaries. In effect, IIOP acts as an Internet application, using the TCP/IP network as a medium for linking objects by defining a protocol for passing object requests and responses over TCP/IP internetworks.

In effect, the intranet, Internet, or extranet (or any TCP/IP network) becomes an intermediary through which ORBs (themselves intermediaries between clients and servers) can pass requests and responses.

A Web server might support IIOP and use it to pass requests from an object on the Web server to objects on other servers supporting CORBA. The object on the server might accept information requests from end users, submit them to databases on other servers, and then return the results. The browser client accesses the Web server through standard HTML, CGI, or JavaScript pages; and the Web server does all the IIOP work. In this case the Web server and the database servers interoperate with IIOP, while the browser simply supplies information.

Another scenario plays out when the browser is equipped with IIOP support. In this case, as with Netscape Communicator, the browser supports IIOP directly. For example, a Java applet could generate object requests directly and thus completely bypass the Web server when accessing databases on servers that support CORBA.

OLE, ActiveX, COM, and DCOM

Microsoft has developed its own set of specifications for distributed objects. Starting with OLE, which at first simply supported the creation of compound documents, Microsoft developed the COM to specify the way software components fit together in a single system. OLE, and later ActiveX, came to specify the way application functions could be implemented as components so that those functions could be called from whatever software was being used at the time to manipulate the data in question. In other words, rather than run a complete spreadsheet program to display or edit tabular data in a word processing document, a subset of spreadsheet functionality can be implemented as an ActiveX control and used to perform those more limited functions. DCOM developed to allow the use of components across system boundaries, across networks using remote procedure calls (RPCs).

Rather than joining the open-standards effort to develop CORBA, Microsoft has developed its own distributed-object architecture. This project represents a significant opportunity for Microsoft, probably the only company with sufficient resources, presence, and clout to create such an architecture on its own, to dominate the market. Chapter 3 includes a more detailed description of Microsoft's standards, as well as a discussion of how, and on what terms, COM and CORBA can coexist.

Extranet Topologies

Most extranets are created with existing intranets, the Internet, and standard internetworking tools. Rather than attempt to strictly categorize extranet topologies, it is wiser to identify the different topological approaches used to create extranets. Two basic approaches, the private extranet and the public extranet, are sometimes joined through the agency of the virtual private network (VPN).

Private Extranets

The private extranet operates under the same principles as the private intranet: restricting access to the network protects data transmitted across the network and stored on systems connected to the network. The difference is that the private intranet is a closed network within a single organization, and the private extranet is a closed network connecting all or part of two or more organizations.

Internetworks with No Trespassing

Strictly speaking, a private extranet, like a closed intranet, will have no points of access for outsiders. The only links will be those connecting member intranets, generally through a backbone network to carry extranet traffic between participants. The objective, of course, is to protect the data traveling across and the systems connected to the extranet from outside tampering.

At one end of the spectrum are extranets that simply link two organizational intranets. If neither intranet has any Internet connectivity (e.g., firewall gateways or Internet routers), creating the extranet may require no more than a single router linking the two intranets.

The other end of the spectrum begins to look very much like the Internet itself. Arguably, the Internet 2 initiative by educational institutions, the government, and industry to reinvent the Internet in parallel could look like a private extranet with many member organizations.

The Internet 2 initiative began in 1996 as a project to bring high-speed, high-availability internetworking to universities and other research organizations. In effect, its purpose is to reinvent the Internet. The initiative is discussed in greater detail in Chapter 4.

Keeping Out Intruders

Strictly private extranets, like their intranet counterparts, will have no outlet to external networks. However, like intranets, extranets cannot really function in total isolation, so firewalls and gateways are permissable to allow communication with outsiders through e-mail and newsgroups and to permit publication of organizational Web sites.

Firewall systems, an important part of any internetwork topology, and other extranet security mechanisms are discussed at greater length in Chapter 5.

Costs and Benefits

Private extranets can cost a lot of money, particularly if they link many organizational intranets. Private extranets require building a private backbone, with all the headaches of dealing with bandwidth, availability, and other performance issues. They also require investing in routing technologies to link all parties together. Firewall systems and gateways to external networks like the Internet, if desired, add even more expense. You can hire a networking service provider to build the backbone infrastructure, which will likely cut costs in the long run, or you can try to build it yourself, but in either case a private backbone is expensive.

Private extranets provide an overwhelming benefit to security-conscious organizations—they bar outside intruders. Whether this protection mechanism can ensure complete security is debatable, particularly because insiders, rather than intruders, commit most computer crimes. However, the isolation of a private extranet may be important for some applications, particularly for defense industries, government agencies, and the military.

Another compelling reason to build a private extranet is to guarantee network availability, bandwidth, and performance. Trying to run an extranet over the Internet makes sense for far-flung extranets reaching users connected to many different networks, but those users must cope with the same issues of variable performance that all Internet users face. A private extranet gives the participants greater control over the quality of the links and performance issues like the number of simultaneous users that can be supported.

Public Access Extranets

As the number of potential buyers and sellers with links to the Internet continues to grow, the potential benefit of deploying extranets across the Internet also grows. As noted earlier, many companies have been using their Web servers to offer the kind of services we are coming to expect from extranets. As distributed objects proliferate to the desktop and to the typical Internet server, true extranet services will also proliferate.

Companies choosing to build public access, or open, extranets tend to be in businesses that depend on providing many instances of an information product or of a service to their many customers. The ability to distribute a product or service quickly and cheaply is crucial to keeping costs down; automating the process with objects can help reduce the losses associated with billing problems, accounts falling through the cracks, and "shrinkage."

An open extranet is simply a projection of part of an organization's intranet into the Internet—alternatively, it might be viewed as opening up part of an organizations's intranet to let the Internet come inside the firewall.

Expanded Intranet/Internet Access

The combination of objects, firewalls, and encrypted channels (discussed below) allows an organization to safely project outside the organizational intranet a significant subset of its legacy and operational systems. Adding an extra layer of abstraction between applications and the underlying information systems can protect the underlying systems from unauthorized access or modification. By requiring all extranet applications to operate within the object architectures, firewall systems can allow object requests and request fulfillment to flow across the intranet/Internet border while protecting organizational systems inside the intranet.

Opening parts of an intranet and including them in a public extranet makes sense for applications that benefit from wide and open distribution. One method is to simply open up the intranet to the outside world—not usually a good choice. A more attractive option is to provide the public services through servers located outside the firewall and allow those servers to use objects inside the firewall to access legacy data.

Controlled Intranet/Internet Access

Another approach to opening up an extranet is to control *who* has access to it. The simplest way to do this is to put access controls on the system using password and user IDs (or some other authentication method, as discussed in Chapter 5). Many limited-access Web sites, whether they are limited to paying customers, members of a particular group, or simply users who have gone to the trouble of registering their names and contact information, use this approach.

The latest round of Web client and server upgrades will see increasing support for client-side certificates, offering a more sophisticated approach to limiting access to extranets. Previously, only servers made available their public key certificate so that client software could use it for encrypted key exchanges and digital signatures. With client certificates, authentication between consumers and merchants can be a two-way street: merchants will be able to certify themselves to their customers, and customers will be able to certify themselves to the merchant. Consequently, you can charge something to your account with a merchant that you have already done business with and exchanged a digital signature: the merchant certifies your signature and can extract your account information (like billing name and shipping address) from his or her database.

Keeping Out Intruders

Even when access controls are used, the public extranet calls for extra vigilance over the integrity of corporate information resources. Legacy information may be made available through intermediary systems using distributed objects or with various traditional and nontraditional access controls. In any case, firewalls will still be required to protect legacy systems not related to the extranet as well as to keep employees out of trouble on the Internet by blocking access to recreational Web sites, for example (and to protect personal workstations from intruders too).

Costs and Benefits

Open extranets need not be significantly more dangerous than closed ones, particularly if the firewalls are carefully engineered and constantly monitored, the extranet infrastructure is well designed, and the extranet applications and supporting objects are securely implemented. The cost for these components, therefore, shouldn't be very different from their cost in private extranets. Security should certainly not be given short shrift, however, and will almost certainly add some expenses to the cost of deployment.

The cost of building and maintaining a data communications network, however, is usually matched by the savings you incur by using public, rather than private, networks. The high degree of redundancy in the Internet should also cause overall network reliability to be higher in the event that any single link goes down—but other factors, like overall Internet congestion, routers with more traffic than they can handle, and other problems at intermediary Internet service providers will also affect the overall reliability and availability. A further benefit of the open extranet is that it is, in fact, open. The more people who can connect, the more useful the extranet can be.

Virtual Private Network Extranets

When an organization desires to build a private network without rebuilding its Internet infrastructure, one approach is the virtual private network (VPN). The VPN combines the flexibility, reliability, and economy of the Internet with the security of a private extranet. By building special systems capable of tunneling encrypted channels across the Internet, you can keep private information private while you are using public networks.

Using the Internet as a Private Backbone

The Internet functions much like the publicly switched telephone network (PSTN). And as more and more organizations and individuals get connected, it becomes more important for everyone else to get connected. However, the problem with using an open, public network like the Internet for transmitting your organization's proprietary information is that it *is* an open and public network with very few ways in which you can control how your data flows across it.

The Internet does not tell you when or whether your data has been scanned as it passes through intermediate networks.

You have no way of knowing whether your "private" Internet communication has passed through a network or router controlled by a business competitor.

In short, communicating over the Internet provides the same degree of security as talking business in any other public place. Most of the time, no one else is listening, but prudence dictates that you shouldn't shout out private information in public places. The problem is that the most crowded places make the best markets.

To get around this problem, the underlying protocols of the Internet allow the *tunneling* (see following sidebar) of data streams within other data streams. Encrypting a data stream and then transmitting it from one system to another across the Internet in an IP tunnel allows individuals to communicate securely. This method also allows you to establish a secure link between two or more networks by using the Internet as a virtual private backbone to carry encrypted traffic among those networks. The traffic itself is an encrypted data stream, which, when decrypted, can be forwarded to the intended networks and systems.

Network Tunneling

Network tunneling is a method of treating data transmitted between two hosts, including all the protocol headers, as an ordinary stream of data to be carried between two other intermediary hosts. Virtual private networking relies on tunneling to encrypt a transmission stream between two hosts and treating that encrypted data as if it were just some data to be sent from one VPN gateway, over the Internet, to another VPN gateway. An originating host sends data in the clear to the originating VPN gateway, which encrypts the data and encapsulates it within the IP datagrams it sends to the receiving VPN gateway. The receiving VPN gateway strips off the IP headers, decrypts the encrypted data, and sends it off to the receiving host. Tunneling is discussed at greater length in Chapter 5.

Keeping Out Intruders

Security for VPNs happens through the proper deployment of firewalls, encrypting routers, and client and server software supporting encrypted channels. VPNs go beyond the transport layer's secure channels provided by Secure Socket Layer (SSL). Encrypting at a lower network layer means that more of the communication is obscured from view. The less a potential eavesdropper can know about an encrypted data stream, the harder it is for that eavesdropper to break the encryption. Another benefit of using a VPN is that it securely supports any type of TCP/IP application, so end users can use Web services as well as services like FTP and Telnet that are not always enabled to use SSL.

Secure Socket Layer (SSL) is a protocol first defined by Netscape to allow Web browsers and servers to establish an encrypted data stream. Widely implemented on Web browsers and servers, SSL can also be incorporated into other types of Internet applications to secure a communication channel.

Costs and Benefits

Privacy is expensive, whether you are buying real estate or data communications. If you use encryption to keep your information private, you have to pay not only for the processing power to do the encryption but also for the encryption technology and software. Because public key encryption is computationally intensive and internetwork routing depends on processor power for acceptable performance, combining the two functions can require some very hefty hardware.

Another expense is software. Most of the adequately tested and proven encryption technologies require licenses from their patent holders as well as very careful implementations by cryptographic professionals to prevent the introduction of security holes. Finally, VPNs, like any product that incorporates strong cryptographic tools, may be strictly controlled by many governments. For example, the United States has to date restricted export of any general use encryption software using strong cryptography and keys longer than 40 bits. Therefore, implementing an international VPN may be difficult or impossible to do with software created in the United States, although using products originating from other countries and importing them into the United States may be legal.

The costs of implementing a secure VPN can easily be offset by its greatest benefit—an almost instantly extensible backbone that can carry sensitive information at a much lower cost in money and time than would otherwise be possible. VPNs can be the simplest way to link physically separated intranets and may be the most effective way to provide access to mobile users.

A VPN may look like an extranet from a topological view, but without distributed objects, it remains an extension of the intranet.

Security Facilities

Providing security can sometimes attract unwelcome attention. When two men with big guns jump out of an armored car carrying a big, bulging bag, it's a safe bet that the bag's contents are worth a pot of money. (Some people are more comfortable transporting their valuables in a greasy brown paper bag. They assume the crooks would rather try for what the armed guards are carrying than what more than likely will turn out to be a tuna sandwich.)

Nevertheless, just as large banks must have armed guards and armored trucks for their currency pickups and deliveries, so too must large organizations maintain a security infrastructure to protect their information assets from theft and vandalism.

Three pieces of the security puzzle that have been mentioned already (and that will be discussed in greater detail in Chapter 5) are firewall systems, secured access to systems, and the use of encrypted channels.

Firewall Technologies

In general parlance, a *firewall* is a barrier: something to keep the bad stuff out and the good stuff in. Internet firewalls are meant to keep intruders outside the organizational internetwork; they also keep organizational users from getting into "forbidden" territories. Most firewalls use similar tactics to perform these functions; they may differ, however, in the implementation.

The accepted firewall philosophy is to forbid anything that is not explicitly permitted. In theory, strict firewalls mean that hackers cannot enter a network through back doors that the person building and configuring the firewall has not anticipated. This strictness is exemplified by the four basic tools that firewall designers use to deny access that is not otherwise explicitly allowed:

- IP filtering

- Proxy servers

- Hardened operating systems

- Internetwork isolating strategies

IP Filtering

The most obvious way to restrict access to hosts, networks, and services is by using the protocols themselves. An IP filter is simply a list of host and network addresses to and from which traffic is permitted (or denied). Port numbers may also be included in the filter, indicating "legal" network applications. The IP filtering system checks the headers of every packet that passes in or out of the network against this filter and forwards only those that are explicitly permitted.

IP filtering is often built into other server products and provides some protection against intruders. However, these filters are not sufficient by themselves to prevent unwanted intrusions, particularly when they are built into servers.

IP filters that permit enough traffic in and out to do anything real on the Internet are very complicated to create, hard to maintain, and tricky to edit.

Intruders can defeat IP filters fairly easily in a number of different ways, though IP filtering is still a standard feature of almost every firewall product on the market. IP filters can block incoming as well as outgoing packets, so they are often used to keep employees out of non-work-related Web sites or network applications.

Proxy Servers

A more effective means of preventing unauthorized access is the use of proxy servers. Virtually all IP applications communicate in two directions: Requests for information go from the client to the server, and fulfillment of those requests goes from the server to the client. These links can sometimes be subverted for nefarious ends, a problem that proxy servers are meant to solve. Instead of allowing direct access to external services through standard client programs, users within an organization use special versions of the client that can communicate only with the proxy server. The proxy acts on behalf of those internal clients when communicating with servers outside the organizational internetwork. By acting as an intermediary, the proxy server can prevent unauthorized access and attacks.

Hardened Operating Systems

One way to limit access to an internetwork is by denying attackers any foothold on the systems through which the network is accessed. Attackers often search visible systems for network programs with known security holes and then attempt to exploit those holes to gain control over the system or as a stepping stone to attack other systems. The more programs you have on such a system, the more likely that one of them may have a bug or a backdoor through which an attacker can sneak in. Although many firewall products are available as software installed on top of standard shrink-wrapped operating systems, others include their own "hardened" operating systems. These products are often rewritten versions of standard operating systems with extraneous or unnecessary programs removed.

Internetwork Isolating Strategies

Internetworks are connected through routers. The router has two or more network interfaces, and it forwards packets from those interfaces when appropriate. However, a router that has been compromised may mean that every network to which it is connected has been compromised, too. To avoid this problem, firewall designers have produced a number of strategies for isolating the protected internetworks.

One approach is to connect the protected internetwork to a firewall network on which the firewall system is installed. The firewall, in turn, is linked to a router that links an unprotected network to the Internet. (Further refinements are discussed in Chapter 5.)

Another strategy is to use the firewall system as a single point of contact for the organization's Internet presence. A server sitting outside the firewall handles all inbound requests, and that single host mediates all outbound communication. This approach hides the network structure of the internal network, including host names, IP addresses, and services offered internally.

Finally, organizations not using IP as their networking protocol may opt for a protocol gateway, rather than a real firewall. These gateways also act as the single point of contact for the organization's Internet presence but convert IP to IPX (the most common protocol—used in Novell NetWare and other proprietary network operating systems) as data comes in to the organization and convert IPX to IP as data flows out.

These gateways have an added attribute, which may or may not be considered a desirable feature. Servers on the inside cannot offer Internet services because the internal hosts cannot be directly pointed to with their own IP address. For organizations that want to make sure none of their internal resources are available directly through the Internet, this attribute is a positive feature. For organizations that might at some time want to host an Internet service internally, this attribute is a bug.

Secured Access

Finding ways to keep all unauthorized people out without denying access to all authorized people is an age-old problem, probably as old as the caveman. The three solutions to this problem are to let someone in based on the following:

- Something they know (a password, for example)

- Something they have (a backstage pass, for example)

- Something they are (a fingerprint, for example)

Passwords have always been a mainstay of computer security, but they are not enough. Increasingly, tokens that generate pseudorandom numbers in synchronization with programs running on access control systems—sometimes called *one-time password systems*—are used, particularly for controlling access to firewalls. Biometric access controls, based on fingerprints, voiceprints, and retinal scans, are still rare but will probably become more popular because they are easy to use. You don't have to remember to carry your card-key, you don't have to remember a password—all you must do is display your hand (or eyes, or voice).

Secured Channels

Restricting access to information, particularly if it is to flow across a public network like the Internet, does not afford adequate protection. The way that data flows across IP internetworks makes it fairly simple to intercept a data stream and interpret it. The best way to demonstrate this concept is with a protocol analyzer: Hook up to a LAN and turn on the protocol analyzer; then browse through the results. You can strip off the link layer headers of each chunk of data flowing across the LAN to expose Internet layer headers, strip off Internet layer headers to expose transport layer headers, and remove transport layer headers to show application headers, the last veil. Shedding the final layer reveals the actual data. Application data includes such tasty tidbits as terminal session and file transfer session passwords, user IDs, text of e-mail messages, and anything else that gets transmitted in the clear—which, over the Internet, means just about everything by default.

Application Layer Encryption

Some protocols attempt to encrypt information at the application level. In other words, the application protocol specifies how application data is to be protected, and the application software does the encryption. Security is one of the services that early TCP/IP researchers and developers thought should be performed higher up the network protocol stack, but so far this approach has not been very popular. The problem is that plaintext attacks are easier when more is known about the communications channel.

A *plaintext attack* against encrypted data can be used when the attacker knows (or can correclty guess) the unencrypted contents (or plaintext) of part of the encrypted data.

When application layer encryption is used, eavesdroppers can, usually correctly, assume that the first exchange between client and server will be an exchange of user ID, password, or key information. Knowing, for example, the user ID that is being sent enables criminals to chip away at the security of the protocol.

Also important are the protocols that will use encryption (as well as other cryptographic tools) at the application layer to support Internet commerce, allowing credit card and digital cash transactions. Applications like those from CyberCash and DigiCash, used for transactions and digital cash, respectively, use encryption at the application layer. The Secure Electronic Transaction (SET) protocol will also make use of application layer encryption.

Another important protocol at the application layer is Secure MIME (S/MIME), which is useful for encapsulating information securely in a standard format accessible through a variety of applications. Some other application layer encryption protocols that come to mind are Secure HTTP (a standard that was eclipsed by SSL and the various e-mail privacy tools, including Pretty Good Privacy [PGP], which is also used in many other applications, and Privacy Enhanced Mail [PEM]).

Using application layer encryption does not rule out the use of encryption at lower layers, and in fact, some applications may call for the use of encryption at two or more protocol layers for extra security.

Transport Layer Encryption

Application protocols package information to be sent between processes by the transport layer protocols. Transport layer protocols package application layer data, often as data streams, and send it to its destination. Consequently, the transport layer is a logical place to encrypt data before sending it onto a public network, and SSL performs this job.

Even though it was first introduced for use with Web browsers and servers, SSL can be adapted for any TCP/IP application. Operating just below the application, SSL can be used to obscure many of the details of the application data. Operating at the transport layer means that SSL can take a stream of application data and produce a stream of encrypted data for transmission across an internetwork.

Encryption at the transport layer, however, still reveals some potentially useful data to criminals. The transport and internetwork protocol headers include the internetwork address of the sending and receiving hosts; the headers also provide the information to identify individual communicating processes on the two communicating hosts.

Internetwork Layer Encryption

The idea of encrypting data at the Internet layer of the protocol stack has long been resisted by purists who believe that the only task appropriate at that level is the movement of datagrams from one host to another. The number of people clinging to that viewpoint is dwindling, particularly as the IPv6 upgrade implementation of IP level security is being embraced. Part of the reluctance to encrypt at the Internet layer has been that systems must operate efficiently there, to avoid losing too much data at peak periods. However, the advantages of IP-level encryption can be significant. The most important advantage is that it allows you to create VPNs as long as you can pair up routers (to connect separated intranets) to encrypt and decrypt IP datagrams.

Extranet Applications

Any application that runs across an internetwork and integrates information from sources that cross organizational boundaries can be considered an extranet application. Simply extending an intranet physically is not enough to create an extranet, though it does provide the infrastructre upon which extranet applications can run. This section discusses the context in which extranet applications operate and how they are implemented; much more will be said about these applications in Chapter 7.

The Networked Desktop

Currently, the typical desktop system includes some or all of the following connectivity tools and applications:

- Access to local area network resources

- Access to organizational intranets

- Access to the Internet

- GUI clients for legacy data and systems

- Organizational e-mail services

- Internet e-mail service

- Private information services

- "Push" broadcast services

Sorting through the information entering the desktop from all these sources (and more) and keeping on top of all the important items without losing track of less critical information is becoming increasingly difficult. The problem is that we have too many sources of information and too few applications capable of consolidating the deluge of data in a single place.

During 1997 Netscape and Microsoft are releasing products that will be able to consolidate information from all connected sources on the desktop. Distributed-object components are also making an appearance. IBM and other vendors are introducing significant component tools for Internet commerce, both as Java Beans and as ActiveX controls. Applications built from either Java or ActiveX will almost certainly be stunningly useful, as they can integrate disparate information and facilitate complex transactions.

For now, we can expect two basic sets of standards for distributed computing: one from Microsoft and one from the rest of the industry. Having only one standard, particularly at this early stage, would probably be a less-positive development. Competition should be a healthy process for the consumer of the technology, at least in the long run, but that is cold comfort for anyone who chooses the wrong standard. The possibility exists that the two competing models will ultimately converge and grow together into a single set of standards or that both models will share the market and provide reasonable mechanisms for interoperability.

What Makes an Extranet Application

Typical and recognizable extranet applications will be those that could not have been implemented using an intranet or the Internet alone. They faciliate relationships across organizational boundaries, and they do so by permitting access to resources across organizational boundaries. They also tend to be based upon some distributed-object model. For examples, see the case studies describing actual extranets in Chapter 7.

If an organization reengineered the way e-mail was delivered, moving from isolated intranets linked through e-mail gateways to an extranet topology using centralized e-mail services, one might argue that the result is not a real extranet application.

Whether an application is written as an ActiveX control or as a Java applet (or implemented using some other developmental framework) is less important than how the application functions and how it fosters interaction with other applications, users, organizations, and audiences.

Extranet Services

As a TCP/IP internetwork, an extranet requires certain basic services to operate. Just as the DNS translates human-accessible host names to network addresses, additional services built on top of standard TCP/IP services are necessary within extranets to help identify entities. Essentially, these services fall into three categories: directory services, key management, and certification.

- **Directory services** allow users, entities, or objects to locate other users, entities, or objects across the extranet.

- **Key management services** allow interacting entities to exchange cryptographic keys across the extranet, use those keys securely, and administer those keys securely.

- **Certification services** allow entities to certify the identity of other entities they are interacting with.

Directory Services

The millions of people with e-mail addresses often have trouble finding each other simply because no centralized repository for e-mail addresses exists, at least, not yet. Even though every e-mail system has its own method of providing directory services, without a universal standard for compiling, storing, and retrieving directory information, users will find it difficult to get to that data.

E-mail is not the only application that depends on directory services. For example, distributed objects in extranets need directory services so they can locate resources (in the form of other objects) without knowing exactly where they are. Directory services simply map information about objects to the objects. An e-mail directory maps an e-mail address to a person's name; a network directory service maps resource location information to the resource name.

There is no shortage of directory services, particularly if you don't mind tying yourself to a single vendor's view of the world. Among the choices are the Windows NT directory service, Sun's Network Information Service (NIS+), and Novell's Novell Directory Service (NDS).

The problem with proprietary solutions, however, is that they tend to favor the owner of the standard, thus alienating providers of alternative products. The solution is to use a vendor-neutral standard. The X.500 directory services standard, developed by the CCITT (now ITU) in 1988, provides a set of standard procedures and protocols for network and database application directory services. X.500 defines how directory systems can share information and how systems can use other systems to discover new directory information.

Retrieving information from distributed directories requires a set of procedures, or a protocol, to define how that information is to be retrieved. A protocol called Lightweight Directory Access Protocol (LDAP) provides this type of access to X.500 directories and is increasingly being implemented as part of e-mail clients.

Unification and simplification of directory services are key to developing extranets, both as a means to simplify access to information about people for other people and as a means to simplify access to information about distributed objects for other distributed objects.

Key Management and Certification Authorities

Internet applications from digital commerce to e-mail encryption to encrypted channels require keys—increasingly public keys from a public key pairing. (Public key cryptography is discussed in Chapter 5.)

Extranets currently rely heavily on cryptography. Whether to secure data channels traversing the Internet or to protect proprietary information or to complete commercial transactions, public key and secret key encryption and digital signatures are vital mechanisms in the extranet infrastructure. With this increased reliance on public and private keys, even individual users need additional services to deal with all the different keys. Extranets require mechanisms for securely exchanging secret keys between two entities on the same network, as well as for distributing and reliably ascertaining the validity of public keys.

A public key infrastructure (PKI) is necessary to deliver public keys to distributed users and to systems so that all parties are satisfied that the distribution can be trusted. Another ITU standard, X.509, defines the format in which public key data is to be expressed as well as a procedure for distributing such data using certificates that contain the digital signatures of trusted certification authorities (CAs).

Certification authorities are important because key management involves more than just obtaining keys. For example, keys are sometimes revoked, and the entities using the keys need to know when that happens. Extranets must support these services because they support many of the interorganizational activities that extranet applications provide.

CHAPTER

3

The Extranet Object Architecture

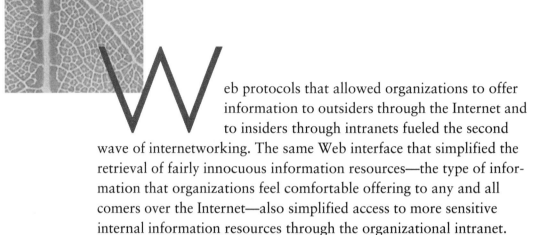

eb protocols that allowed organizations to offer information to outsiders through the Internet and to insiders through intranets fueled the second wave of internetworking. The same Web interface that simplified the retrieval of fairly innocuous information resources—the type of information that organizations feel comfortable offering to any and all comers over the Internet—also simplified access to more sensitive internal information resources through the organizational intranet.

However, Web designers found themselves working very hard to implement two functions:

- The ability to provide internal information selectively to certain individuals but deny it to others

- The ability to allow users to generate transactions over the Web medium

Web designers needed to allow outsiders to interact securely and reliably with internal resources through the World Wide Web. Designers have found ways (albeit with a certain amount of difficulty) to implement these features within the constraints of the basic Web protocols. However, solutions that work for dozens, hundreds, or even thousands of end users often break down with relatively small increases in simultaneous user loads.

A new set of protocols that simplify the task of allowing outsiders to interact with organizational resources securely and reliably is now enabling the third wave of internetworking, or the extranet. Deploying solutions using objects, components, and a distributed computing architecture permits a whole new world of complex interactions for the extranet. As of mid-1997 the extranet implementer needs to deal with two groups of standards: those originally offered by Microsoft and those originally championed by the Open Management Group. The market, consisting of vendors who must sell extranet-related software, is still attempting to embrace both Microsoft's ActiveX and Distributed Common Object Model (DCOM) and the OMG's Common Object Request Broker Architecture (CORBA).

This chapter introduces the concepts behind distributed objects and explains why objects can be useful. It also introduces the major object architectures now available for deploying extranet applications.

Distributed Objects and Extranets

Microsoft offers a full range of tools and support of the Active Platform throughout its product offerings, making it very easy for developers to create and for content providers to host Active Platform–enabled content. These products have much to offer in terms of flexibility and potential for building interesting and useful applications; however, they have been developed specifically to help Microsoft sell software. Even though Microsoft has offered to open up some of these specifications to standards bodies, it still retains enough control over them to make many competitors uncomfortable. Microsoft's Active Platform provides significant advantages for usability and ease of development of applications. However, the platform is generally more fully featured at the desktop end and becomes somewhat less impressive as one moves down through the architecture to the distributed-object model that it uses. The great strength of Microsoft's Active Platform is the ease with which designers can create and deploy very impressive applications.

The alternative, using open protocols from the OMG, can be more difficult for the developer but can also offer greater flexibility at the heart of the distributed-object architecture. Compared with DCOM, CORBA was developed over a longer period, with input from more sources. However, fewer tools are available to simplify design and development of CORBA-based applications, which means that developers must do more hand coding. An application layer protocol, the Internet Inter-ORB Protocol (IIOP), is part of CORBA and is a mechanism by which clients can easily access data and resources through a browser, independent of the details of the actual resource implementation. Even though it is now a part of every Netscape browser, IIOP is still less widely deployed than the Active Platform now available on virtually every personal computer running Microsoft's Windows operating systems.

Why Use Distributed Objects?

The arguments for using distributed objects are so compelling; the more puzzling question is why distributed objects haven't been used all along. The computer hardware world has long accepted the idea of using modular components that fit standard interfaces, but this concept is only now gaining widespread acceptance in the software market. The reason for the lag in the software industry probably has much to do with the relatively low capital cost of software fabrication. (Unlike hardware manufacturers, software vendors don't have to build chip-fabrication plants or processes to produce their goods.) Without widely accepted standards, software vendors have little reason to use someone else's interface standards.

However, the cost of building software capable of exploiting the latest high-performance computers and networks is rapidly rising. Network-aware applications require significant "plumbing" software to handle common tasks like database queries, file manipulation, and transactions. Building support for these tasks for each network application is costly—some estimates put the plumbing portion of these applications at between 40 and 60 percent of the cost of developing the application. Building network awareness from scratch for each application also opens the door to an entire set of possible security risks and application bugs. Building and maintaining dozens or hundreds of versions of what should be relatively standard code is much more difficult than building one or two sets of secure, reliable, and robust network application plumbing.

Interoperability

Objects are aptly named, although they could just as easily be called "things" or "units" or anything else similarly neutral. However, more important than the actual guts of the object (which is some kind of compiled or executable code) is how the object behaves through its interface. Neither the system on which the object resides nor the language in which the object is programmed are important to applications using the object. System and language independence are possible because the behavior of all objects must conform with their underlying protocols and architecture.

An Interface Definition Language (IDL) defines an object's interface, which includes information such as what the object is, what it does, and how to get it to do what it does. An object repository makes this information available, so external processes that need to access the object can simply query the repository to find out how the object works. For example, a database query object might return the results of a database query as shown in Figure 3.1.

This explanation is an oversimplification, of course. The object model must make available a way for objects to advertise their interfaces and must also support a wide variety of services pertaining to functions such as security, name binding, life cycle management (creating, moving, copying, and removing objects), event management (notification of when "things" happen with other objects), and transactions (robust and reliable interactions between objects that are rolled back when not properly completed). A fairly simple object bus with

FIGURE 3.1

An object accepts information from outside and can return results from inside.

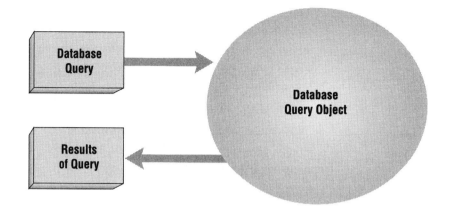

standard inputs and outputs handles all this functionality. As shown in Figure 3.2, a client application on a host can generate a request to a server through the distributed-object architecture. Neither side needs to know the specifics of the other side's implementation.

FIGURE 3.2

Distributed objects allow disparate hosts to interoperate as long as they all support the same architecture.

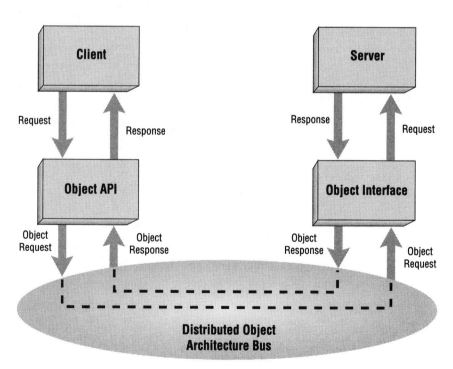

An object application programming interface (API) interprets the client request; that is, the object API translates the client request into a standard format for use within the distributed-object architecture and passes the translated request through the object architecture to the server's object interface. The server object interface accepts the request, which is processed inside the server object, and the object generates a response.

Just as internetworking protocols enhance interoperability by enabling any two systems that support the same set of protocols to interoperate, distributed-object architectures provide the same type of lingua franca support to connected systems. The client illustrated in Figure 3.2 could have been developed in C++ on a UNIX workstation, in Visual Basic on a Wintel PC, or in COBOL on a Unisys mainframe. As long as the client is written to the object API, it can use other resources that have also been adapted to the same object architecture.

For the extranet, therefore, the object architecture can simplify and streamline access to existing legacy databases. Extranet applications can be built by interfacing the existing legacy systems to the object architecture of choice, thereby making the information available to anyone running client software that conforms to the chosen object architecture. Security is handled within the object architecture, using standards-based authentication and encryption mechanisms (see Chapter 5). Interoperability within the object architecture is assured, freeing the extranet developer from concerns about writing applications to specific platforms and handling security, reliability, and robustness issues.

Software Reusability

Using standard interfaces for hardware has been a tremendous boon to manufacturers of hardware devices. Being able to design, build, and sell a hard drive, internal modem, or video controller, confident in the expectation that it will fit perfectly on the system board of any personal computer, is a huge benefit to vendor and consumer alike: standardization lowers the cost of production. Standardization also means that vendors can cut their costs even further by reusing those devices and designs.

Using a distributed-object approach to developing software can bring some of the same benefits to the software industry. Building "componentware" to accomplish basic functions, much like the object described above for database access, provides benefits beyond the off-loading of network application plumbing to "middleware" within the distributed-object architecture. The components themselves are built upon basic functions, like database accesses, with business logic and other specifics added on top of the basic components, resulting in more complicated components. More information about components and middleware appears later in this chapter.

Middleware Explained

Middleware is a type of software that sits in between clients and servers and manages their interaction. Most often found in mainframe shops, middleware is especially useful for handling applications that support many users. The middleware interfaces with the mainframe (or other large system), running some number of processes on the application server; for example, perhaps 50 instances of a client process might be running on the application server to service a population of 10,000 application users. Those clients connect to the application through the middleware, which maintains the state for each client and shares the 50 processes out among all the concurrent clients. So if a system supports 250 concurrent users, the middleware would share the 50 processes among the 250 clients.

This approach supports increasing user populations much better than the direct, two-tier approach that stresses servers unable to handle more than a hundred or so concurrent sessions before being overwhelmed by the tasks of network connection and session state management.

Using and reusing components is one benefit of object architectures, but the ability to continue to use existing legacy applications within the object architecture is an added benefit. Rather than redesign and redevelop existing applications, the extranet designer can build adapters to provide an object-compliant interface to the legacy system, making it easily and securely accessible to extranet users.

Object Options

In the middle of 1997, designers still have two options for building distributed object applications as discussed in Chapter 2.

DCOM

Microsoft's OLE is one strategy for simplifying the interaction between objects on the same desktop; OLE has been implemented on Windows desktops since 1990. Microsoft later rolled out Network OLE as a means of supporting interaction between objects across a network. Network OLE was renamed the Distributed Component Object Model (DCOM) in 1996.

CORBA

The Common Object Request Broker Architecture (CORBA) protocol specification is the work of the Object Management Group (OMG). The protocol revolves around the concept of the Object Request Broker, or ORB. The ORB is simply a broker, passing requests from outside to the objects it is responsible for, and passing responses back outside from those objects. Part of the latest revision of the CORBA specification is the Internet Inter-ORB Protocol (IIOP), which is an application protocol that defines how clients can pass requests through the Internet to ORBs and the objects represented by those ORBs.

Transactions

The notion of a *transaction* is central to the extranet. However, transactions have not been easy to implement in Web environments largely because of the nature of the protocols used to build Webs. HTTP is a stateless application protocol, and the underlying protocols (especially IP) are not sufficiently reliable to support traditional transactions. Although an informal sense of transaction exists—meaning the kind of exchange that can occur between a browser and server, where a request is made and response is elicited—a more formal definition of transaction must be deployed before extranets provide them in a real business environment.

The difference between *stateful* and *stateless* application protocols lies in the amount of information the server retains about the application session. In a stateless application, the state of the server does not change after an interaction with a client. Since nothing the client does to the server will change anything on it, the server will always produce the same result when responding to an identical request. This attribute is desirable for applications that use unreliable networks, such as HTTP. If a client request is lost (to network noise, for instance) it can simply be sent again. Although you could use HTTP to interface to stateful systems to support transactions (for example, using the Common Gateway Interface, or CGI, to connect to database applications), the technique is not efficient.

A *transaction* consists of an exchange; for example, a consumer might want to give money to a merchant in exchange for a product. If both consumer and merchant are operating through computers, the transaction can be considered complete when each party's database has been updated to reflect the exchange. In other words, the consumer authorizes the release of digital currency, and the merchant authorizes the release of a digital product, for instance a copy of a research report, only on the receipt of the currency.

Transactions are difficult to implement not only on the Web but also in private networks because two systems have to be synchronized. It is not enough for the merchant to know that the customer's account holds enough money to cover a charge at a precise moment if the owner of the account can shift the value in the account before the merchant can collect for the current transaction. The crux of the problem is that both databases must be updated at the same time. If one part of the transaction happens but the other half does not, the result is unacceptable. The system requires a mechanism to ensure that both parts of the transaction are completed correctly or that both parts fail.

That mechanism is called a *transaction monitor*; it can mediate transactions through a two-phase commit process and allow completion (commitment) of the transaction by both sides only if both sides agree, as shown in Figure 3.3. During the first phase, the transaction monitor gets the participants to change their databases; in the second phase (assuming that all has gone well), the transaction monitor notifies the participants of the success, and they commit the changes as permanent. Each participant has the opportunity after the first phase to abort the transaction, and if either participant does abort the transaction, both participants roll back their databases to their previous values.

Transaction monitors are also important for solving the problem of *scalability,* or handling ever-increasing numbers of simultaneous users of a single-server application, as discussed next and again at the end of this chapter.

FIGURE 3.3

A two-phase commit transaction requires a mediating structure to ensure that both participants in a transaction hold up their respective ends of the bargain.

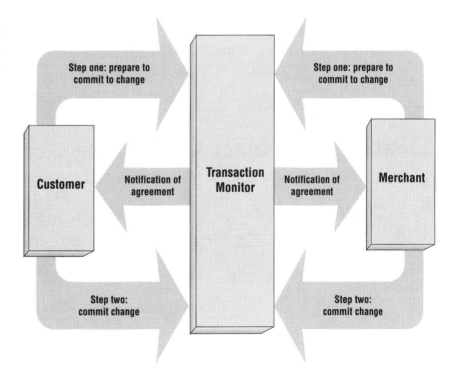

The ability to make transactions happen over the Internet is a critical component of extranet implementation, since transactions are the medium through which organizations interact with their customers and suppliers. *Nonfinancial interactions* can also be modeled on this type of transaction, so transactions are clearly fundamental to the way organizations interoperate over internetworks.

Although the importance of transactions to digital commerce over the Internet is fairly obvious, implementing interactions in a transaction model has some subtle aspects. More complex, nested transactions can also occur once a robust infrastructure is in place, and they are increasingly important to extranet designers (see Chapters 7 and 10).

CORBA provides transaction services, and Microsoft markets a Transaction Server product for use in the DCOM architecture. Other middleware vendors offer transaction monitors as well as *middleware message queuing software* that manages the transmission of messages between processes connected to the most heterogeneous and tenuous of wide area networks.

Distributed-Object Computing

The foundation of distributed-object computing includes the concepts of distributed computing and object computing. By themselves, these areas have produced many important advances in practical computing, but together they are revolutionizing the way in which we use computers and the way in which we build and use software applications.

Distributed Computing

Distributed computing happens whenever two computers process shared information. Distributed computing usually happens in the context of a client and server model, as described in the following examples:

- A personal computer (the client) accesses data stored in a file on a LAN file server (the server).

- A Web browser (the client) displays data that has been retrieved from a Web server (the server).

Two sequences of events need to be happening for distributed computing to occur:

- Application programming, that is, the code that handles functions such as data displays on the client and reliable retrieval of data from the server

- Network programming

That extra network programming allows the information to pass over the network, between possibly dissimilar computers, and still be recognizable to the machine receiving it.

Traditional distributed computing used two approaches to program such applications: the remote procedure call and the network application programming interface. Each methodology provides a framework in which distributed computing can happen relatively easily, but each has its drawbacks.

Remote Procedure Calls

When accessing remote resources, one method that has been used with a lot of success is the remote procedure call (RPC). The client computer sends an RPC that contains a request to the remote server; the server accepts and processes the procedure locally and then returns a result to the requesting system as shown in Figure 3.4.

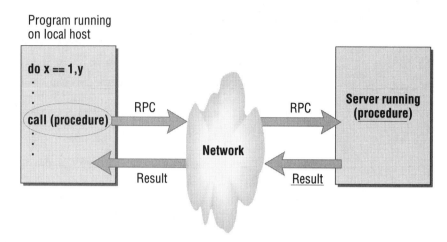

Building applications on RPCs deployed across large internetworks is complicated by the fact that RPCs usually work synchronously. Therefore, the client usually has to wait for a response from the server before it can move on to the next step of the process. TCP/IP over the Internet or extranets can be subject to long or unpredictable delays, so the result can be very spotty performance.

Network Application Programming Interfaces

Using RPCs can simplify matters when the alternative is to use a network application programming interface (network API) because they have even less infrastructure than RPCs. Network APIs may require programmers to code almost down to the wires, often dealing with matters like the way each communicating computer represents data. Whether using a network API or RPCs, the programmer must do a lot of work to make sure that data is moving around the network the way it is expected to. In addition, much of the code must be modified or replaced in the event that a new system is put into the loop, a new platform is to be supported, or the existing network is modified (by adding servers, for example).

Object Computing

Distributed computing, despite the difficulty involved, produces lots of big wins in leveraging computing power across a network. Distributed computing is a way for many users (through their computers) to use the same network resources simultaneously. *Object computing* is way of allowing many processes (programs running concurrently on one computer, or on different computers) to use the same programs simultaneously. Distributed computing helps achieve economies of scale, for example, by providing a group of users with shared access to one big file server and a high-performance printer instead of forcing them all to equip their personal computers with their own printers (probably not as nice as the shared one) and hard drives (somehow kept up-to-date with shared data). Object computing allows many computers—and not necessarily all using the same operating system or end-user application software—to simultaneously use a single piece of code (an object).

Objects have been developed in response to the need to create software that can be reused even when client software changes or when end-user populations migrate away from mainframe systems but still want to have access to programs running on the mainframe.

What Are Objects?

An *object* is simply a chunk of code that does the things that an object can do and that can be manipulated as an object. More specifically (and less recursively), objects are entities that have some particular set of attributes: The object's *attributes* belong to the object, and the object's *methods* allow the object to do things (which are also often called the *functions* or *operations* of the object). Objects operate on their own private data, which may be called the object's *state* or *instance data*. Objects have their own unique reference IDs, so they can be identified from among all the other objects in use on a system or in a network.

Differentiating an object from many other programming constructs are three characteristics that also make objects particularly useful:

- Polymorphism

- Encapsulation

- Inheritance

Understanding these characteristics is fundamental to understanding objects.

Polymorphism *Polymorphism* has Greek roots, and means "many forms." Polymorphism is the characteristic of objects that allows the same object to produce different results depending on how the object is used. One simple, concrete example is the standard wall switch, which is an interface object that controls the flow of electricity. The wall switch is most often interfaced with an electric device, usually a light. However, the result from switching it on depends on whether the switch is connected to a standard filament light bulb lamp, a fluorescent tube fixture, or a halogen lamp. In fact, it will produce a very different result when connected to a vent fan, a heater, a radio, or a television. And of course, there is the mysterious instance of the wall switch that seems to produce no result whatever when switched on or off.

Software objects behave similarly: Double-clicking on a file representation, an action associated with the opening of the file, will produce different results depending on the type of file clicked on. The interface is the same, but the results are different.

Encapsulation Objects provide a public interface to the universe and keep the gory details of what they are doing private and to themselves. This characteristic is *encapsulation*. All the interesting stuff happens inside, where it is hidden from the rest of the world. Users needs to know only what the object's interface is and what the object does with it.

To put it into the context of the electric switch example, encapsulation is the property of the switch that actually hides its inner workings. All you know about the switch is that it is a lever with two positions that somehow controls a device. To use the switch you do not need to know anything about how the switch is cabled to the device. You can use the switch even if you are ignorant of the principles of electricity—even if you are completely unaware of the existence of electricity.

Inheritance   *Inheritance* allows you to create new objects that are based on existing objects, rather than requiring you to reinvent every object from scratch. Inheritance allows programmers to create parent object classes that can produce children classes that do all that the parent objects can do in addition to performing their own specialized functions appropriate to the task at hand.

The inheritance process is somewhat akin to building a line of computers on a standard system board. The top-of-the-line computer will share base functionality with the base computer, but each incremental model adds some new functions. When you upgrade the base model (like modifying a parent object class), all the related models (all the children objects) gain the same new features or improved performance.

Advantages of Objects

Because objects present a standard external interface to the world, in theory any other object that knows how to work that interface can access them. This huge benefit means that programmers do not have to re-create the same type of function for every new platform that an application supports, for every instance of a new function applied across platforms, or for applications being ported to a new programming language or operating system.

Extranet developers can leverage the modularity of objects to respond to one of the greatest challenges they face: how to scale up an application that worked perfectly well with 100 users to work well for 10,000 users? Because objects communicate with the outside world through a standard interface, the underlying code can be replaced whenever it needs to be upgraded or modified in any way. This modularity means that extranet developers can build application interfaces that connect to application objects that are actually just mapped to very basic application implementations or existing legacy systems. As those underlying systems are upgraded, the application interfaces remain exactly the same, communicating with what they believe to be the exact same application objects. However, those objects can be upgraded transparently to use newly designed applications, or even to interface to some other application.

Two-Tier and Three-Tier Applications

Traditionally client/server applications have been implemented in a two-tier architecture. The client sends requests directly to the server, and the server responds directly to the client, as shown in Figure 3.5. This architecture works reasonably well for a number of reasons:

- It is relatively simple to implement, since programmers need to deal only with interactions between the client and the server.

- Plenty of development tools are available, and the issues are relatively well understood.

- Performance (up to a point) is acceptable, as long as the server has sufficient processing power to support the necessary number of simultaneous users.

Two-tier client/server applications are widely deployed for access to legacy systems in all types of organizations.

Unfortunately, two-tier applications do not usually scale well as more and more simultaneous users are added to the application. Even very high-performance servers have a limit to the number of simultaneous sessions they can manage. As the number of processes the server has to manage increases, response times for any particular session

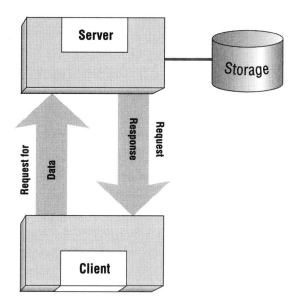

begin to lag. Managing all the different process threads can also
present a problem, as can handling simultaneous network connections
from many different hosts.

The problem is not so much insufficient resources to handle all the
requests, but the huge amount of overhead in dealing with direct connections with all the clients. If 10,000 simultaneous client users are connected to a server, the server would have to maintain 10,000 separate
sessions, each with some or all of the application functions running separately and simultaneously—even though *most of the time* any given session does not need to use more than one function *at a time,* and a lot of
"dead air" occurs as the end user looks at the computer screen, drinks
coffee, or stops to think. Even so, managing 10,000 separate and simultaneous user sessions would bring most servers to their knees.

Looking at the application itself, you can see that if multiple clients
can share any particular server application function, you could get along
with significantly fewer instances of that function. In other words, if you
could share 100 instances of a file read process among 10,000 clients,

none of the clients would notice any difference. Only the server, which would suddenly have to manage only 100 copies of the process instead of 10,000, would notice a change.

The solution is to add a tier to the two-tier client/server architecture. In three-tier applications, something sits between the mass of clients and the server. This "something" is often called *middleware,* and it maintains a limited number of connections to processes running on the server, as shown in Figure 3.6. (See "Middleware Explained" sidebar earlier in the chapter.) When a client request comes in to use a function running on the server, the middleware hooks up that request with one of the processes it is managing. That way, the server just has to run its processes, not manage hundreds of connections; the middleware takes care of storing state information about all the connections from clients. The middleware also correlates that state (e.g., the client's user ID, authentication, and session information) to the process being run. In fact, the system designer can even allocate more than one physical server to the application, with the middleware taking care of managing the process connections.

Middleware does such a good job of handling multiple connections through the process of load balancing; that is, inbound requests may be routed to a single server, but they may be referred to another host for session processing. All clients for a particular application point to a single host name or address to initiate a client session. The host at that address accepts each request, checks to see which server is currently available to process a session, and then refers the client to that server.

Middleware and Object Request Brokers

Transaction monitors, as mentioned above, help solve the problem of connecting many clients to a single server or of connecting many clients to several servers through load balancing. However, this solution means that the application must be built from top to bottom as a monolithic project. If you use objects to build an application, you can solve this problem by adding ORBs to the system.

FIGURE 3.6

The three-tier
architecture moves
responsibility for managing
many simultaneous
connections from the
server to the middleware
system.

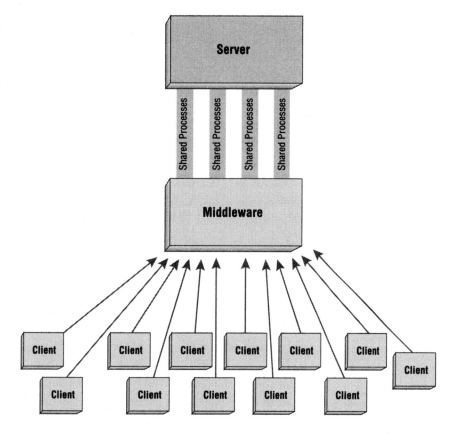

The ORB provides a certain set of baseline services, including functions related to the completion of transactions, maintenance of transactions, handling of queries, and interfacing to objects. The ORB also acts as an "interface bus" for software in the same way that a hardware interface bus acts to allow the connection of different pieces of hardware.

An ORB can be implemented on a single system to act as the common bus for software components on the system so that any object on the system can access any other objects on the same system. The OMG CORBA model provides this type of service (as does Microsoft's COM to a certain extent) as discussed in the next section. Extending the ORB beyond the local system, however, allows objects to interact seamlessly across system boundaries; the CORBA IIOP enables this type of interaction (as does Microsoft's DCOM to a certain extent).

CORBA and IIOP

The OMG started work on the CORBA in 1989 and released the first version of the CORBA specification in 1990—well before TCP/IP had emerged as the clear choice for interorganizational networking and communication. The implication, of course, is that the participants in the OMG were building the infrastructure for distributed-object computing independently of any network infrastructure. By the end of 1994, OMG was starting to publish CORBA 2.0, which included the Internet Inter-ORB Protocol (IIOP): an application layer protocol defining the way that clients and servers could interoperate through the CORBA architecture over an Internet backbone.

CORBA's advantages over the DCOM model derive mainly from the fact that CORBA is an open specification, designed over a period of years by a large group of software vendors whose goal was to allow their software to work together.

CORBA

The CORBA reference model defines how ORBs interact, what services ORBs provide, and how to build interoperable objects within the OMG Object Management Architecture.

The concept of an ORB is central to the CORBA architecture model. The ORB itself sets the rules for interaction among and between objects; on top of the ORB are application objects (the actual objects that people create to solve specific business problems). Parallel to the application objects are the common facilities (basic tools that can be used to build solutions). These common facilities can include vertical application facilities, which are useful to specific industries, and horizontal facilities, which are useful to anyone building applications, such as systems management tools and user interface primitives. Underneath the ORB are the object services that provide services related to working with objects. The basic architecture is shown in Figure 3.7.

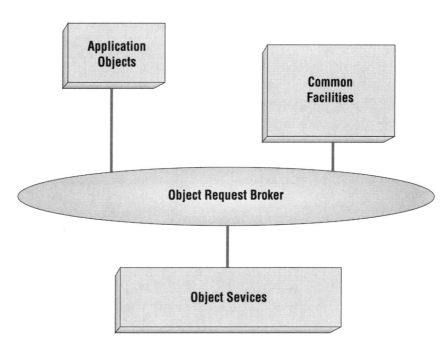

The object services accessible through the ORB are interfaces and objects that support the most basic functions required for building and using objects. No distributed application can be built without using these services, and the services themselves are independent of any particular application, server, or system. The object services defined by the CORBA specification are listed in Table 3.1. The result is that any ORB component can be accessed by any other component or object stored in the ORB.

	Service Name	Description
TABLE 3.1 Object services provided within the CORBA specification	**Naming Service**	Makes it possible to bind a name to an object.
	Event Service	Allows objects to request and receive event information; the relatively simple basic event-related functions can be combined for flexible and powerful results.
	Life Cycle Service	Defines how objects are created, deleted, copied, and moved.
	Persistent Object Service	Defines how objects manage and store their own state.
	Transaction Service	Provides support for handling transactional interoperability, in other words, allowing transactions to be completed across networks, as well as across different transaction programming models.
	Concurrency Control Service	Allows multiple clients to have read-only access to the same shared resource through the use of locks. This service permits one client to update while others can still use the resource.
	Relationship Service	Makes it possible to explicitly represent relationships between objects.
	Externalization Service	Defines how objects can be expressed as a stream of data (externalized) for storage on a disk or in memory or for transmission across a network. It also defines how such externalized representations of objects can be turned back into operating objects (internalized) once they arrive at their destination.
	Query Service	Provides a query syntax and mechanism allowing objects or users to request object information, invoke object operations, and set object attributes.
	Licensing Service	Enables object developers to collect fees for the use of their components. The mechanism is flexible enough to support charges each time the object is used, each system on which the object is used, and each time the object is initialized, as well as site licensing.

	Service Name	Description
T A B L E 3.1 (cont.) Object services provided within the CORBA specification	Property Service	Makes it possible to attach specific values (properties) to objects. The property may be assigned dynamically based on some attribute of the state of the object itself. For example, the date of the object's creation or the object's author name.
	Time Service	Keeps track of when things happen and provides the current time with an estimate of accuracy. This service is useful for dealing with events: determining in which order two or more events occurred, time-stamping events, and determining how much time elapsed between two events.
	Security Service	Fulfills several functions relating to security, including user and object identification and authentication, authorization and access control, security auditing, security of communication between objects, nonrepudiation and administration of security policies.

IIOP

An ORB helps achieve a higher degree of interoperability across an internetwork as long as the ORB can interact with other ORBs. The latest revision of CORBA, version 2.0, provides for just such interoperability through the General Inter-ORB Protocol (GIOP) and the Internet Inter-ORB Protocol (IIOP). GIOP defines how messages can be sent between ORBs and provides for common data representations for inter-ORB communication. IIOP is an application protocol that sits on top of TCP/IP and can turn any TCP/IP internetwork into an ORB backbone.

CORBA objects speak directly to their local ORB, which then passes off to the GIOP, which in turn interfaces directly with IIOP. The object interactions are then carried over a TCP/IP network and can be passed through it to other ORBs. The ORBs handle all the plumbing of the interaction while at the application level the application itself needs to worry only about object requests and transmissions.

CORBA and IIOP Products

The 700-plus members of the OMG have produced many, many products that support the Object Management Architecture, CORBA, and IIOP. Prominent among the members are some of the biggest names in software, including Microsoft, IBM, Lotus Development, Apple Computer, Novell, and Computer Associates. The following sections present a very abbreviated selection of the types of products that support CORBA.

Netscape

```
http://home.netscape.com
```

CORBA and IIOP have been a big part of Netscape's strategy for some time, and IIOP is supported directly in the latest versions of Enterprise Server and Communicator client, as well as in the Netscape ONE platform.

Lotus

```
http://www.lotus.com
```

With the addition of the Domino server to Notes, Lotus (now a division of IBM) transformed its proprietary network workgroup product into an enhanced Web platform. Domino can serve both Notes content and enhanced Web content, all accessible to any standard Web browser, but with extra features available to Notes clients. Both Domino and the Notes client, as well as other products from Lotus, support CORBA and IIOP.

Visigenic

http://www.visigenic.com

Visigenic Software, Inc., offers a full line of middleware and tools for developing CORBA applications, particularly database connectivity tools. One product is VisiBroker for Java, the first CORBA 2.0 ORB written completely in Java. VisiBroker for Java is a development tool for building, managing, and deploying distributed Java applications. Visigenics also offers other products, such as CORBA development tools, and has licensed some of its CORBA technologies to Oracle Corporation for use in Oracle's Network Computing Architecture.

Oracle

http://www.oracle.com

Oracle Corporation has committed to supporting CORBA and IIOP, in addition to HTTP, in its Network Computing Architecture. Oracle Web Application Server 3.0 shipped in early spring of 1997, and includes native support for CORBA and IIOP.

Distributed COM and Active Platform

Vendors very much like proprietary standards because (when they are successful) they help to sell the vendor's products. Examples of this type of success abound in the computer industry; they include character representation schemes (EBCDIC used on IBM mainframes); proprietary networking protocols and architectures (IBM's SNA, Novell's NetWare and IPX, Apple's AppleTalk, and Microsoft's NetBIOS and NETBEUI); and end-user application file formats (everything from database to spreadsheet to word processing).

The protocols underlying the use of the Internet (and other TCP/IP internetworks) have been, by definition, open standards developed in a collegial environment designed to generate the best possible results for all. Proprietary standards tend to undermine the objective of interoperability because they lock out competitors. With open standards, vendors' products must compete strictly on their merits: performance, robustness, reliability, completeness, and comprehensiveness of the protocol implementation.

Product differentiation through the creation of a new standard is hardly unheard of in the TCP/IP market. Well before Netscape's Secure Socket Layer (SSL) started out as an alternative to the slowly developing Secure HTTP standard for secure commerce, Sun Microsystems developed the Network File System (NFS). Since then, many other vendors have developed their own standards and subsequently donated them to the appropriate standards bodies (including Sun's Java development language and Marimba's Castanet protocols).

Microsoft is hardly the first company to take this step, which it is doing with DCOM and the supporting technologies, but it may be the largest company to do so. Microsoft certainly stands to profit handsomely from success. Its gains will be shared by everyone else who can benefit from the rapid and easy implementation of extranet applications over an object architecture that is already almost universally deployed on tens of millions of Windows desktops around the world.

DCOM

Software components use DCOM, which in turn uses any underlying network transport protocols (including TCP/IP and HTTP), to communicate with other software components. DCOM is based on the Open Software Foundation's Distributed Computing Environment (DCE) Remote Procedure Call (RPC) specification, which provides a method for objects on one host to call procedures running on other hosts connected to the same network.

Figure 3.8 shows how DCOM facilitates the sharing of resources across the Internet. A COM component on one host can request services from another component on another host, using a TCP/IP network as the transport medium. DCOM can operate as the application protocol, or DCOM activity can be encapsulated within another application protocol like HTTP.

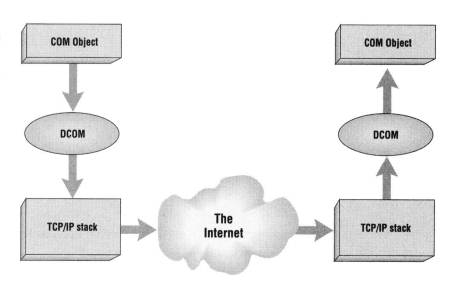

FIGURE 3.8

DCOM allows components on different hosts to interact across a network link.

Microsoft stands to gain the most from industry acceptance of DCOM as the distributed object architecture, and DCOM support is integral to the Microsoft product line. Acceptance of DCOM means acceptance (or at least tolerance) of Microsoft operating systems as the default network client and server platforms. Although Microsoft has submitted DCOM and many of the supporting technologies in its Active Platform to standards bodies for consideration, the company continues to add proprietary extensions to protocols, as well as proprietary features and products. The results are specifications that work best when used with Microsoft products, particularly its Internet Explorer Web browser, Internet Information Server (IIS) and related server products, and the entire Office 97 productivity suite, as well as virtually all other Microsoft applications.

Opting for the DCOM solution does not exclude the implementer from the CORBA world, particularly since the announcement early in 1997 that Microsoft would actively support full interoperability between CORBA and DCOM and that the DCOM and some related specifications would be put into the open standards stream. Although performance should be best when data does not have to cross object architecture boundaries, Microsoft has committed to supporting all open standards and to opening many of its own standards.

Active Platform

Microsoft's *Active Platform* is a family of client and server technologies that enable integrated connectivity across the Internet and other TCP/IP internetworks. Active Platform is based on Microsoft's implementation of HTML, as well as open scripting and the COM component architecture, and includes the technologies that run within the Active Client browser (Internet Explorer) as well as technologies built into the Microsoft server offerings (Windows NT Server and Internet Information Server). The platform also includes the development technologies that enable component-based applications and that allow the client and server to interact seamlessly.

ActiveX

ActiveX was originally built on OLE as part of Microsoft's Internet strategy; its purpose is to extend the COM to enable Web applications to use components. ActiveX also includes Distributed COM support, enabling the use of components on other systems across internetwork links. As ActiveX has gained prominence, it has increasingly supplanted OLE as the general term referring to Microsoft's component technologies; for example, what used to be known as OCXs or OLE controls are now referred to as ActiveX controls.

Microsoft introduced the term *ActiveX* in 1996, and it has gradually replaced OLE as the term describing things built with COM. OLE is now more frequently being used in its original sense, to refer to the linking and embedding of objects.

Microsoft has opened up the ActiveX specification for use as a standard interface to get into Active Platform servers and clients. Consequently, developers can use certain programming interfaces to build ActiveX controls and other mechanisms to integrate their products into the Active Platform.

Not all Active Platform specifications are open; the client and server pieces remain under Microsoft's control—it has not opened up the specification enough for other software vendors to build their own Active-compatible servers or clients. Microsoft has been opening up many of the specifications for application programming interfaces so that others may create programs that work with their servers, but so far has stopped short of opening up the specifications enough to allow a competitor's server to provide Active Platform services.

Active Platform Products

COM and DCOM are incorporated into Microsoft's ActiveX and Active Platform. This platform includes a full line of products upon which extranet applications may be built.

Microsoft Internet Explorer

The basic client product for the Microsoft Active Platform is the Internet Explorer browser. It supports DCOM, COM, and ActiveX, as well as other open Internet standards. In addition to support for Dynamic HTML and standard HTML, Microsoft includes a Java virtual machine (VM) to run downloaded Java applets. Although Active

Platform works best when accessed with the Microsoft client, developers can also adapt Active Platform content for access by "lowest common denominator" clients, in other words, non-Microsoft clients that support HTML, Java, and JavaScript.

Dynamic HTML is a set of extensions to basic HTML supported by both Microsoft and Netscape browsers released later in 1997. Microsoft developed Dynamic HTML in concert with the World Wide Web Consortium (W3C) to expand the ability of Web designers to build pages that can reflect user updates and changes without requiring extra "round trips" to the server. In other words, users can directly manipulate objects on a page rather than click on an object (or attempt some other action) and wait for that action to be sent to the server and refreshed by the response from the server—a big time saver.

Microsoft Internet Information Server (IIS)

Microsoft's Internet Information Server (IIS) is a full-featured Web server that is integrated with Microsoft's Windows NT Server product, which means that it ships with NT Server and also uses NT Server system services for most administrative tasks. For example, user access to Web pages is built on the basic NT Server access and authentication procedures. Other IIS features that pertain to the building of extranets include Active Server Pages (see the next section) as well as support for the Active Directory interface (ADSI, see below and Chapter 6).

Microsoft Active Server Pages

A new feature of Microsoft's IIS 3.0 is the Active Server Page (ASP) feature. ActiveX components are stored on the server and combine with HTML and scripts (Microsoft's VBScript and Jscript) to generate custom HTML output on the fly to deliver targeted content to users. The scripts call the ActiveX components in the context of a standard HTML page. The developer builds a basic HTML page, but instead of attempting to build complicated scripts or CGI routines, uses simple scripts to call ActiveX controls that are stored on the server. The server interprets the scripts and controls and generates Active Server Page output, which is pure HTML that any browser can view.

This feature of IIS 3.0 and later helps users interface to legacy systems through the Web or use some external information to generate a customized page. For example, instead of building a static page that contains links to product descriptions and graphics for an online catalog, an ASP application might build a catalog by defining a set of database queries to retrieve the most current products from a legacy database, along with the most current prices. A user could generate a catalog page by requesting a product category from a list of current product categories. The result is that pages will always be up-to-date and will always reflect the current prices—no one has to manually update the catalog pages every time the product line changes.

Microsoft Active Directory

Microsoft is positioning its *Active Directory* as the directory solution for use in NT networks and internetworks. The product will be implemented as part of Windows NT Server 5.0. Active Directory will be based on the X.500 directory standards and will be interoperable with that standard as well as other open standards for directory services.

The Active Directory interface is referred to as *ADSI*.

Directory services are an important part of any object architecture because it must have some central and authoritative source for information about where to find things like the distributed objects themselves and the systems on which they are running. Active Directory is an important part of Microsoft's object architecture strategy. Directory services are discussed in greater detail in Chapter 6, and deployment of Active Server Pages (as well as other Active Platform products) is discussed in Chapter 7.

Microsoft Transaction Server

Another issue raised by the use of extranets for commercial transactions is scalability. Web protocols (HTML, CGI, and HTTP) are not suited to building applications that can support robust transactions or tens or hundreds of thousands of concurrent users.

Developers working on mainframe systems intended to support transactions in mass quantities have already faced, and solved, scalability problems. Examples include airline reservation systems and banking applications.

Transaction monitor products like Microsoft's Transaction Server (formerly code-named "Viper") work by managing the inbound requests for services from Web users and using a pool of processes running on the server side. Transaction Server acts as an intermediary for the client requests, managing many requests and sharing a limited number of processes. In addition to managing processes like a traditional transaction monitor, Transaction Server also functions like an object request broker for the DCOM architecture, allowing servers to register in a directory and making sure that requesting clients can get to the object processes they need.

As of the middle of 1997, Microsoft had not implemented all the functions of either a transaction monitor or an object request broker in its Transaction Server product. Full support for transaction monitor functions are, at least for the moment, available with much larger and more specialized products. Likewise, complete object request broker services are still more completely available through true ORB products, as discussed in the next section.

What Does the Future Hold?

CORBA's greatest advantages over DCOM derive from CORBA's longer history as an open specification, built by hundreds of software vendors. With more than seven years' tenure (CORBA is roughly twice as old as the World Wide Web), CORBA has a significant installed base in heavy-duty applications and database products, as well as reasonably widespread deployment in TCP/IP internetwork client and server applications such as those from Netscape. With its longer history comes a more mature specification that has been tested by time and many different implementations. A more important benefit comes from CORBA's more complete distributed-object architecture, which is a result of its extended life span.

To some extent Microsoft's DCOM architecture enjoys a significant advantage purely from a marketing standpoint. Microsoft owns an installed base of roughly 100 million Windows desktops, all of which support, or can support, DCOM. With a compelling presence in the server market, both on LANs with Windows NT Server and on TCP/IP internetworks with the Internet Information Server, DCOM becomes even more attractive. To further enhance its Active Platform as the platform of choice for extranet development, Microsoft offers a full range of Active-enabled tools for users and developers of all skill levels to create both extranet content and extranet applications.

From a purely technical viewpoint, however, Microsoft has yet to deploy the same depth and breadth of distributed-object functions that users can find in CORBA implementations. Also, platform support for DCOM is still largely restricted to Windows. This status will change, however, as Microsoft is moving very quickly to announce, develop, and release new products, and to add new distributed features to existing products.

Although some software vendors—particularly the larger firms with deeper pockets (e.g., Lotus)—may be able to afford to develop components for two distributed architectures, most smaller organizations must make a choice. Software vendors that have already built ORBs continue to deploy them with their products while vendors building new extranet application products seem to be heading in the direction of DCOM. Further complicating matters, Microsoft's move to put DCOM onto an open-standard track means that DCOM is likely to continue to gather momentum, as well as to catch up to CORBA in terms of implementation and interoperability. Finally, DCOM-to-CORBA bridges have been announced and will improve the interoperability of systems across the two architectures (although these bridges will undoubtedly be subject to performance issues).

Therefore, the future of distributed architecture is likely to continue to be some mixture of the two models. One of them will eventually prevail in some form or another, even if the two are somehow merged. At this point the contest is probably too close to call, but as Damon Runyon said: "The race may not always be to the swift nor the victory to the strong, but that's how you bet."

CHAPTER

4

Extranet Infrastructure

Ⓐll networks require some sort of infrastructure across which data actually flows. Extranets can have particularly interesting (that is, complicated) infrastructures because they can span so many different boundaries. Extranet topologies may be modeled on traditional internetworking structures, or they may cross and overlap intranet and Internet boundaries. Finally, even though we have only a handful of basic models upon which to build extranets, each implementation will be different in some way from every other extranet.

This chapter introduces basic extranet *topologies,* or the forms extranets take as they relate to existing internal and external networks. Among the basic building blocks that designers use to build extranets are backbones and virtual private networks (VPNs); neither is a prerequisite, and both are discussed in this chapter. Firewall gateways are also important extranet components; they are discussed in Chapter 5.

Extranets have many other physical components, like routers and servers, but these are well documented in texts covering intranet and Internet implementation issues, and their use does not change significantly when deployed in extranets or in other internetworks. Likewise, although this chapter includes a brief survey of backbone design, the specific technical details are best documented in data networking design texts. One good introduction is Darren Spohn's *Data Network Design 2nd edition*, (McGraw-Hill 1997).

Although every extranet does not require a private backbone, organizations seeking some degree of security from external attack will at least consider this approach. This chapter discusses how to approach the task of building a private backbone for an extranet linking two or more organizations' intranets. Extranet backbone design is discussed in the context of backbone topologies used for internetworks designed for local, regional, and national internetworks.

Virtual private networks can function as supplements to or replacements for extranets. This chapter introduces virtual private networks, explains what they are, how they work, and how they are built.

Interorganizational Internetworking

From a networking perspective, extranets can be considered *interorganizational internetworks*. Consequently, extranet designers and administrators can draw on their experience working with other types of internetworks: intranets and the Internet. Seen in this light, designing and implementing an extranet should be no more (and no less) difficult than building an intranet. In fact, however, extranets require considerable attention to issues like security and sharing network administration duties across organizational boundaries.

A Very Big Extranet

To get an idea of what is involved in building an interorganizational internetwork, consider the Internet 2 project. In 1996 representatives of 40 educational institutions announced this project to create a high-performance internetwork linking universities and related research organizations. As of March 1997, the project had about 100 charter member institutions and more than a dozen affiliate and corporate members.

The objective is to create a high-performance, broadband internetwork to link these organizations and to foster the use of applications suited to such networks. For example:

- Multimedia, multicasting applications required for distance learning and remote classroom applications

- Virtual access to national laboratories and supercomputing facilities

- Access to large bodies of simulation or observed data of the type required for astronomical, geophysical, or meteorological research

- Remote medical consultations and diagnoses for research purposes

- Access to large volumes of financial and commercial transactions for real-time economics analysis

The Internet 2 project includes the following design specifications:

- Support for high-bandwidth networking applications

- Use of IP version 6 (but with backward compatibility to IP version 4)

- A high degree of interoperability by providing access to a wide range of client devices

More to the point, Internet 2 will be interoperable with the existing Internet, use object brokering services and software components to foster interoperability across a large population of users, and connect as many as 100 or more educational and related organizations from its start.

Although its purpose is to provide faster, more reliable internet-working to its members, Internet 2 is not intended as a replacement for the Internet. Member institutions will still use Internet access, but Internet 2 services will supplement the Internet applications already in use. Internet 2 applications will go beyond those possible on the Internet, supporting applications like remote learning and helping develop new applications that require high bandwidth, reliable services such as distance medicine.

In other words, the Internet 2 project is very much a model for extranet designers. Internet 2 is being designed to support a largely new set of applications to be deployed within the research community. However, the intention is not to build a computer science research test bed (as was the original Internet for much of its existence), but to develop a practical tool for conducting research in a wide range of fields. Internet 2 is a production extranet.

The Internet 2 project maintains a Web site at `http://www.internet2.edu/`. Full details of the project, as well as the latest news about the project, are published here.

The rest of this section will refer to some aspects of this project as it relates to the development of more modest extranets.

Design Principles

In the Internet 2 project preliminary engineering report, the following principles were presented as having come out of the Engineering Working Group's initial deliberations:

- Use available, well-supported, and reliable technologies instead of creating new ones wherever possible.

- Use open standards instead of proprietary solutions and generally maintain the network as openly as possible. This principle includes sharing performance information with other members.

- Build the network as reliably as possible through redundancy. The objective is to avoid any single point of failure that might result from reliance on any single service provider, hardware manufacturer, or software publisher by building in backup routes and using alternative vendors to the greatest extent possible.

- Build the basic network functions (as defined in the project specifications) before adding more-advanced functions. The project is sufficiently complex that it would be counterproductive to start adding advanced new features before implementing the base set of features.

- Become a production network, not an experimental research test bed. Although technical innovation may be impossible to avoid, the network is an engineering project, not a computer science project.

- Complement, do not to compete against, commercial networks. Any Internet 2 services provided by, for example, commercial Internet service providers, must remain separate from access to commercial networks like the Internet.

These principles are well worth following for almost any networking project, but particularly when planning a project that will affect more than 100 very large participating organizations. Extranet designers would be well served by at least considering these principles when formulating their guidelines for new extranets.

Linking Organizations

Building Internet 2 requires the cooperation of many organizations. For the Internet 2 project, charter members were required to make commitments that included, but were not limited to, financial support of the project. According to the Internet 2 project Web page, estimates of the cost for member institutions could be as high as $500,000 per year for the first few years of the project (although some of that cost may be covered by existing budgets for networking), with a commitment of as much as $25,000 per year to cover administrative and support expenses.

However, participation goes beyond a simple economic commitment. Charter members must also commit to these additional tasks:

- Providing executive-level support to the project management effort

- Helping to build applications development and network services project teams to support the Internet 2 project

- Implementing end-to-end broadband Internet access so that project developers can build, test, and use Internet 2 applications

The Internet 2 project is huge and requires significant allocation of resources. In the tradition of Internet development, much of this activity is delegated to member organizations through a steering committee. The project has working groups for applications development and for engineering, and member organizations can participate in various project meetings, depending on membership level.

An Overview of Internet 2 Architecture

As of the project's start in 1997, the Internet 2 architecture looked something like what is shown in Figure 4.1. A connectivity cloud provided some yet-to-be-determined high-speed, high-bandwidth data communication service. Access to the connectivity cloud is through "gigapops" (gigabit-capacity points of presence) that serve Internet 2 members within the same region. Each member organization installs a high-speed circuit to link itself to the local gigapop, and the gigapops provide access to other member organizations using other gigapops across the connectivity cloud.

If the architecture for this huge project appears to be a bit vague, that impression is deliberate. Rather than attempt to specify all the details before determining the best architecture, technology, data communication media, and protocols, the Internet 2 planners have begun instead by specifying the objectives of their project in the most basic and general terms of functionality. By first specifying the network's functions, the designers will be able to make the best choices for implementation technologies. This approach avoids the problem of choosing technologies first and later finding that the project is tied to an inappropriate design that will be incapable of achieving the project's goals.

FIGURE 4.1

The Internet 2 project architecture uses high-speed, high-bandwidth gigapops to link campuses to a connectivity cloud.

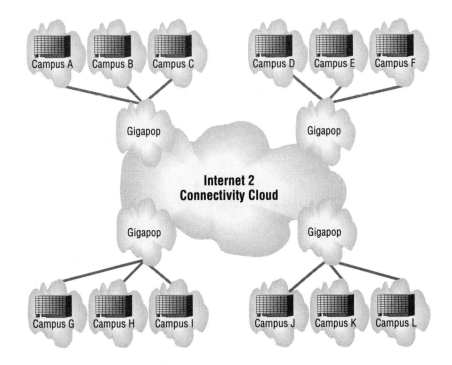

FIGURE 4.1

The Internet 2 project architecture uses high-speed, high-bandwidth gigapops to link campuses to a connectivity cloud.

Extranet Topology Options

Building any kind of network requires making many decisions that will affect the network topology: what kind of LAN medium to use (Ethernet or Token Ring; 10Mbps or 100Mbps Ethernet) and how to connect those LANs (with repeaters, bridges, routers, simple backbone, or collapsed backbone). In practice, these decisions are rarely irrevocable and often must be revised from time to time as needs change: departments expand or contract; organizations merge or spin off subsidiaries.

Moving across a continuum of extranet implementations produces the following general types of extranets in the space between private and public:

■ Private extranet, for members only

- Hybrid extranet, using the public extranet as a channel for private data

- Extranet service provider, offering customer organizations extranet services over their own infrastructure

- Public extranet, open to all users

The details of extranet implementation are much like the details of other internetworks. However, two very different approaches to the overall extranet structure are of interest to us here. As mentioned in Chapter 1, an extranet can be entirely private, completely disconnected from any other networks (like the Internet). A public extranet, on the other hand, uses public networks (the Internet) and provides resource access to any user.

The Internet 2 project can be considered a private extranet (of a sort). Even though its users will probably be able to access it from the Internet, and access the Internet through it, the project is an entirely separate network entity that is open to its members and to authorized users only.

Between these two extremes is an entire rainbow of intermediate options, all with more or less restrictive policies depending on the needs of the sponsoring organizations.

Another option, the *hybrid extranet*, is based on a virtual private network, which is a network that uses encrypted channels across a public network to connect physically separated parts of an extranet.

One last option for organizations wishing to create extranets, but without the resources or expertise to do so, is to purchase extranet-working services from a network service provider. These vendors may be networking providers, with extensive private data communications networks of their own, who are able to sell their excess bandwidth to other organizations. Network service providers may also operate as consultants, setting up leased lines to create a private extranet for each client and using their own staff to maintain and manage all their clients' extranets.

The Private Extranet

Figure 4.2 shows a typical private extranet. Its structure resembles the structure of the Internet: a central cloud of connectivity across which users within connected organizations can communicate. A private extranet and the Internet are functionally identical: Both link organizations across heterogenous data communications networks using open networking protocols.

FIGURE 4.2

A typical private extranet

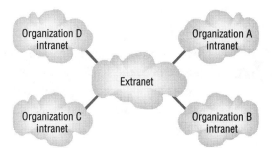

The primary difference between a private extranet and the Internet is a matter of scale and exclusivity. The private extranet links member organizations, for example, the educational and research member organizations of the Internet 2 project; on the other hand, the Internet is a global and inclusive network. Most organizations belonging to a private extranet will likely have some link to the Internet. However, the Venn diagram in Figure 4.3 shows that Internet connectivity is not a prerequisite for private extranet connectivity. Although most organizations either are connected or are planning to connect to the Internet, some organizations may prefer to join private extranets to meet their interorganizational data communications needs.

FIGURE 4.3

F I G U R E 4.3

Many, but not all, organizations connected to a private extranet will also be connected to the Internet.

Why Build a Private Extranet

Building a closed-system, private extranet provides the following advantages to the participants:

- Greater protection from unauthorized uses of the extranet because there is no "public entrance" via the Internet, for example, to the private extranet

- Greater control over performance variables, including end-to-end performance, throughput, and latency

- Greater confidence in sharing sensitive or proprietary information with business partners across a nonpublic network

- Improved protection against denial of service attacks that can be relatively easy to perpetrate when a network or system is exposed to the Internet or other public networks.

The number of organizations that share the need for the same or similar applications limits the size of the private extranet.

As the number of organizations sharing a private extranet increases, the expectation of security implicit in a private network decreases.

The Internet 2 extranet brings together a relatively large number of organizations sharing the same goals for educational applications, but all participants will continue to maintain their own security programs. There is little or no expectation that Internet 2 will be a totally private and inaccessible network. The potential for vastly improved network performance is the driving force behind the project.

A word of warning to organizations considering buying extranet services from Internet service providers with their own networks. As with all products and services, conditions change (and change rapidly in the world of internetworking), so you must be very much aware of what service you are buying and monitor that service closely. AT&T's Worldnet Intranet Connect Service (AWICS) was originally designed to be a "secure" Internet for company-to-company communications. However, that goal has since mutated somewhat, and a number of subscribers were surprised to learn that AT&T connected the Internet to the AWICS cloud with no provision for security, other than that which the subscriber may (or may not) already have in place. (Thanks to technical editor Morgan Stern for this information.)

Implementing a Private Extranet

The Internet 2 project is worth examining as an example of how to approach the creation of any extranet, but particularly an extranet providing services to member organizations only. The high cost in money, networking resources, and network personnel of such an endeavor makes it imperative for all participants to believe that they are getting their money's worth. Building an advisory committee with representatives from all member organizations, or at least a representative sampling for larger extranets, is an excellent first step. Likewise, the sponsor must get full corporate support for this type of project from all participants because a long-term, infrastructure-building project could easily be viewed as dispensable unless it has high-level backing.

Disadvantages of the Private Extranet

Although private extranets provide the potential for great control over the performance characteristics of the network, this advantage comes at a price: Members of the extranet must build—and pay for—this control. Designing, provisioning, deploying, and managing a high-performance, high-traffic extranet backbone can be dizzyingly expensive. Without a strong organizational resolve to participate, the private extranet is unlikely to be a good option for most extranets.

Another potential drawback for some organizations is that membership in a private extranet may bind the organization to a group from which it can be difficult to extricate itself. This shortcoming will be particularly true for companies in fast-moving industries where today's business partner may be tomorrow's competitor.

The Open Extranet

As the number of organizations and individuals connected to the Internet continues to grow, so does the incentive for organizations wishing to link to many other entities to create an open extranet. You might want to build a private telecommunications network if you and your friends desired to maintain complete control over who can use the network, how they can use it, how it works, and who pays for it—this is like building a private extranet. On the other hand, if you prefer to talk to anyone, even people you don't know—and allow them to contact you—then you would call your local telephone company and have them connect you to the global telecommunication network.

The same goes for extranets: if you prefer to be exclusive and need to retain control, you would build a private extranet. If you prefer to be as inclusive as possible and don't mind using public networks, you would build an open extranet. Figure 4.4 shows how the open extranet works. The open extranet itself is simply an intranet (offering some form of a distributed application, of course) that has been connected to the Internet. (It may or may not have a firewall gateway, even though firewall gateways are strongly recommended for all networks connected to the Internet.) Any client that is connected to the Internet, whether directly (through a dialup link, for example) or indirectly (through an intranet connected to the Internet by a firewall gateway, for example), is able to access extranet resources.

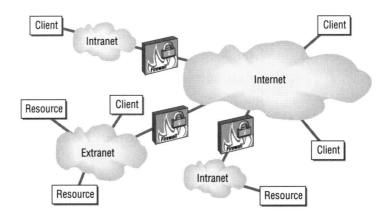

Another feature of an open extranet is that clients and resources connected to it may use resources outside the boundaries of the designated extranet; for example, a client connected to the extranet might use resources resident on an intranet, another extranet, or the Internet. Furthermore, resources connected to the extranet may point to other resources at other organizations or on other networks.

The diagram in Figure 4.5 shows that open extranets tend to be inclusive rather than exclusive. Almost all organizations that are connected to the Internet could potentially connect to an open extranet. Exceptions might be those that do not permit use of extranet applications across a firewall, those that do not permit use of external applications at all, and those that exclude access to the networks or hosts on which the extranet resources are stored. (See Chapter 5 for more information about how firewalls can exclude access in these ways.) For the most part, the open extranet is open to all users.

FIGURE 4.5

All open extranet users will be connected to the Internet, and almost all users connected to the Internet at least have the potential to connect to an open extranet.

Extranet Technology on the Internet

One of the most important applications of extranet technologies is to Internet commerce. By definition (at least, when it is done correctly), Internet commerce invites outsiders into an organization's network resources to make modifications: preferably, to cause an order system to generate fulfillment orders and an accounting system to note an increase in income due to a sale.

As will become apparent throughout the book, although not always explicitly, implementation of an extranet largely addresses the problems of Internet commerce. Extranets solve the following Internet commerce problems:

- How to keep customer payment information secure (especially credit card numbers and personal information)

- How to handle complicated transactions with multiple participants (like those involving credit card payments)

- How to speed up the completion of a sale (integrating the Internet commerce stream directly into the order processing stream)

- How to streamline customer service operations (putting the customer directly in touch with account, ordering, and support information)

Why Build an Open Extranet

Whereas control is the key to most of the reasons to build a private extranet, openness is the key to most of the reasons to build an open extranet. Here are some reasons that organizations build open extranets:

- Accessibility to the widest possible body of business partners (customers or suppliers) for extranet resources (very important to companies wishing to sell to mass markets through a value-added extranet).

- The cost of distributing applications to the widest possible body of potential business partners is relatively small.

- Changes in extranet structure, including improvements and additions to services or expansions in network access performance, are relatively easy.

- Availability of alternative and complementary resources through the Internet enhances the value of the services provided.

Examples of open extranets are many and varied, though the details of implementation may not always be available. For instance, in 1995 Federal Express began offering its customers access to package-tracking services through its Web site. Any user with access to the Internet and a browser could enter a package-tracking number and other shipping information, and be rewarded, instantly, with the status and location of the package. The functional diagram in Figure 4.6 shows how a delivery company might reproduce this service (which other delivery companies quickly did).

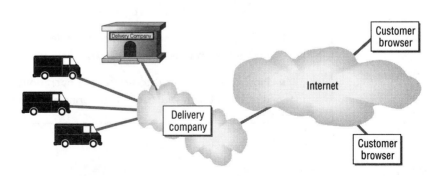

FIGURE 4.6

A delivery company gathers information from drivers and other staff and then makes that information available to customers through the World Wide Web.

Delivery information generated in the field, as packages are picked up, moved, and finally delivered, is sent directly to the delivery company. This data may include everything from shipper and recipient information to accounting and billing data and the name and employee number of the driver of the delivery truck. Some of the information will be made available to customers through the Web page. The delivery company is shown in this figure with clouds connecting it both to the field, from which it gathers data, and to the Internet, over which it distributes data.

The exact mechanisms by which these functions are completed can vary. In one approach, the field data is transmitted directly to a large mainframe database that is connected directly to the Internet, with all customer queries handled directly through SQL queries. Alternatively, the field data could be transmitted to the mainframe database, which periodically replicates only relevant data (removing billing, accounting and human resources information) to a system accessible only by the Web server.

You can find somewhat more complicated examples at many online stores. The most sophisticated stores can be linked to various corporate systems, including inventory (to indicate the availability of products on sale), fulfillment (to initiate shipments immediately upon receiving the electronic order), accounting, billing, accounts receivable, marketing, and sales.

Implementing an Open Extranet

The simplest, and least desirable, way to implement an open extranet is to simply build a Web site with links to extranet resources and plug it all directly into the Internet. This process would open the organization to an entire universe of trouble. Criminals could break into sensitive corporate systems, vandals could "edit" product descriptions (or write their own), and other evil-doers could shut down services, systems, and even networks. At the very least, some form of firewall protection (as described in Chapter 5) is absolutely necessary.

Developing an extranet application that permits outsiders to access organizational resources is a basic requirement for building an extranet, but it is not the only prerequisite for an extranet. At least as important as building the application is building in security for the application. Also important is security through constant vigilance (in the form of monitoring log files for suspicious activities) coupled with intelligent deployment of systems. Protecting sensitive systems while still providing access to some of the information on those systems through application servers is the goal of the successful extranet.

Disadvantages of the Open Extranet

Anything that relies on an open or public network is always at the mercy of that network. The telecommunications networks in some less-developed nations are neither sufficiently reliable nor sufficiently widespread for working people to use them to perform their jobs. Likewise, the public transportation networks in some American cities are neither sufficiently reliable nor sufficiently widespread for working people to be able to use them to commute to and from work.

Whether or not the Internet is sufficiently reliable for companies to base their businesses on its availability depends on a multitude of factors, but the answer to this question underlies the basic disadvantage of implementing an open extranet. Undoubtedly, Internet service will eventually improve, perhaps to the point at which it is as reliable as the North American telephone system. However, until that day, businesses may not be able to afford to rely on the Internet too much.

The Hybrid Extranet

At this point, it should be obvious that no extranet is likely to be purely open or purely private. Private extranets may offer some services to outsiders, through gateways, and almost all open extranets will use some form of exclusionary device like a firewall system to keep out

Who Controls Your Extranet?

One of the biggest problems with using the Internet for mission-critical extranet applications is that you have direct control over (at most) only the parts of the extranet that are internal to your organization (or that are under the control of the central extranet committee). You have indirect control, through your Internet service provider, over only those links connecting your extranet to the Internet.

Who actually handles the rest of the network can vary from moment to moment. There is no certain way to predict the path your data may be taking, and there is no way to hold any single entity responsible for that path.

The result is that your provider may be doing a wonderful job of providing service, but when a backhoe severs a backbone circuit maintained by some regional, national, or global operator halfway across town or halfway around the world, it will stop your extranet dead in its tracks and there is nothing you or your Internet service provider can do about it.

undesirables. Likewise, private extranets may permit or even encourage Internet connectivity for members, while open extranets may use private data communication conduits for backup or parallel services to key extranet users like preferred customers and business partners.

Extranets, just like other networks, must be designed around the requirements of their users, rather than around a technology. This approach gives the extranet designer full latitude to choose the most appropriate method of deploying services to fulfill application requirements as they relate to security, availability, and functionality.

Electronic Data Interchange

Electronic Data Interchange, or EDI, is an application for business-to-business digital commerce. Its basic premise is that the primary barrier to electronically transacting business is the incompatibility of formats used to represent information in purchase orders and sales orders. In other words, the buying organization uses its own formats for representing the important information about a purchase it wishes to make, including special items like department numbers and special chargeback information, while the selling organization has its own set of information that relates to each sale. Many of these data items overlap (e.g., quantity, price, item number, and description), but even these items may be stored in incompatible formats.

Solving this problem is increasingly important, as the actual cost of processing a purchase order for many companies has risen to as high as $100 or more for every purchase made by the organization. There are similar costs to the selling organization.

The EDI solution uses special software that helps each participant link its internal data items to a set of universal data items. Each participant then translates its proprietary information into the universal standard and exchanges that data. When the buyer submits a purchase order through an EDI system, the seller can immediately process the order automatically.

One major sticking point for EDI is building a framework for transmitting this information between organizations. Companies that buy from only one vendor and sell to only one customer can solve the problem with a pair of dial-up lines. In the real world, however, that solution probably won't work. Most organizations either have many suppliers, many customers, or both. The result has been the value-added network (VAN), a private network linking all the organizations that subscribe to that network.

A VAN is very much like a private extranet. However, another problem that arises is that there are several very large VANs and not all your trading partners will belong to the same VAN as you do. The result is a need for multiple VAN memberships.

Increasingly EDI vendors are making their software and services available over the Internet, usually by providing a secure channel over the Internet that links their users to their EDI servers.

Extranet Service Providers

Organizations offering extranet services fall into three categories:

- Consulting firms that offer intranet and Internet connectivity services in addition to extranet services

- Communications firms that sell connectivity, for example, America Online, which offers private networking services

- EDI and other special purpose networking organizations that offer value-added network (VAN) services

The services these companies offer can be invaluable, although no organization should delegate all its extranet tasks to outsiders. Even if outside consultants are called in to build the corporate extranet, the organization should also create its own team to be responsible for managing and coordinating its extranet development.

Virtual Private Networks

A virtual private network uses strong encryption and authentication to secure a private channel across a public network like the Internet. These private channels, as shown in Figure 4.7, can link two remote networks or connect a host to a remote network. When linking two networks, a virtual private network provides a channel that can carry all traffic between the two networks. Virtual private networks usually operate by encapsulating regular IP traffic inside an encrypted IP channel. The virtual private network host or gateway transmits the encrypted, encapsulated packets directly to the remote virtual private network gateway, which decrypts the datagrams and forwards them to their final destinations on the remote segment of the virtual private network.

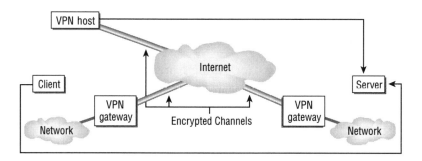

Tunnels and Gateways

Virtual private network products come in two flavors: those delivered as part of a firewall gateway and those delivered as stand-alone tunneling solutions. In either case remote access to the main network is possible either from a satellite network (e.g., a branch office or a business partner) or from an individual host (e.g., a telecommuting employee's home PC or a traveling employee's laptop).

AltaVista Tunnel (from AltaVista Internet Software) is one tunnel solution for virtual private networks. It operates independent of any firewall gateway and supports connections between two networks or between a host and a network. The rest of this section discusses the AltaVista Tunnel implementation of virtual private networks. A list of some other virtual private network software products appears in Appendix A.

How the Virtual Private Network Works

Under normal, non-tunneled, circumstances, a host can connect to a remote network through the Internet without any special arrangements, as long as both ends support TCP/IP. (See Appendix B for more details about the TCP/IP protocol suite.) Data is simply packaged into IP datagrams (also sometimes known as packets), which are sent in the clear across the Internet for delivery to the remote network. The same arrangement is in place for two networks. Any data that one network's router is willing to forward to the other network's router will pass through the Internet. Delivery is based on IP addresses, with each network connection getting a unique IP address. For example, each router shown in Figure 4.8 has two network connections. Therefore, each will have two separate IP addresses: one for the link that connects it to the Internet and the other for the link that connects it to its own local intranet.

FIGURE 4.8

Non-tunneling IP connectivity across the Internet is simple, but not secure.

IP addresses can normally be assigned only where a corresponding network link exists, whether it is a point-to-point dial-up link, an Ethernet adapter connecting to a LAN, or a connection to an ATM network. This attribute of IP addresses comes about because they are ordinarily used to bind a logical (network layer) host address to a physical (link layer) address, enabling the IP network software to transmit data across a physical medium.

To create a virtual private network, however, AltaVista Tunnel creates a software-only pseudonetwork adapter that uses its own IP address while the tunnel is in operation. The tunnel server also uses a pseudonetwork adapter, with another IP address, to serve as the other end of the tunnel. When the remote user wants to connect to the network securely through the tunnel, the upper layers (application and TCP) send their data streams to the tunnel IP address's TCP/IP network protocol stack for processing.

Sending the datagrams to a pseudonetwork adapter on the same host is functionally equivalent to sending those datagrams to some other host. In both cases an entirely different set of programs will process the datagrams, encrypt them, and forward them to the other end of the tunnel.

Once the datagrams arrive at the pseudonetwork adapter's protocol stack, the tunnel software encrypts them and forwards them to the other end of the tunnel through the real, physically connected TCP/IP network protocol stack. Remember that each datagram has two sets of endpoints; the originating host's tunnel IP address and the destination host's normal IP address are both associated with the unencrypted datagram. They are encrypted and encapsulated inside a datagram that is addressed from the real IP address of the tunneling workstation to the real IP address of the tunnel server. Figure 4.9 shows how the tunneling effect is achieved.

FIGURE 4.9

A datagram being sent through a virtual private network tunnel is encrypted before being sent over the Internet.

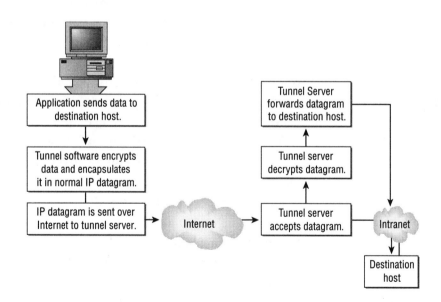

The originating host generates a datagram, using the tunnel IP address as the source address and the destination host's IP address as the destination address. This datagram is encrypted and can be treated as if it were the output of any other network application process on the host. It is packaged into other datagrams, which are sent out to the Internet with the originating host's hardware-linked IP address as the source and the tunnel server's IP address as destination. Once the tunnel server receives this datagram, it strips off the protocol headers to reveal the encrypted datagram, which in turn is decrypted to reveal the original datagram, intended for a host local to the tunnel server. The tunnel server then forwards that datagram to its destination.

When the destination host responds to the originating host, it addresses its datagrams to the originating host's tunnel IP address. These datagrams will be routed to the tunnel server, which encrypts them and encapsulates them into datagrams addressed to the remote host. The process is reversed when the remote host receives these datagrams. (The remote host performs the same decryption functions as the tunnel server.)

The tunnel server behaves like an IP router, accepting datagrams intended for the other end of the tunnel, packaging them, and forwarding them. Although the example above shows how the tunnel works for an individual host connecting into a remote network through a tunnel server, the principles are the same for network-to-network tunneling. Each network has its own tunnel server, and hosts on either network communicate with hosts on the other network by forwarding all packets to the local tunnel server, which encrypts and encapsulates those packets into datagrams to be delivered to the remote tunnel server. When the datagrams arrive at the remote tunnel server, the outer IP headers are stripped away, the encapsulated datagrams are decrypted, and those datagrams are forwarded to their destination host on the remote network.

Microsoft Point-to-Point Tunneling Protocol (PPTP)

Starting with Windows NT version 4.0, Microsoft began shipping its own tunneling protocol, the Point-to-Point Tunneling Protocol (PPTP). The goal of this protocol is to protect data streams passing between hosts connected using the Point-to-Point Protocol (PPP) for remote network access. PPTP simply uses the facilities inherent in PPP for authentication (the Challenge Handshake Authentication Protocol, or CHAP, is described in Chapter 5) and encrypts and encapsulates the resulting data stream between the systems.

Virtual Private Network Security Issues

A recent National Computer Security Association (NCSA) report indicates that virtual private networks may provide sufficient encryption and authentication protections for most uses. However, just as high-security, high-profile systems, like those maintained by the government, military or telecommunications industry, often attract attackers because of their perceived inaccessibility, virtual private networks may attract intruders. Their vulnerability increases as large volumes of encrypted data begin flowing across the Internet.

Another, more disturbing, potential problem for virtual private networks is the *denial-of-service attack*. Organizations wishing to deploy production applications across a virtual private network must be very careful to consider the consequences of an intermediate network outage or a denial-of-service attack against virtual private network nodes, both of which can bring an extranet down for hours or even days. Although most firewalls have been enhanced to deal with the most typical denial-of-service attacks—which are also the easiest to launch—you will very likely always be somewhat vulnerable to such attacks as long as you are connected to a public network. (For a description of two of the most common denial-of-service attacks, SYN flooding and the Ping of Death, see the sidebar to the firewall software roundup article in the June 1997 issue of *BYTE* Magazine.)

Extranet Design Structures

Although you could build a very simple extranet from a pair of routers linking two organizations' intranets over a modem connection, the result would be far from robust, scalable, or reliable. More serious interorganizational internetworking—that is, linking more organizations with better performance and more traffic—over a private extranet requires a significant resolve from all parties to commit time, money, and resources to the effort. Private extranets, being special cases of large-scale data communications networks, are usually approached in three sections:

- End-user or application section

- Network access section

- Backbone section

The end-user or application section is submerged within the intranet clouds in most of the diagrams in this book. This section is the part of the network with which the user interacts: the personal computer, workstation, or terminal; network interface card; and all the supporting network software and LAN media that carry data to and from the user.

The network access section defines the interface between the application layer of the network and the backbone layer of the network— the part of the network that passes data between an intranet and the extranet, for example.

The backbone section is the part that passes data between different network access points, backbone section usually refers to a very high-performance network that can handle a lot of bandwidth. Figure 4.10 shows how the three sections fit into the typical private extranet.

The extranet designer does not necessarily have to be concerned with the specifics of the underlying network structures of the component intranets, since these will likely be the domain of their respective

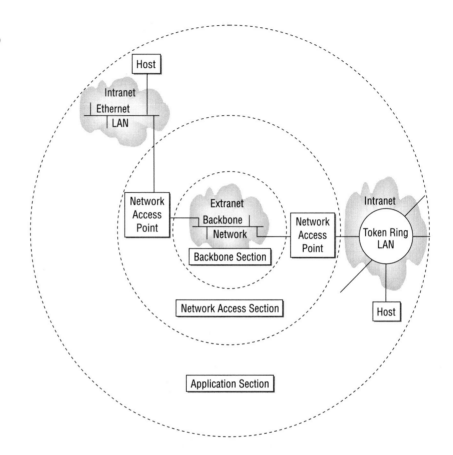

organizations and are also likely to already be in place and operational. The network access design, to link the intranets to the backbone, is very much part of the extranet design. The Internet 2 project
pays considerable attention to the network access portion of the program, for example. Finally, the backbone gives the private extranet its
structure and makes it useful, carrying all interorganizational traffic.
Should the backbone fail, be unreliable, or be unable to handle all
extranet traffic, the extranet itself will fail.

   If network access and backbone design could be explained completely in a single book (let alone chapter), demand for experienced

designers would very likely plummet. The rest of this section introduces some of the issues and options available to extranet designers. (For more in-depth coverage of these topics, a book like Spohn's *Data Network Design 2nd edition*, [McGraw-Hill 1997] is a good place to start.)

Access Network Design Issues

This piece of the puzzle provides the interface from the LAN to the WAN. The network access points of any extranet (or intranet or the Internet) need to accept data generated by users and the processes they run and then forward the data to the network backbone for delivery across the internetwork. Access networks have the following components:

- Routers to pass IP datagrams

- Switches and other network transmission devices to move the bits across wires

- Protocols to properly package all the data being transmitted.

The access network design solves all the issues involved in moving IP datagrams off LAN media, encapsulating them into the right data transmission units for the backbone network, and transmitting them onto a high-speed backbone medium.

Determining how network access works means analyzing the extranet requirements, with special attention to these issues:

- Volume of data expected

- Routes the data takes to get from desktops to network access point

- Network and application performance criteria

- Budgetary considerations

- Structure of the network backbone

Extranet Structure and Backbones

Simple extranets don't necessarily require backbones. Linking two intranets with a point-to-point link (preferably a monitored leased-line solution) is one alternative. Linking all participating intranets with point-to-point links is an acceptable solution in certain situations. This approach, which results in a *full-mesh network*, is illustrated in Figure 4.11. The full-mesh approach provides reliability because it connects every participating network directly with every other participating network. If one network goes down, no other network will be affected by its failure.

The full-mesh network approach is not very scalable—each participating network must build and maintain a separate point-to-point link for every other network. Therefore, with three participants, each network must manage two links; with 10 participants, 44 circuits are linking the networks.

FIGURE 4.11

The full-mesh internetwork uses direct links between every participating network.

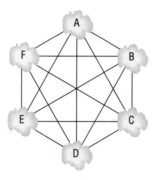

You can achieve some of the benefits of the full-mesh approach, like the ability to withstand circuit failures without affecting interconnectivity, at much lower cost with partial-mesh solutions. As shown in Figure 4.12, a six-network routing extranet can easily operate with nine point-to-point circuits instead of the 15 of a full-mesh network.

Traffic going from network A to networks B, D, or F is transmitted directly; traffic from A to C or E is routed by B or F, respectively. And if the A-to-B link fails, traffic between the two networks could still be carried by routing it through network F.

F I G U R E   4.12

The partial-mesh network reduces the number of point-to-point links without significantly impairing connectivity.

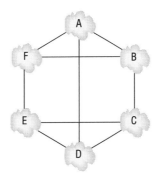

The partial-mesh network is somewhat more scalable than the full-mesh approach, but as the number of networks attached increases, the amount of traffic that must be routed by intermediate networks increases. This increased burden limits the degree to which these networks can expand. Likewise, as the number of networks increases, the number of point-to-point links will also increase to an unacceptable level (albeit more slowly than the full-mesh network).

The solution is to build a backbone—a high-speed network where all participating networks are equidistant, at least conceptually as shown in Figure 4.13. Every network in this extranet is a single hop away from any other network, and the member networks are not burdened with routing traffic between two or more other networks.

The actual configuration of the backbone network will vary depending on a variety of factors, including

- Geographic distribution of member networks

- What type of network medium is required to meet bandwidth needs

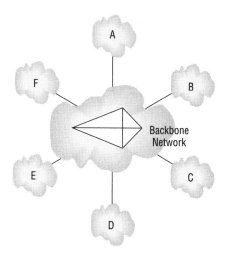

- Number of member networks

- Application performance criteria

- Budgetary considerations

Whether the backbone is deployed as a set of high-speed, point-to-point links to whose endpoints member networks connect (resembling a bus network), as a collapsed backplane to which all members connect (producing a sort of star structure), or as some other configuration will vary from extranet to extranet.

Private backbones solve many of the problems of running a mission-critical application over the extranet, but they pose a new one: The backbone itself becomes a single point of failure for the extranet. When using the Internet as the backbone, you can bypass most failures within the network cloud by routing within the Internet. You can resolve problems with Internet service providers by maintaining a backup or parallel link with another provider, but when the extranet backbone goes down, the entire extranet goes with it. Another drawback to the private extranet backbone is the expense. The backbone usually calls for a significant outlay of capital to build it, as well as the ongoing expense associated with hiring the necessary technical expertise to keep it running.

Ultimately, most extranets won't fit precisely into these categories, but will be implemented with some blend of technologies—mostly because no single solution is applicable to every extranet problem.

PART

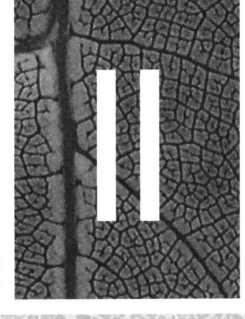

II

EXTRANET BUILDING BLOCKS

CHAPTER

5

Extranet Security

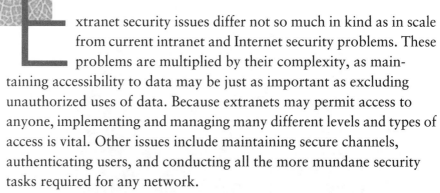

xtranet security issues differ not so much in kind as in scale from current intranet and Internet security problems. These problems are multiplied by their complexity, as maintaining accessibility to data may be just as important as excluding unauthorized uses of data. Because extranets may permit access to anyone, implementing and managing many different levels and types of access is vital. Other issues include maintaining secure channels, authenticating users, and conducting all the more mundane security tasks required for any network.

As should already be apparent, security issues permeate the design, implementation, and management of any internetwork. By definition extranets provide connectivity across organizational boundaries and often across open networks, a condition that requires even greater attention to security details than closed systems do.

This chapter examines the specific mechanisms, technologies, and procedures that extranets require to maintain security, as well as some of the solutions to these issues. Security issues as they relate to the use of virtual private networks (VPNs) were raised in Chapter 4; they will be discussed again in the context of extranet services (Chapter 6) and extranet applications (Chapter 7).

Extranet Security Issues

As internetworks, extranets raise the same security issues as any other internetwork—only more so. When building an intranet, the explicit goal is to keep it a closed system; the security task of protecting resources is very clear. When using the Internet, the explicit goal is to maintain connectivity with users outside the organization; the lack of control over who uses Internet resources is also very clear. When contemplating an extranet, the goal is very nearly the same as when using the Internet; however, the security task is very much like that in an intranet.

The goal of security for any kind of network is to protect the organization's networked resources. Fully developed security plans go way beyond instituting a password access point on an intranet: resources can be harmed by physical catastrophe (flood, fire, and earthquake, for example), as well as by theft or vandalism of equipment, failure of key equipment or software because of manufacturing flaws, software viruses and bugs, or even unauthorized use of systems or data by employees. Unfortunately, although you can plan for those risks, technology alone cannot provide adequate protection. For example, although predicting when an earthquake will hit is difficult, developing backup facilities is relatively easy. Background security checks may screen out the most obvious criminals, but trying to identify and remove employees who pose real security risks is probably impossible.

This chapter addresses only security issues that apply directly to extranets and that are susceptible to technological solutions:

- Limiting extranet access

- Protecting networked assets

- Securing open channels

- Authenticating users and data

Although a certificate authority function is an important security-related service, it is an extranet service and is discussed at greater length in Chapter 6. Authentication of extranet application program code is also discussed in Chapter 6 as well as in Chapter 7.

> Network security is a very complex and difficult field—hardly a subject to be completely covered in a single chapter. Many excellent books on security are available, including Kaufman, Perlman, and Speciner's *Network Security: Private Communication in a Public World,* (PTR Prentice Hall 1995).

Cryptographic Tools for Extranets

Developments in the field of cryptography over the past 20 years have, when coupled with expanding computing power, resulted in nothing less than a revolution. Public key cryptographic tools allow us to transmit encrypted information over open networks and to be confident that only the intended recipient will be able to decrypt the information. *Digital signatures* allow us to know with certainty which entity has produced the information we receive, exactly as we receive it with no changes, over open networks. *Nonrepudiation*—positive and undeniable proof that an entity generated signed and encrypted data— is another by-product of public key cryptography.

Public key cryptography is an integral part of securing extranets, just as it is for securing data passing across the Internet. Without public key cryptography, Internet and extranet commerce and transactions are virtually impossible. The actual mechanism by which it operates is relatively straightforward mathematically and has been explained clearly and completely elsewhere (see preceding sidebar). This section introduces public key encryption and digital signatures.

Public key pairs are sets of two numbers that can be used together in asymmetrical functions. Data processed with either one of the numbers (the key for encrypting the data), can be returned to its original form only by reprocessing it with the other member of the pair (the key for decrypting the data). Just as important, knowing one of the values of

---

The Story of Public Key Cryptography

The story of public key cryptography—how it works and how it came about—is an interesting one, and the mathematics behind it is relatively accessible even to nontechnical readers. To find out more, try the following sources:

- This author's *TCP/IP Clearly Explained* (AP Professional, 1997) includes a very brief introductory discussion of public key cryptography.

- *Network Security: Private Communication in a Public World* by Charlie Kaufman, Radia Perlman, and Mike Speciner (Prentice-Hall, 1995) is an excellent introduction to the mechanisms underlying most of the security tools in general use today. Although it includes fairly detailed technical discussion, it also provides readable introductions to the technologies used.

- *Applied Cryptography* by Bruce Schneier (John Wiley & Sons, 1996) is an excellent resource for programmers and developers interested in building software that uses cryptography. It includes sample source code as well as discussion of the relative merits of different cryptographic algorithms and protocols.

---

the public key pair does not significantly enhance the ability of a criminal to determine the value of the other value. Thus an entity can publish one value of a public key pair (the public key), which other entities can use to encrypt messages. As long as the private key (the other member of the pair) is kept secret, the only entity able to decrypt the messages will be the holder of that value.

This quality of public key pairs enables a bank, for example, to accept transactions from an account holder who has encrypted them using the bank's own public key: Only the bank can decrypt the transactions. Figure 5.1 shows how this asymmetric function operates.

Another function that derives from the asymmetric function associated with public key pairs is that an entity can encrypt data using its private key and make that data available to anyone who is using the entity's public key. Anyone decrypting the information must use

FIGURE 5.1

Data encrypted with a public key can be decrypted only with the private key of the public key pair.

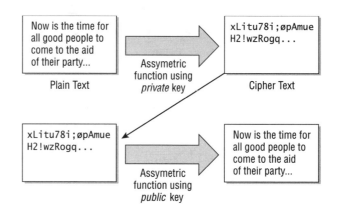

the entity's public key—and in that way can be sure that only the holder of the private key associated with that pair could have been the source of the data. Digital signatures are based on this approach, but instead of encrypting the entire message, the digital signature is based on a hash or digest function that summarizes the message and is then encrypted with the signer's private key. A digital signature is validated by running the same hash function on the message and using the entity's public key to decrypt the signature. If it matches the calculated value of the hash function, the signature is valid.

This use of public key cryptography is the feature that allows a bank to confidently accept transactions transmitted over an open network as coming from a valid account holder. The account holder digitally signs the transaction, which makes the transaction *nonrepudiable;* that is, the account holder cannot deny having originated the transaction without also admitting that his or her private key had been lost or stolen.

Secret key cryptography, the more traditional method of encryption that uses a single shared secret key to encrypt messages, is still very important. Whereas public key cryptography requires relatively intense computation even for short messages, secret key cryptography is usually performed more efficiently and tends to be used often for stream encryption (often using public key encryption to pass session keys between the communicating entities).

Strong encryption requires the use of key lengths sufficiently long to prevent brute-force attacks against the encrypted information. Determining the proper length tends to be a function of estimating how much money and time the most determined attacker (which may often include governments of large nations) is willing and able to spend to break the encryption. Of course, this effort also depends on the value of the information the code breakers are seeking. For example, to protect the design of my 200 mpg carburetor from the oil industry, I must determine how much it would be worth to my adversaries (say, $100 billion) and then encrypt it with a key that is long enough to deter a brute-force attack against the encrypted design—perhaps requiring a trillion dollars' worth of computers running nonstop for the next 20 years would be sufficient.

Because governments have traditionally used cryptography to protect their military and diplomatic communications, cryptographic tools are often classed as armaments. Therefore, political rather than technological considerations often limit the strength of commercially available cryptographic tools. Increasingly, cryptography is making the news pages, but for an interesting and complete overview to the political aspects of cryptography, see *Building-in Big Brother* edited by Lance Hoffman (Springer-Verlag 1994).

Limiting Extranet Access

Limiting access to intranets with no external access points is easy: Simply keep unauthorized users out of the building, and they cannot get into your intranet. Limiting access to your organizational resources through an Internet connection is similarly simple: Put your Internet services on dedicated systems sitting outside the organizational firewall with no direct access inside. In reality, protecting resources is almost never this cut and dried, but because the TCP/IP protocols are so open, the strongest defense against intruders is isolation.

Limiting access to extranets is a much more complicated process, largely because extranets cannot operate in isolation. Even in closed extranets linking only member organizations and individuals, access to certain resources may need to be restricted. Extranets that enable communications through the Internet or that use the Internet as a transport medium have even tougher access problems. Designers need to consider several levels of access:

- Access to the extranet itself

- Access to resources connected to the extranet

- How much of the resource is permitted (e.g., names but not salaries)

- Degree of access permitted (e.g., read only or read/write)

This section examines how to limit access to networks, how to limit access to resources, how to define permissions, and how to use some of the mechanisms that can limit access to extranets.

Three Access Control Mechanisms

The easiest way to limit access to something is to lock it in a safe and throw away the key, ensuring that no one will ever be able to get at your treasure without blowing up the safe. However, although this approach may provide greater confidence in the resource's security, it lacks something in terms of utility. Unless the "right" people (those with authorization) are able to use a resource, you might as well just throw away the resource.

Keeping out unauthorized users and allowing in authorized users is a problem that predates computers, probably by many thousands of years.

Whether dealing with a network or a building or anything else with an inside and an outside, entry control can depend on three things:

- What you know

- What you have

- Who you are

What You Know

Whether you call it a shared secret, a password, or something else, this approach works well in certain situations and less well in others. Problems abound, particularly when an individual needs to use passwords to access many different systems or resources. Passwords need to be changed frequently so that the system will not be compromised if they are lost or stolen. Passwords must be random enough so that they are not easy to guess but simple enough for users to remember without writing them down (thereby, risking loss and theft). Password length is also important; longer passwords are generally more secure than shorter ones, which can be guessed more easily.

The more entities that use the same password, for example, when using a shared secret key to encrypt data that several entities will use, the more likely that password is to be compromised. Whether an entity stores the password insecurely on a computer, writes it on a piece of paper taped next to a terminal, is convinced to divulge it to a "social engineer," or sends it in the clear over a monitored circuit, one instance of loss can easily compromise all users of that password. Password storage, both for system managers and for end users, constitutes a significant risk to those passwords.

On balance, the greatest advantages of using passwords to control access are that users are familiar with the process and that passwords are implemented almost universally on computers and networks.

Social Engineering

Social engineering is the application of social solutions to engineering problems. Computer criminals and other types of criminals are applying social engineering to the problem of getting access to a system when they attempt to persuade a person to divulge a password or permit them to enter a restricted system. Typical techniques include

- Calling a network or system administrator and posing as an irate executive who can't access a corporate system. The criminal may threaten the administrator with dire consequences for holding up a project critical to the organization.

- Calling an end user and posing as a system administrator who needs to diagnose a problem with the network. The criminal may ask the user to provide a user ID and password for system-testing purposes.

- Calling a consumer and posing as a long-distance telephone service security officer. The criminal may ask for calling card numbers or PINs on the pretext of doing a security check.

Other social engineering methods include theft of mail, breaking into offices and searching for passwords or security badges, even extortion and bribery of key personnel. The lesson of social engineering is that no matter how strong the encryption and authentication mechanisms are, there are always other ways to get access to a secured system or resource. Very simply, relying solely on technology to protect a network or system is not enough. Users and employees must also be educated to avoid falling prey to social engineering.

What You Have

Tokens, such as physical keys, backstage passes, ATM cards, and phony IDs, are in some ways an attractive alternative (or supplement) to passwords for controlling access to extranet resources. Until special card-swipe boxes are attached to every network computer, magnetic card tokens won't become common to control network access—but token cards are in general use today. These tokens use on-board processors to generate pseudorandom sequences that are synchronized with systems running on the network. The devices display a sequence for some brief period (often 30 seconds), after which a new sequence is displayed. When a user attempts to log in to the network, a challenge prompt asks for the current output of the device (and sometimes a passcode as well). If the user enters what the authentication system expects from the token, access is permitted; if not, access is denied.

The chief advantage of using this type of token is that it virtually eliminates the risk of having passwords stolen because, in effect, the token generates a new password every few seconds. Although lost or stolen tokens don't necessarily prove identity, assigning a simple passcode to each user can help reduce this risk.

Who You Are

Entering a secure facility should require some method of authenticating that you actually belong there. For example, some sites employ security guards who scrutinize every employee and make sure that no one enters without a matching photo ID or security badge. Other sites may simply use an unattended locked door through which you can pass only if you have the key—or if you walk in behind someone else who has a key. However, the field of biometrics has produced several more promising methods, including the use of fingerprints and retinal scans. Although further from mass market adoption than tokens, biometrics can also be used in combination with passwords and tokens for enhanced security.

Differentiating Internal and External Resources

When designing your extranet security infrastructure, you should be careful to identify and separate the resources that are intended for external (extranet) use and those intended only for internal consumption. You may be able to structure the extranet so that internal systems are protected while external systems are exposed. For example,

Figure 5.2 shows how one organization segments its intranet into two parts, separated by a firewall system. (The firewall itself sometimes includes several physical components.) The portion of the intranet intended for external use sits behind its own firewall gateway and is also set off from the part of the intranet intended for internal consumption by another firewall gateway. The outermost firewall will be more permeable, as it is intended mostly to protect the external resources against gross misuse rather than more insidious attacks. After all, the resources within this external portion of the intranet are intended to be shared. The inner firewall, however, protects more sensitive resources, including production systems and proprietary data resources, and will therefore be considerably more restrictive in the packets it allows to pass.

FIGURE 5.2

Segregating internal and external resources can simplify extranet security considerations.

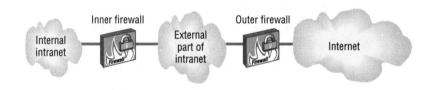

Exposing any more of the organizational intranet to the outside can be quite risky. When the resources to be shared on the extranet must be maintained on more sensitive internal systems, one approach is to simulate the structure shown in Figure 5.2 using an object request broker (ORB) sitting outside an inner firewall and accepting—and handling—requests for resources through the ORB. The ORB responds to requests from the outside by relaying them inward using Internet Inter-ORB Protocol (IIOP), connecting to an ORB on the inside of the intranet. By designing the interacting objects correctly, outsiders will be able to access only that data for which they are authorized. Figure 5.3 shows how this mapping works.

FIGURE 5.3

Distributed objects allow
an extranet to seem to
encompass the private
portions of a member
intranet.

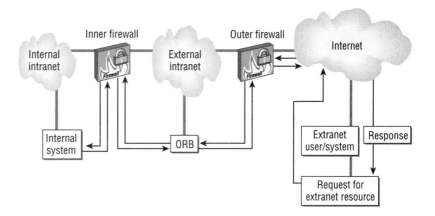

Using ORBs allows extranet users to have limited access to information and processes that live inside the private portion of an intranet, even though the actual systems through which this information is distributed live outside the physical borders of the extranet.

Authenticating Extranet Users

One of the first things the extranet implementer must do is to determine who will be using the extranet. This group may include anyone, all customers, or all customers who subscribe to a particular service that includes access to the extranet; on the other hand, it may be limited to an even more exclusive group. No matter how the extranet user population is determined, defining the population should be one of your first tasks. The user population will very likely be the most important factor driving extranet security, infrastructure, and applications.

Most extranets have a mixed user group ranging from potential customers to existing customers to business associates, trading partners, and organization employees—all requiring varying levels of access. Mixed security environments are common; various resources can be available at differing levels of access for different sets of users based in different locations.

Simple user ID and password access control are sufficient to protect resources as long as the transmission of the password and user ID can be kept private. As more resources are made available through networks, particularly open networks, plaintext (unencrypted data that can be viewed by anyone) transmission of passwords and user IDs becomes less acceptable. Using the Internet to transmit passwords and user IDs is an invitation to attack by eavesdroppers who can intercept them unless you take measures to protect this access control.

Some approaches that take user authentication beyond the simple password and user ID pairing are discussed next. Access control encryption (ACE) is the system used in the Security Dynamics SecurID hardware token system. SecurID tokens are about the size of a credit card (though noticeably thicker) and have been used for secured access to organizational networks since the 1980s.

Another authentication technology is S/Key, a system devised by Bellcore for generating and authenticating one-time passwords through software-only implementations. Users generate a database on the S/Key server, which verifies one-time passwords (OTPs) based on a secret code known only to the user and not stored on any system.

Password Authentication Protocol (PAP, RFC 1334); Challenge Handshake Authentication Protocol (CHAP, RFC 1994); and Remote Authentication Dial In User Service (RADIUS, RFC 2058) are related protocols that authenticate users connecting to resources across a dial-up or other point-to-point link. These protocols are of particular interest to people wanting to implement secure extranetworks without denying dial-up access to remote users and sites.

User authentication tools are necessary but not sufficient to protect valuable resources from unauthorized access. They can be vulnerable to man-in-the-middle eavesdropping (an eavesdropper intercepts and manipulates messages sent between the user and the system being accessed), to social engineering, and to other routes of attack. However, authentication tools can help keep out most casual attackers and can also keep track of resource use.

SecurID ACE

When SecurID ACE users attempt to connect to a protected resource (usually a network, through an ACE server), they are prompted for their user name and a passcode (the number currently displayed on the SecurID card, or token, and a personal identification number, or PIN). Then the following sequence of events occurs:

1. The server retrieves the PIN and a seed number associated with the SecurID card assigned to the user name.

2. The server uses another mechanism (using data from previous connections) to attempt to estimate the current clock "drift" associated with the internal time keeping of the token.

3. The server calculates the correct token passcode, including the PIN, and determines for how long that passcode will be accepted as valid authentication.

The passcode itself is the product of a hashing function that starts with the token's secret key and the current time to generate a time-limited product. The token generates these values continuously, but the server calculates this value when a user attempts to connect to the resource. The token's secret key, the product of the key, and the current time are never transmitted; rather, a cryptographic hash (or digest) function is applied to the result to produce a much smaller value (though still too large to be susceptible to guessing). If the server comes up with the same value as the user who is attempting to log in, access will be allowed.

The result is a two-part authentication:

1. The user enters a correct PIN to indicate knowledge of a shared secret. (The user and the server share this information.)

2. The user enters a correct passcode to indicate possession of the token.

Strictly speaking, the access control encryption protocol doesn't use encryption (although cryptographic hashes are used). The founder of Security Dynamics merely wanted to create a product name that could use the acronym ACE.

Bellcore S/Key

The risk of using a hardware token for user authentication is that the token can be lost or stolen, and if the PIN (usually shorter than the typical stand-alone password) can be compromised, a criminal can be authenticated as an authorized user. Bellcore's software-only solution, S/Key, generates one-time passwords based on a password known only to the user but not stored on any system.

S/Key requires only that the server side of the resource be modified. It uses one-time passwords that do not require encryption or any other special treatment through the client. Each time the user logs in, a different password is used; intercepting it would be of little use to anyone. A sequence of one-time passwords is generated with a *one-way hashing function;* that is, a function that modifies input so that it cannot be determined simply from the output. S/Key usually uses the MD5 message digest function (sometimes the MD4 function is used) to generate a list of one-time passwords for the user. (These passwords may either be printed out or may be generated on the user's client system.)

The key to S/Key is that it uses passwords in the reverse order from which they are generated so that the one-way nature of the hashing function can be used to authenticate the user. It works like this:

1. The user enters a secret password in a direct (at the host console, for example) or secure (encrypted Telnet, for example) connection with the host.

2. The S/Key host software uses that password and an internal, randomly generated key to create a seed value for the password list.

3. The S/Key host then hashes the seed value repeatedly, storing only the last value calculated. Typically, the digest function is run 99 times, with the S/Key host storing only the 99th value, along with the random value generated to seed the hashing process and the user ID.

4. The user logs in to the S/Key host for the first time and is prompted for the 98th password (if the one stored on the host is the 99th value). The S/Key host runs the hashing function on the 98th password (sent by the user); if the result is the value stored, the user is permitted access.

5. The S/Key host replaces the previously stored password value (the 99th value) with the password just used (the 98th value). The next time the user logs in, the 97th hash value must be used to produce the stored value when the hashing function is run.

Like any security mechanism, S/Key is not 100 percent bulletproof. For example, it can be defeated if a criminal is able to steal the list of passwords or get access to the system storing the user's passwords. However, S/Key is potentially safer than sending reusable passwords in the clear over the Internet.

Password Authentication Protocol (PAP)

Originally designed as a simple method for a host to authenticate itself to another host while using the Point-to-Point Protocol (PPP), the Password Authentication Protocol (PAP) is described in detail in RFC 1334, "PPP Authentication Protocols." Very simply, PAP is a two-way handshaking protocol in which the host making the connection (the *peer*) sends a user ID and password pair to the system it is trying to establish a connection with (the *authenticator*—though not all PPP links require authentication). PAP is two-way because it uses a simple, two-step process. The peer sends its authentication information, and the authenticator acknowledges approval of the peer. PAP authentication can be used at the start of the PPP link as well as during a PPP session to reauthenticate the link.

Once the PPP link is established, PAP authentication can be carried out over that link. The peer sends a user ID and password in the clear to the authenticator until the authenticator accepts the pair or the connection is terminated. PAP is not secure: Authentication information is transmitted in the clear, and nothing protects against playback attacks (repetition of successful log on attempts by an interceptor) or excessive repetition by attackers trying to guess a good password/user ID pair.

Challenge Handshake Authentication Protocol (CHAP)

Documented in RFC 1994 ("PPP Challenge Handshake Authentication Protocol [CHAP]"), which supersedes RFC 1334, CHAP provides a more secure mechanism for authenticating PPP links. Like PAP, CHAP can be used at the start of a PPP link as well as repeated after the link has been established.

CHAP is referred to as a *three-way handshake protocol* because it incorporates three steps to produce a verified link after the link is first initiated (or at any time after the link has been established and verified). Instead of a simple two-step password/approval process, CHAP uses a one-way hashing function in a fashion similar to that used by S/Key. MD5 is specified as a requirement of the protocol, though other functions can be supported. The actual process looks like this:

1. The authenticator sends a challenge message to the peer.

2. The peer calculates a value using a one-way hash function and sends it back to the authenticator.

3. The authenticator can acknowledge authentication if the response matches the expected value.

The process can be repeated at any time during the PPP link to make sure that the connection has not been taken over or subverted in some way. Unlike PAP, which is driven by the client side, the server controls CHAP reauthentication. CHAP also removes the possibility, inherent in PAP, that an attacker can repeatedly attempt to log in over the same connection. When the CHAP authentication fails, the server is required to drop the connection, complicating the task of password guessing.

Remote Authentication Dial In User Service (RADIUS)

CHAP, although a stronger method than PAP for authenticating dial-up users, is not inherently as scalable a protocol as large organizations might need. Even though it doesn't transmit any secrets across a network, it does require lots of shared secrets to be run through the hash function. Organizations with many dial-up users must maintain very large databases to accommodate them all. The Remote Authentication Dial In User Service (RADIUS) protocol, described in RFC 2058, uses a client/server model to securely authenticate and administer remote network connection users and sessions. RADIUS is largely a way to make access control more manageable, and it can support other types of user authentication, including PAP and CHAP.

The RADIUS client/server model uses a network access server (NAS) to manage user connections. Although the NAS functions as a server for providing network access, it functions as a client for RADIUS. The NAS is responsible for accepting user connection requests, for getting user ID and password information, and for passing it securely to the RADIUS server. The RADIUS server returns authentication status (approved or denied), as well as any configuration information required for the NAS to provide services to the end user (for example, what access to network resources is permitted).

By providing a single point of access while supporting multiple authentication schemes out of multiple systems, RADIUS simplifies securing access to different resources within an internetwork. RADIUS clients and servers communicate securely, using shared secrets for authentication and encryption for transmitting user passwords.

Terminal Access Controller Access Control System (TACACS)

Terminal Access Controller Access Control System (TACACS) is a protocol specification, described in RFC 1492, that can administer authentication, authorization, and accounting information for users logging in. TACACS are currently best known as Cisco System Inc.'s server-based security software protocol. All Cisco router and access server product families use this protocol.

TACACS uses a centralized server, either a special TACACS database or the UNIX password file with TACACS protocol support, to which all authentication, authorization, and accounting information is directed when a user attempts to log in. For example, a UNIX server supporting TACACS passes requests to the UNIX database and returns the accept or reject message to the access server.

TACACS, as described in RFC 1492, transmits all information in the clear between the user and the server, but a recent update from Cisco, TACACS+, adds a message digest function to eliminate plaintext transmission of passwords. TACACS+ also supports multiprotocol logins, meaning that a single user ID and password pair can authenticate a user for multiple devices and networks (e.g., an IP network login and an IPX network login). Finally, TACACS+ can also handle PAP and CHAP authentication.

Protecting Corporate Assets

An extranet requires a complete security infrastructure, including far more than the mechanisms by which data and network resources are protected from unauthorized access and improper tampering. For example:

- Contingency plans for catastrophes
- Screening programs for systems employee candidates

- Training programs to keep employees aware of good security practices and proper physical security for information systems

The protective mechanisms discussed here, however, extend beyond the features just mentioned. Two basic strategies are

- Firewall gateway systems

- Virtual private networks

These strategies are most important, and possibly most interesting, from a technological viewpoint. They use various architectural and cryptographic tools to protect data and networks against active attacks. Organizations are increasingly relying on these strategies to keep critical applications safe in an open networking environment (the Internet). Virtual private networks were covered in Chapter 4 because they function as part of the extranet infrastructure and use security tools as enabling technologies. Firewall gateways are covered in this chapter because they have traditionally been considered an integral part of the internetworking security infrastructure.

Firewalls

The goal of keeping unauthorized users out of sensitive networks and systems requires constant vigilance as well as multiple strategies to cover all the bases. This section discusses five of the most important firewall strategies:

- Packet filtering

- Circuit gateway

- Application proxies

- Hardened operating systems

- Network Address Translation (NAT)

The design of the actual firewall system, which can often include several separate systems and physically isolated networks, is a sixth important aspect of effective firewall protection and is discussed in the section "Circuit Gateway." The following section examines functional strategies.

Packet Filtering

Perhaps the most obvious way to keep out unauthorized users (and prevent internal users from unauthorized access to the outside) is the packet filter. In fact, many entry-level LAN-to-Internet access products, such as low-end routers, hardware, and software products, provide a degree of firewall protection through packet filtering. A packet filter can be implemented on any standard IP router, though a filter packet alone will be insufficient protection for most intranet and extranet security applications.

By its nature the TCP/IP protocol suite makes it relatively easy to set up rules for filtering packets, traveling in either direction (in or out) through an internetwork router. Every IP datagram includes information about its destination, its source, and its contents. Because each IP datagram passing in or out of an internetwork can be forced to go through a single point (the firewall gateway), each datagram can be checked against a list of rules to determine whether it should be allowed to pass.

Packet filtering rules use the information in the IP datagram to determine what is permitted and what is not permitted to pass through the firewall. Figure 5.4 shows how this process works. Generally accepted practice is to be strict—prohibiting anything that is not explicitly permitted—rather than to be liberal—permitting anything that is not expressly prohibited. The firewall gateway doing the filtering checks every packet, incoming and outgoing, and compares it to the list of rules. If the packet is for a service (FTP) going to an allowed port (port 23) on a host on a permitted network, then the packet is forwarded; otherwise, it is blocked.

Building a packet filter requires determining what services, ports, sources, and destinations are permitted.

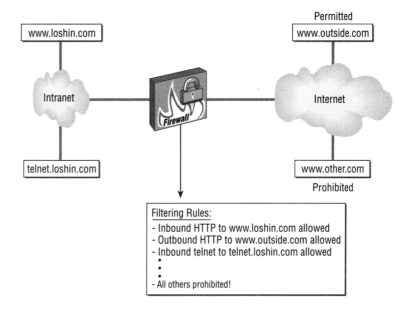

Packet filtering seems to offer an excellent way to ensure network integrity. More difficult, however, is creating a list of rules that can be relied upon to always keep out intruders and to never (or rarely) disrupt normal operations. In addition, people can find many ways to avoid most packet-filtering rules. For instance, some companies use packet filtering to keep employees from accessing the World Wide Web. Devious employees can still do their Web surfing through such packet filters by using an alternative protocol to connect to a host outside the network and tunneling their Web sessions through that permitted link. Figure 5.5 shows how a user can tunnel HTTP transfers with a Telnet connection through a firewall that prohibits connections to external HTTP servers but that permits access to Telnet servers.

Packet filtering will keep out certain types of casual intruders and may slow down more sophisticated intruders; it may also limit use from inside the organization. The way TCP/IP application protocols operate makes filtering of outbound packets as important as filtering inbound packets. For example, FTP uses two virtual circuits during file transfer: one initiated by the client to connect to the server (this circuit

FIGURE 5.5

Tunneling one application protocol inside another can circumvent firewall gateway packet filters.

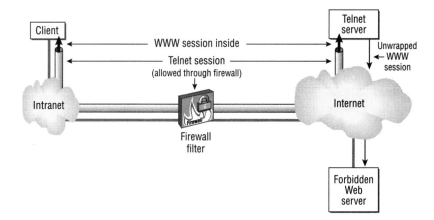

carries control information like client requests and response codes from the server) and the other initiated by the server, in response to a client request for a file, to carry the actual file transfer. If a packet filter permits outbound FTP sessions, it must also permit at least some inbound FTP session traffic. Otherwise, users would be able to open a file transfer session without being able to transfer any files.

Packet filtering suffers other drawbacks as well:

- Once you allow access to an internal host, you cannot control what happens on that host. This loophole permits the remote user to attempt to exploit any security weakness in that host—possibly using that host's access to other hosts on the network.

- Packet filters use the information stored in IP datagram headers, which means that attackers can do *IP spoofing*—counterfeiting the source IP address of the datagram, making the gateway believe it comes from an authorized host (for example, from inside the protected network).

- Packet filters provide no mechanism for user authentication; instead they depend on the security of the remote systems from which access is permitted. Therefore, if an intruder breaks into a remote system that is permitted access by the firewall, that intruder can get inside the firewall without being challenged or detected.

Packet filtering is an important function of the firewall gateway system but is not a complete and secure firewall solution by itself. However, packet filtering becomes increasingly difficult to implement as the number of prohibited and permitted services, networks, and hosts increase. As the number of rules increases, the amount of processing required to determine whether any particular datagram should be passed also increases—as does the likelihood that a permitted datagram may be blocked or that a prohibited datagram may be permitted. Defining and maintaining rules is often quite complicated, and rules do not always have the intended effect—anyone who is building an IP filter should also know a lot about the TCP/IP application protocols and how they work. Finally, some older filtering products do not process rules in order, so when a rule affecting a broad prohibition (e.g., Deny all datagrams from outside the firewall) is executed before a rule permitting some access (e.g., Allow FTP datagrams from host X), the desired effect won't occur.

Circuit Gateway

Another approach to protecting internal hosts from attack is to have the firewall system act as an intermediary for all application exchanges. In other words, internal hosts pass all session requests through the firewall, which forwards them to the remote server as if they were coming directly from the firewall. The remote server then responds to the request by replying directly to the firewall, which relays the response to the internal host. Figure 5.6 shows how this process can prevent any direct links between internal systems and external systems. Both the internal system and the external system connect directly to the firewall, which relays all messages between the two.

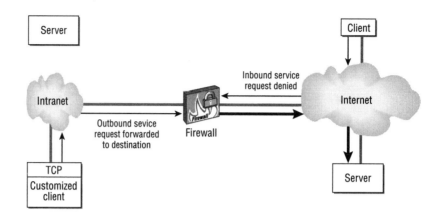

FIGURE 5.6

A circuit-level gateway acts as an intermediary between internal hosts and external hosts.

Circuit-level gateways act to eliminate access to unauthorized servers on the protected network. This security measure provides a certain amount of protection from attacks that originate from within the organization. Server software can be configured to listen to a nonstandard transport layer (where circuits are created in TCP/IP networking) port, allowing access by unauthorized users from outside the protected network even if packet filtering is turned on. Circuit gateways can eliminate this risk because they deny all unsolicited incoming requests (which means that nothing from outside the protected network can gain access to internal hosts).

On the downside, circuit gateways often require that systems inside the gateway use special versions of TCP/IP client application software to support the indirect connection with external hosts through the circuit gateway. Consequently, all users within the organization wishing to access services outside the firewall—through the firewall—need to have special copies of the client application software: standard clients will be denied access through the firewall. And of course, because no inbound client requests are permitted, circuit gateways support a limited level of service. (Some firewalls claim to support circuit gatewaying transparently to end users.)

Application Proxies

Whereas circuit gateways use special software to provide the interface between the application client inside the firewall and the application server outside the firewall, an application gateway provides the same service seamlessly: The firewall acts as a proxy for the client when a service is requested and passes responses from the server back through to the client. A *proxy* is the same as an application gateway and is the most secure type of firewall gateway system. The proxy maintains the state of the TCP connection between client and server and is thus able to make the client program believe it is connected directly to the server. Likewise, the server program behaves as if it were connected directly to a client located on the application gateway. The server program never knows (or needs to know) where the client program is actually located.

Figure 5.7 shows how an application gateway operates. In effect, the proxy acts on behalf of the client when communicating with a server and on behalf of the server when communicating with the client. An advantage of application gateways is that you can configure them to pass external requests in to approved servers. This technique is possible because all requests to open well-known ports are funneled through a single point: the application gateway.

FIGURE 5.7

Application gateways, also known as proxies, maintain the state of TCP connections between clients and servers so that both ends believe they are directly connected.

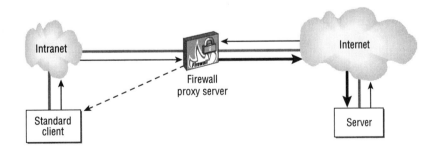

For example, requests to open a Telnet session from an external host to an internal host all are processed through the gateway. If the session request is for a host that is authorized to provide Telnet services to outside users, the gateway will pass the session request to the internal host. If, on the other hand, the request is to open a Telnet session on a host that has not been authorized to provide Telnet services, the firewall will not pass it through.

Because they are involved directly in every application interchange between clients and servers inside and outside the firewall, application gateways can do very detailed logging of all those connections—and of all attempted connections. Logging failed attempts to break into systems on the intranet can be invaluable in tracking down the source of the attacks. And of course, when combined with network administrator notification systems, firewall gateways can alert intranet managers to an attack in progress.

Application gateways mediate all client and server connections to systems outside the intranet, a task that can be very computer intensive. One potential problem is that application gateways may become a performance bottleneck, particularly as the number of simultaneous sessions increases.

Hardened Operating Systems

The more doors a building has, the easier it is to break in. Operating systems don't have doors, but they do have various ways of allowing users (and other programs) to get in to the system and use it. The more functions that are allowed, the more different ways outsiders can get in. Accessibility to computing resources is usually a good thing, as the whole point of computer systems is to allow people and programs to use the resources stored and maintained on the system.

Unfortunately, firewall gateways are not intended to be used as multipurpose computers. The firewall is intended to act simply as a gatekeeper, keeping the inside in and the outside out. Firewalls generally use variations of commonly available operating systems (usually some flavor of UNIX). Some firewalls that use Windows NT require the administrator to configure the operating system to shut down or prevent access to sensitive functions and resources because those operating systems are robust and reasonably well understood. Network managers can be confident that OS security bugs will have been discovered over the years that the OS has been in general use and that any new bugs will be found and fixes made public.

Firewall gateways very often use operating systems that have been "hardened" against attack even further by reducing the number of potential doors to the system. For example, removing the functions that support multiple users on a system (and thus disallowing any access other than through a direct physical connection to the system) improves security. Taking out all nonessential system commands and functions is another important step to strengthening the OS. Firewalls need to implement only enough of the TCP/IP network stack to be able to pass IP datagrams from one network (the intranet) to another (another intranet, an extranet, or the Internet). As Figure 5.8 shows, firewall systems don't need to have client or server software running to provide e-mail, file transfer, or terminal emulation; firewalls also don't need any application software or functions. Removing the functions means that attackers cannot use those functions to subvert the system.

FIGURE 5.8

Hardened operating systems have only enough functionality, through a basic OS kernel and TCP/IP stack, to provide firewall services.

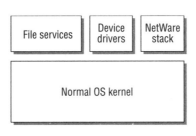

Normal Operating System

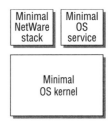

Hardened Operating System

Network Address Translation

Another fairly common strategy for protecting intranets, illustrated in Figure 5.9, is to have a gateway act as a "mailing address" for all the hosts within the network. In other words, network addresses within the intranet are kept entirely private, whereas the addresses advertised to the outside world are maintained and managed through the gateway. All domain names within the protected network are associated with the gateway's IP address; the firewall sorts out requests to the appropriate systems inside the network but never advertises the actual locations or addresses of those systems. The origin of these addresses is explained in the sidebar "The Internet Address Shortage and Private Network Addressing."

FIGURE 5.9

A gateway can perform network address translation to keep intranet addressing information private.

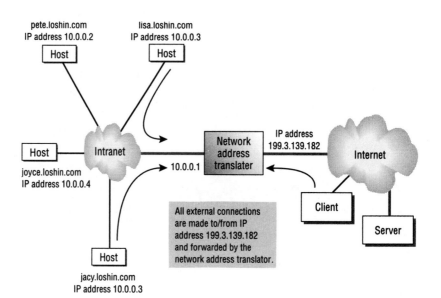

When requests come in to the gateway, it forwards the request to the destination host without allowing the source host know anything about the internal system. Because the internal network uses nonrouting network addresses, no (standards compliant) router will forward packets to the network. And because any number of organizations can use these nonrouting network addresses for their internal networks, a router cannot be certain it is properly forwarding datagrams addressed to these addresses.

Network address translation can be both a blessing and a curse. For example, if you have a NAT product that offers only many-to-one address translation (only one outside address for all your internal addresses), you may have trouble offering services (like HTTP) on more than one internal system. Because the firewall has one port 80 (the port on which HTTP requests are monitored by the server), you may need to use nonstandard ports for the additional HTTP servers.

Another approach to network address translation is to use of protocol gateways to connect non-IP networks. For example, linking a Novell NetWare LAN to the Internet with a protocol gateway guarantees that no direct IP interoperability exists between hosts inside the private internetwork and outside it simply because no host within the internetwork is running IP. These devices are popular for small organizations and offices looking for a simple and economical way to connect a legacy LAN to the Internet—simple because they usually require little installation and configuration; economical because they often allow an entire office to share a single IP address for access to the Internet. Of course, the major drawback to protocol gateways is that they do not support inbound traffic very well, so internal systems will not be directly accessible to anyone outside the organization.

The Internet Address Shortage and Private Network Addressing

By the late 1980s, computer experts realized that the IP address space, thought to be more than enough when it was designed a decade earlier, would soon be exhausted. If the address space were used efficiently, as many as 4 billion hosts could be supported with the 32-bit addresses. However, designing addresses that allowed hierarchical addressing meant allowing the largest networks to "waste" much of the address space.

Proposals for an upgrade to the Internet Protocol version 4 were submitted in the early 1990s, and by 1996 most of the basic specifications for IP version 6 (version 5 was skipped for historical reasons) had been submitted to and approved by the Internet Engineering Task Force (IETF).

One of the proposed stopgap strategies was to use standardized nonrouting network addresses for private IP networks. Organizations using IP for their internal networks had long been encouraged to request and use an official network IP address from Internet registration authorities, whether or not they ever intended to connect to the global Internet. There was no technical reason to use this numbering scheme, and many organizations simply assigned themselves their own unregistered network IP address.

Some organizations using unregistered network addresses subsequently wanted to connect to the Internet, and they had to reconfigure all their systems to conform to their new, official, network IP address. Recognizing that not all organizations using IP would want to open their networks to outsiders—and also recognizing that as the address space was depleted, assigning registered network addresses to these organizations was wasteful—a set of three network addresses (one each for Class A, B, and C networks) was set aside for nonrouting intranets. In addition, all IP-compliant routers are required to not forward datagrams destined for these network addresses.

Firewall Gateway Topologies

Two sets of topologies relate to firewalls:

- Topologies that define the shape of the firewall gateway system itself, which may include several systems and isolating networks

- Topologies that define the way entire internetworks are segmented by firewalls, using layered firewalls to provide added protection to interior networks

So far, this discussion of firewall gateways has been in the context of the firewall functions, rather about specific examples of how they are deployed. Implementing any but the most basic firewall can require two or more separate hardware components and often requires significant expenditures on hardware and software, network implementation, and security consulting services.

This section introduces some of the basic building blocks of the firewall gateway system and examines one strategy for nesting firewalls to provide additional protection to restricted networks within an extranet.

Firewall Gateway Components

Each component of a firewall system fulfills some security function. The most basic component is the *screening router,* which is simply a device that can do packet filtering. Some stand-alone commercial firewall products (or other types of product that claim a firewall function) are simply screening routers. As has been mentioned, simply filtering packets is not sufficient to completely protect an internetwork from attack, though screening routers are vital building blocks of the secure firewall gateway.

Central to most firewall systems is the *bastion host,* a well-protected host placed strategically to guard the internal network. A bastion host and a screening router are often used together. The router forwards packets from outside the network to the bastion host only and accepts outbound packets from the bastion host only. An example of this configuration appears in Figure 5.10. The bastion host is placed inside the protected network, and the screening router funnels all packets bound for or from the external network through the bastion host.

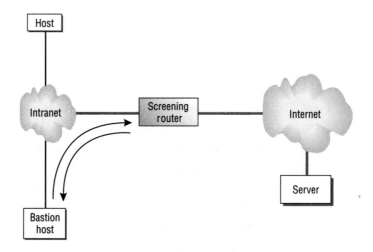

A firewall can be implemented using a combination of these components to enhance security. Sometimes referred to as a "belt and suspenders" or "screened subnet," the firewall system shown in Figure 5.11 uses two screening routers on their own subnet, shared only with a bastion host, to separate inside from outside. The subnet itself is sometimes called a "DMZ," or demilitarized zone, because it provides a space in which all traffic can be minutely examined before being allowed in or out. The advantage of this approach—as long as all components are securely configured and managed—is that it requires intruders to break through three layers of protection.

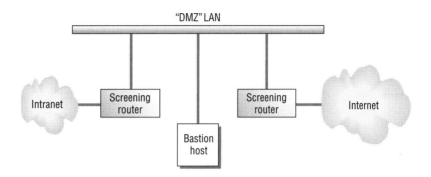

Nested Security Zones

The purpose of traditional firewalls is very simple: to separate an intranet from the Internet. Extranets, however, are often designed to provide some degree of permeability to access via the Internet. Using multiple firewall systems within an organizational extranet allows the organization to selectively open only part of its internetwork to the Internet. Figure 5.12 shows a simple example of how nesting firewalls can produce two security zones: one for internal, proprietary systems and the other for open, shared extranet systems.

In general, as you move inward into an internetwork across firewalls, the level of security should be constant or increase rather than decrease. In other words, the inner firewalls should be stronger than the outer firewalls. When stronger firewalls are used for the outermost perimeter, intruders able to pierce that perimeter will almost certainly be able to easily bypass internal firewalls. On the other hand, when firewalls increase in strength as they move inward to more valuable resources, intruders face greater obstacles to access as they attempt to attack those resources.

Extending this approach to larger organizations and to extranets reveals added benefits. By properly nesting firewalls and combining them with virtual private networks, it is possible to partition intranets into security zones within the extranet. Internal peer networks and

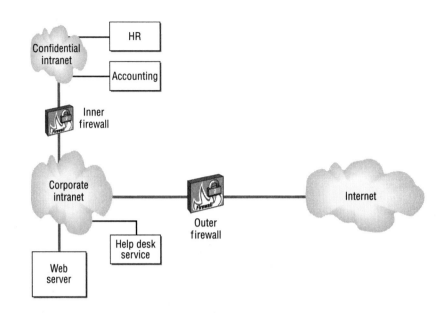

FIGURE 5.12
One firewall restricts access to proprietary resources while another allows limited but open access to resources across the Internet.

intranets can maintain interconnectivity within security zones while restricting access to outsiders. For example, a corporation's branch sales offices can be kept in an outer security zone with easy access to each other but somewhat restricted access to outsiders; marketing, accounting, and finance intranets can be put behind a more restrictive firewall, each using its own, even more restrictive, firewall for further protection, as shown in Figure 5.13.

Auditing Extranet Access

No security infrastructure can reliably and securely operate by itself. Until true artificial intelligence—capable of making reasoned decisions affecting all extranet users—is developed, an experienced human should be in the decision loop. Network auditing is a requirement, though, to allow automated systems to monitor all extranet access, flag suspicious activity, and notify the human network manager appropriately.

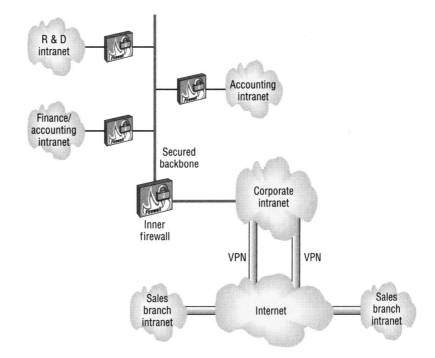

The extranet manager is responsible for determining what to audit, what to record, and what type of event should trigger a notification (and what type of notification the event deserves: e-mail, wireless page, weekly status report). Being too cautious can be costly in time wasted on false alarms, hardware required to store excessively detailed audit data, and time spent on keeping track of all the audit information. On the other hand, lack of caution can allow intruders to slip in unnoticed.

Deciding how to audit extranet access and what to audit are important decisions that should be made with the informed participation of all responsible parties—and probably a security consultant. As with any other aspect of extranet security, all parties should be aware both of the cost of implementation and of the risks related to foregoing the security feature. The final decision should balance both sets of costs.

Securing Open Channels

The TCP/IP protocol suite is a set of open standards designed for interoperability. This openness can pose a security risk because TCP/IP data is generally transmitted in the clear, often across public networks, and usually across networks about which the source and destination systems have no knowledge. The range of data that is vulnerable to eavesdroppers runs the gamut from basic network service user IDs and passwords (for example, Telnet and FTP logins are transmitted in the clear) to credit card numbers (easily identified by their format when sent in the clear) to confidential e-mail and attachments (also usually sent in the clear).

Within the TCP/IP architecture, one might consider protecting channels at any of the four internetwork layers. (See Appendix B for more details of the Internet model and TCP/IP networking.) However, by definition it would be fruitless to attempt to encrypt all data link layer transmissions, since they would have to be decoded once they reached a router—otherwise, a remote host could never receive the transmission. Although encryption can be accomplished at the network layer (IP layer) or at the transport layer, TCP/IP networking engineers and computer scientists traditionally eschewed encryption and most other security measures at these levels. They argued that these functions cost too much processing overhead and were best provided by the applications themselves at the application layer.

The networking engineers have long believed that the best place to do encryption (as well as other security and integrity functions) is the application layer. They reasoned that using an end-to-end encryption scheme put the task of encrypting the data in the hands of the application generating the data and put the task of decrypting the data in the hands of the application using it at the other end of the pipe. This arrangement removed the burden of cryptographic processing (increasingly large, particularly as key sizes grow) from any part of the networking stack.

Moving the task down the stack to the transport layer might slow down network processing while keeping encryption as an end-to-end process (of a sort). The data stream is encrypted by the transport layer software and decrypted only upon reaching its destination by the destination host's transport layer implementation. One advantage of encrypting at the transport layer is that many details of the application that would otherwise be sent in the clear can be hidden. Application protocol headers proclaim the contents of the data portion of application messages, including user authentication information. This information exposes the users of the application to known-plaintext attacks, where the attacker knows or guesses some bit of the transmission, such as a user ID, and may be able to break the security in that way. Encrypting the entire application data stream at the transport layer can reduce the risk from this type of attack.

Moving the encryption task further down the stack to the network layer also causes changes. Encrypting IP datagrams further obscures their contents (though this technique is not effective against all traffic analysis attacks) and allows routers to directly exchange encrypted datagrams. Although the use of encryption on IP datagrams is particularly useful for building a virtual private network, generating a stream of encrypted datagrams requires more computational resources than sending plaintext datagrams. When a router is used to do encryption of IP datagrams, this extra computation may affect the ability of the router to process regular network traffic (depending on the router and the normal network traffic load).

The following sections introduce some of the security and encryption protocols currently implemented or in development for use at the application layer, the transport layer, and the network layer. This list is not comprehensive, and it includes protocols that have been approved by standards bodies, protocols that are still being developed, and widely used nonstandard protocols.

Most of these protocols provide for some sort of negotiation between client and server to determine which cryptographic functions (digital signature or encryption, for example) and which cryptographic algorithms (RSA public key or DES secret key encryption, for example) are necessary to complete the connection. The various methods of doing this negotiation, and of exchanging key, signature, and cipher-text data, vary depending on the protocol.

RSA is a public key cryptography algorithm named after its developers, researchers Ron Rivest, Adi Shamir, and Len Adleman. RSA is now also a company, offering cryptographic products and services based on this algorithm.

DES stands for Data Encryption Standard. It is a symmetric key algorithm developed for general purpose use for the U.S. government, as well as for commercial users.

Application Layer Security

Virtually any application that requires a password for access could be said to provide some application layer security, but fewer applications actually use that password to secure the information passed back and forth between client and server. This section introduces some of the more popular applications that implement security of this type at the application layer.

Secure Electronic Transaction (SET)

MasterCard International and Visa International, after much work and some apparent disagreement, released a specification for the Secure Electronic Transaction (SET) in 1996. Developed with input from GTE,

IBM, Microsoft, Netscape, SAIC, Terisa, and Verisign, and eventually supported by American Express and other credit and charge card issuers, SET defines how transaction data flows among card users, merchants, and banks and also defines the security functions (digital signatures, hashes, and encryption) that must support these transactions.

The major card issuers have been urging their cardholders not to use their cards for Internet transactions unless they use SET. (Some issuers have also supported the CyberCash service.) Most organizations providing Internet commerce services and software have committed to supporting SET when it is completely specified, with widespread deployment of SET-enabled commerce applications by the end of 1997.

Secure HTTP (S-HTTP)

The Hypertext Transport Protocol (HTTP) upon which the World Wide Web is built does not include any mechanisms for security. The Secure HTTP (S-HTTP) protocol was developed as an extension to HTTP and is documented in IETF working group documents. S-HTTP described a mechanism for using standard cryptographic tools to encrypt HTTP data transfers. Although S-HTTP was widely implemented in Web server software by 1995, few browsers that implemented this protocol were available. The popularity of Netscape's secure browser and server offerings has largely eclipsed S-HTTP.

Pretty Good Privacy (PGP)

Pretty Good Privacy (PGP) is not, strictly speaking, a network application. PGP is a program that can be used to create and verify digital signatures, encrypt and decrypt data, and compress data. It is widely used to encrypt, decrypt, sign, or verify data that has been transmitted or is about to be transmitted across an open network, and has gained considerable popularity. The PGP file formats are described in RFC 1991, and PGP has often been grafted on to other network applications to provide security.

Secure MIME (S/MIME)

MIME stands for Multipurpose Internet Mail Extensions, is documented in RFC 1521, and defines an orderly method of attaching files for transmission over the Internet. The Secure MIME (S/MIME) specification adds a hierarchical approach to security, providing a formal definition of users and certifiers and making it more scalable to large organizations.

MIME Object Security Services (MOSS)

Another approach to security with MIME is described in RFC 1848. MIME Object Security Services (MOSS) describes how encryption and digital signatures can be added to MIME objects.

CyberCash

The CyberCash Internet commerce application protocol, described in RFC 1898, has been used since 1995 to process credit card transactions on the Internet. This protocol is notable because it is implemented at the application layer, encrypting and digitally signing credit card transaction information so that consumers are notified of their transaction approval (or denial) and merchants are able to complete the transaction within seconds. Transactions are encrypted from the consumer to the card processor, and all transactions and approvals are digitally signed. The CyberCash protocol is similar to the SET specification.

Transport Layer Security

With no widely accepted secure protocol for Web commerce, and with few prospects for early completion the S-HTTP project, Netscape seized on the opportunity and developed its own security protocol, which the company deployed widely in freely distributed browsers and in a line of commercial Web servers. Later released for use in standards development, the Secure Socket Layer (SSL) operated between the transport layer and the application layer, offering a protocol for negotiating a secure connection between client and server.

By using the transport layer, SSL can encrypt the application data stream between any application clients and servers, not just Web clients and servers, as long as they have been designed to interface properly with TCP through SSL. Although SSL and its apparent failings have received much attention, most of the deficiencies have been related either to problems with the way SSL was implemented (Netscape has been extremely responsive in fixing security bugs) or to the length of the keys used. (Forty-bit keys are relatively easy to defeat but are at present the longest permitted for export from the United States.) To date, SSL continues to be a reasonable—and widely implemented—mechanism for encrypting streams of data from applications.

Network Layer Security

The IETF formed the IP Security Protocol working group (IPSEC) to develop methods to protect IP client protocols at the network layer. As of early 1997, its efforts had produced IP Authentication Header (HA, described in RFC 1826) and the IP Encapsulating Security Protocol (ESP, described in RFC 1827). Some other protocols described by this working group are

- Simple Key-Management for Internet Protocols (SKIP)

- Internet Security Association and Key Management Protocol (ISAKMP)

- Internet Key Management Protocol (IKMP)

These are described in draft documents available at the IETF web site.

Security Trade-Offs

The importance of extranet security cannot be overstated. However, it is rare to find extranets, or any internetworks, protected by every security tool, firewall, user authentication system, and cryptographic utility described here. Such networks might be secure (but not necessarily), but they would almost certainly be unusable. The features that make networks secure are also the features that make them hard to use. For example:

- Use of very long, very random passwords

- Frequent changing of passwords

- Prohibition against writing or storing passwords

- Use of authentication for access to all network resources

- Frequent reauthentication of users during network sessions

- Restriction of external access through approved hosts and clients

Making the extranet easy enough to use but secure enough to protect the organization's assets is an important design consideration.

Finally, extranet security cannot be limited to technological mechanisms simply because the most dangerous security breaches are still the result of nontechnological attacks. Insiders, whether disaffected employees or greedy employees, are still more likely than outsiders to break into organizational resources. Networking resources are also vulnerable to fires, floods, and other natural (and unnatural) causes and require security planning both to prevent them and to continue operations in spite of them.

CHAPTER

6

Extranet Services

n extranet must provide many traditional internetwork or intranet services, such as file services through Network File System (NFS), file transfer through File Transfer Protocol (FTP), and Web services through the Hypertext Transport Protocol (HTTP). In addition, a number of services that are not typically installed in organizational intranets are integral building blocks of extranets. These services enable you to locate a person, a network resource, a system, or a piece of data or program function, associating a name with a resource or entity across a network. The services include

- Directory services

- Key distribution

- Certification authorities

- ActiveX and Java code-signing security

This chapter discusses services and protocols, including X.500 (an international standard for directories), X.509 (an international standard for digital certificates), and the Lightweight Directory Access Protocol (LDAP). This chapter also considers key distribution mechanisms and certification authorities, including what they are and how they work, as well as Java and ActiveX code authentication.

Introduction to Extranet Services

Without services, a network is only a group of computers connected to the same piece of wire (or fiberglass cable, wireless medium, or other networking medium). Services enable sharing of data and make networking valuable. Many of the services that constitute the typical extranet are relatively familiar, for example, Web services as well as other TCP/IP application services such as e-mail and network news. Protocols for other services such as collaborative computing, group scheduling, and multimedia are still developing but will certainly figure in many extranets. These services, both new and old, are easily understood insofar as they are TCP/IP applications and provide platform and network independent interoperability.

Other types of services are less visible but perhaps more important to the seamless interoperation of any internetwork, and they *are* more important to most extranets. Directory services, comprehensively providing access to named resources, are vital to the operation of an extranet. Once you locate a resource, you may have to exchange cryptographic keys to initiate a secure link or to securely access the resource. Key distribution services fulfill the function of keeping secret keys secret; certification authorities, which distribute and authenticate public keys, provide another cryptographic service. Finally, securely distributing software components, applications, or applets calls for a very specific set of procedures to ensure that all software is downloaded intact and to provide a means of certifying the originator of the downloaded software.

Directory Services

Vendors usually provide directory service software to work with networking products, particularly with server products. The basic need is to provide some way of linking users with user IDs and passwords and to provide account authorization. Essentially, a directory service is a database, containing a user name, account ID, password (or authentication information), system access levels, and perhaps some other supporting information.

Ask anyone who has been using a networked computer lately about how many passwords and user IDs he or she has, and chances are the response will be, "Too many." The problem is that the average information worker in an organization with a large network infrastructure may have to access as many as a dozen or more systems and services. For example, I currently use at least 10 user IDs and passwords on a regular basis. I also maintain (and store in a safe place) a "secret notebook" with literally dozens of rarely used ID and password pairs.

Software and network product vendors have traditionally implemented their own password/ID solutions so that the Novell NetWare login ID and password could not be linked to access another network server. The same went for workgroup application vendors, who required administrators to rebuild workgroups and user profiles for all users. Even though many utilities and migration tools are available, they still mean that databases are replicated rather than leveraged.

At least one product does provide a gateway between Novell's Novell Directory Services (NDS) and Microsoft's NT Server directory service, but it is merely an automated method of replicating one database onto another database and remains susceptible to the same types of problems relating to the need to synchronize two or more separate and distinct databases.

The movement toward open standard directory services means that administrators can build a single database of users and groups. When a new server or service is brought online, the database can build its list of authorized users and groups from the existing list of authorized users and groups. Open standard directory services also solve the basic problems of directory service more elegantly and more effectively, as discussed in the next section.

The Issues of Directory Services

Back in the mythical golden ages, locating someone was a simple matter of going to the place where that person lived and asking for him or her by name. Everyone knew everyone else. There weren't too many people in any given place, and most people pretty much stayed put.

Of course, this scenario is an oversimplification because we live in a big, untidy, and dynamic age where nothing stays the same for very long; and as soon as you think you have it all straightened out, things start changing around on you. Even 50 years ago people knew the local telephone operator by name, and long distance phone calls meant that one operator called another operator and figured out how to locate the party being called. As the world becomes increasingly connected, bringing millions of new networked souls together means a much more complicated task of figuring out which one of those souls is the one you want to talk to. The objective of directory services is to simplify that process.

The traditional approach, as codified in the way telephone companies provide subscriber listings, is not sufficiently scalable to make it work well in large systems that need to keep track of potentially hundreds of millions of entities.

Local Solutions to Global Problems

The traditional approach to directory services was to solve the problem locally. This method works relatively well as long as the directory information you need is available in only a few places, such as when everyone you are trying to reach works for very large corporations or when one service provider maintains directory information for a large area. The problem is illustrated in Figure 6.1.

FIGURE 6.1

Using local directories means checking many different places to find one person.

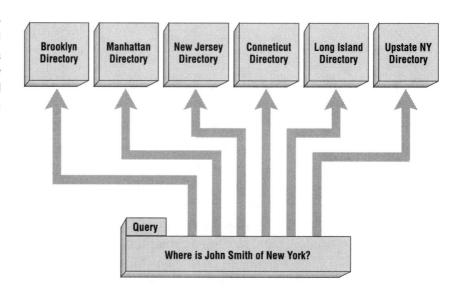

For example, the telephone company compiles a list of telephone subscribers and makes it available to the public. The telephone company is the central authority through which all telephone numbers are assigned (although this system may change quite soon, at least in the United States, as local telephone service is deregulated). NYNEX, for example, can make its listings available for New York City, Boston, and any other city or area it serves. However, if you only know that someone lives in the state of New York, no single source of information can find the number for you: you must call directory information in every area code until you finally locate your party.

This solution is inefficient (and frustrating), particularly as the number of area codes increases. As of early March 1997, New York

City was facing the possibility of another area code partition (its third), which means that even if you know that someone lives in Manhattan, you might need to know which half—or else call information in two area codes.

The local approach to solving the directory problem also tends to breed homegrown solutions. Organizations may maintain many different sets of directories, all in different formats and sorted on different values. For instance, a corporate telephone directory may list people alphabetically within their organizational unit or branch office, while an e-mail directory may contain (and index) addresses based on the users' first initials with no reference to organizational unit.

Change: The Only Constant

A telephone directory is essentially a database, stored on paper and ink instead of on magnetic media, with a single query method. All updates are entered to the phone book in batch mode, once a year, when the database is updated by replacing it with the new directory. This method works fine when people don't move too often, but works less well as people move around more frequently. If you move just after the directory publishing deadline, your new address won't appear in the "new" directory. Move out just after the deadline, and your out-of-date, incorrect listing is enshrined for an extra year. Even calling information may not yield the latest number, depending on how frequently the information operators' database is updated.

The problem accelerates rapidly as the number of directories you are listed in increases. With more organizations to notify of a move, the likelihood of forgetting to notify one of them increases. The problem is also amplified by a higher rate of change, as is often seen inside large organizations where reorganization, downsizing, and upsizing run rampant.

At the root is the problem of propagating database changes across multiple copies of one database (the phone book-revision problem) and across many different databases (the multiple-listing problem) as shown in Figure 6.2. Database replication is hard enough when the databases are all stored in the same format, using the same application software, and connected to the same network; attempting to replicate databases and propagate changes across dissimilar systems is much more difficult.

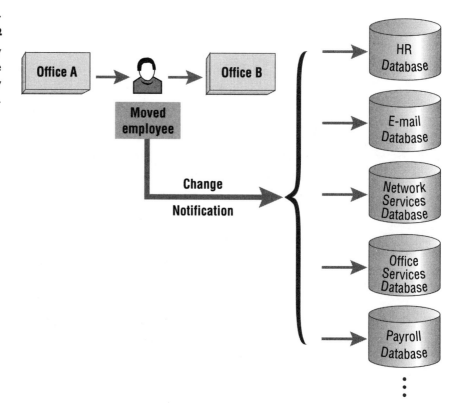

One of a Hundred Needles in a Haystack

Another problem that crops up more and more often as the size of the population listed in the directory increases is that of multiple, identical hits. Finding a needle in a haystack is actually not such a hard task if you've got a good mechanism to sort all the hay to one side and leave only one needle. If you have 2, 10, or 100 identical needles, the task of determining which one is yours is far more complicated.

This type of problem arises when a telephone directory lists more than one person with the same name, as shown in Figure 6.3. Some additional information is necessary when your search yields more than one database hit. However, a telephone directory doesn't give you much to go on, other than full name and initial, the telephone number itself, and (usually) the person's address and town.

F I G U R E 6.3

Finding more than one database hit complicates the job of tracking down a person.

Public, Helen F. .... 24 Ma...
Public, John J. .... 3567 N. Riu...
Public, John Q. .... 869 First Ave.
Public, John Q. .... One Avenue ...
Public, John Q. .... Windor Arms, ...
Public, John Q. .... 67 Wells Ave, San...
Public, John X. .... 901 Fifth St., San...
Public, Joseph .... 486 Beasley Rd, C...
Public, Kelvin R. .... 8457 Marina Villag...
Public, Linda Z. .... 459 Di...... Ct Sa...
Public, Lori ...

Distributed Directory Services

One sort of solution to some of the problems raised above is to use a global centralized authority that manages all directory services, as shown in Figure 6.4. With this approach, the database is never out of synchronization with the main database because there is only one instance of the database (more likely, one primary database with a backup or two, just in case). You don't have to search through more than one database because there is only one: if you don't find what you are looking for, it isn't in there.

FIGURE 6.4

A single, global directory service database simplifies the problem of knowing where to look for directory information.

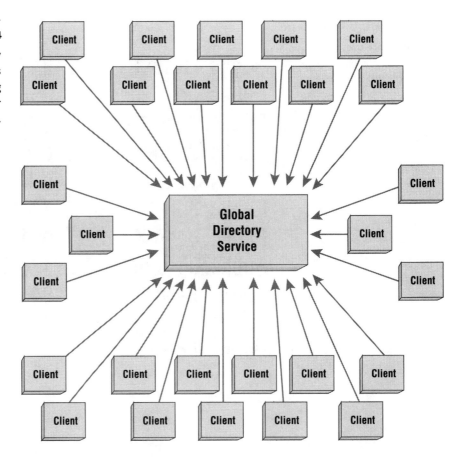

On the other hand, such a global service raises other problems. For one thing, it probably will not scale well as the number of users increases—or as the number of listings increases. Providing services for a billion-entry database is probably at least 1,000 times more difficult than providing services for a million-entry database. And serving a billion users is likewise probably at least 1,000 times more difficult than serving a million of them.

At issue are things like response times for retrieving data, as well as the problem of building a computer powerful enough to handle the flood of requests. Mundane issues of database administration, record updates, and backup just add to the headaches.

Another problem inherent in such a solution is that it is hugely inefficient for dealing with local directory requests and directory administration. Most directory requests are for local services and systems rather than for remote ones, but in this scheme *all* requests have to be channeled to the global directory. Not only does a global directory add significant network load, it also ensures that response times for all directory requests will be long, even when requesting information on a system just a few feet away.

The alternative that the market is coming to accept is a hierarchical solution that allows local directory management to be handled locally while using a global standard for storing, retrieving and disseminating directory information in what is, in effect, a distributed database that spans the globe. If a directory request concerns a local system, it is handled locally; but when the request concerns an external system, it is forwarded through the distributed database to the appropriate directory database.

One problem not addressed directly so far is that of the duplicate match, which can be resolved by building into the global standard the capacity to store more detailed information about directory entries. A discussion of how to implement this type of storage, as well as the deployment of the distributed directory, follows.

Directory Service Options

Directories are for pointing to resources as well as for pointing to people. Some of the more important proprietary solutions include

- Sun Network Information Service (NIS+)

- Novell Directory Services (NDS)

- Microsoft Active Directory Services

Open standards include

- X.500

- Lightweight Directory Access Protocol (LDAP)

- Directory Service Protocol/Directory Access Protocol (DSP/DAP)

- Domain Name Service (DNS)

- Universal Resource Locator/Universal Resource Name (URL/URN)

Some of the proprietary standards are increasingly moving toward compliance or at least some degree of interoperability with open standards, yet even noncompliant directory services continue to be important because of their deployment in legacy systems and local area networks. For now, software vendors are building products for use in extranets that can gateway to legacy directory services. For example, gateway services are available to translate between both Novell NDS and Microsoft NT directory services and X.500.

The most important directory services protocols are open, although Microsoft's Active Directory Services Interface (ADSI) is likely to be a significant factor for many extranets if only because of the degree to which Microsoft is marketing its Active Platform (see Chapter 3) as an extranet development and deployment environment. Two other important directory services, Network Information Service (NIS) from Sun and Novell Directory Service (NDS) from Novell, are discussed briefly.

Open directory protocols include the DNS, which is a distributed database approach to linking host names to network addresses in TCP/IP internetworks. Over the past two decades, TCP/IP has been deployed widely and has scaled up reasonably well, both as the number of host names and addresses has increased and the demand for host name resolution services has increased. The uniform resource specifications, Uniform Resource Locator (URL), Uniform Resource Name (URN), and Uniform Resource Identifier (URI), are also discussed here because they demonstrate how a directory name service can track resources across a heterogeneous network.

The X.500 directory service standard and implementation protocols, including Directory Service Protocol (DSP), Directory Access Protocol (DAP), and Lightweight Directory Access Protocol (LDAP), are of the greatest importance to extranet implementers. To greater or lesser extent, vendors are building in support for at least part of the X.500 specification. This implementation is increasingly necessary as all vendors are moving away from wholly proprietary solutions to interoperable solutions.

X.500

Originally specified by the CCITT (now the ITU) as a method for building a global distributed directory, X.500 appears finally to be succeeding in that role only after ubiquitous TCP/IP internetworking has created a dire need for such a global service. X.500 uses a distributed database structure similar to that employed by DNS, providing many of the same advantages. In particular, the benefits of using X.500, rather than some other directory service, include the following:

- Local organizations and entities maintain their own local directories, so updates need not pass through any intermediary organizations to be recorded and information is added or modified most accurately and quickly.

- With local management, the organization maintains control over the directory and can use it for internal purposes (for example, to maintain account administration information) as well as for external purposes (for example, telephone or e-mail directories).

- With its highly structured information representation model, X.500 supports simple commands that can be combined to build quite complex database queries.

- With its open data representation specification, X.500-compliant directories can be built with extensions that enhance their ability to meet specialized local needs while not impairing their ability to interoperate with other X.500-compliant directories.

- Using a single, global, naming space means that X.500 will unambiguously locate the exact object (person, program, component, data item, or entity) being searched for.

X.500 Fundamentals

The X.500 specification represents the distillation of work done in two dimensions:

- Information representation

- Directory architecture

These two areas are referred to as X.500's information model and its directory model.

Information Model   The simplest way to begin explaining the X.500 information model is to look at the most basic entity, the directory. A *directory* contains directory entries. An *entry* contains information about a single object, which could be a person, a software component, a computer, an organization, or just about anything that is being tracked through an X.500 directory. The entry can be considered, in more familiar database terms, as a record.

Each entry consists of some number of *attributes*, each of which can be compared to a database field. Attributes contain specific information about some aspect of the entry; for example, the object's country, surname, e-mail address, pager number, street address, or birth date could all be attributes of an entry.

Also associated with an attribute is an *attribute syntax*, which corresponds to the database field type and specifies the type and format of the data required for that attribute. For example, the attribute syntax of a birth date attribute might require that the value of the attribute be a valid calendar date; a country attribute might require a two-character valid ISO country code.

With entries, attributes, and attribute syntaxes alone, X.500 would be little different from any other database system. We cannot create a global directory service with just those pieces; at the very least, we need some way to identify precisely what each entry is referring to—particularly if the directory service is to be able to unambiguously locate *any* object, whether a person, a network, or a data file. The addition of *object classes* permits this kind of identification.

Every entry in a directory belongs to an object class; in fact, each entry has an attribute called *objectClass,* which contains the object class to which that entry belongs. Every X.500 object class is defined with a list of mandatory and optional attributes. Once an object class has been defined, it can be used as the basis for building a new object class, which is a subclass of the original object, but which inherits all of the original object's attributes and can add new attributes. Therefore, once an object class is defined for keeping track of humans, a new subclass of humans can be created simply by referencing the human object class and whatever additional attributes are to be included in the new class. For example, a human object class might include attributes for first and last name, telephone number, and e-mail address. To create a subclass of humans, for example, humans licensed to operate a motor vehicle, you might simply add a few attributes for driver's license number and date of expiration.

As with other distributed database representations the network professional commonly encounters, X.500 classes are all subclasses of some other class, as shown in Figure 6.5. Ultimately all classes can trace their pedigree back to a single, root class called *top*, which contains only one, mandatory, attribute: the class attribute.

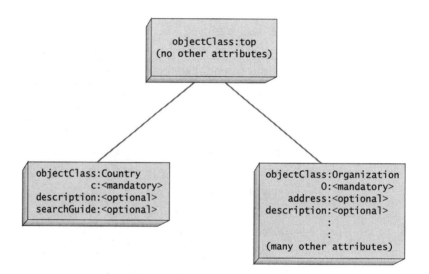

Using these object classes, we can create an X.500 name space in which the object classes are entries themselves (since each has a set of attributes) and are also used to create directory entries of the things each one describes. So the object class C (for country) has entries that correspond to the two-character ISO country code and that may include values for the optional attributes of description and search-Guide, as was illustrated in Figure 6.5. Other common object classes are O (for organization), which usually hangs off a country, and CN (for complete name, an alias for a person's first and last names), which is organized under an organization. An object class for organizational unit (OU) is also commonly specified.

The X.500 name space itself can be represented hierarchically as a *Directory Information Base* (DIB). All entries fit somewhere on the *Directory Information Tree* (DIT). Entries that represent classes that have been used to create subclasses are referred to as *non-leaf nodes,* while those entries that do not have any subclasses are called *leaf nodes*. Each leaf node represents an entry that refers to a directory entity: a person or thing that the directory can point to. Figure 6.6 shows the type of hierarchical structure that X.500 can support.

Similar hierarchical representations can be seen in the Domain Name System (discussed above), the Management Information Base (MIB) used with the Simple Network Management Protocol (SNMP, for more information see almost any text on TCP/IP and network management), and the Usenet newsgroup hierarchies.

FIGURE 6.6

X.500 hierarchies can look something like this, although most of the objects represented here have more attributes than are shown.

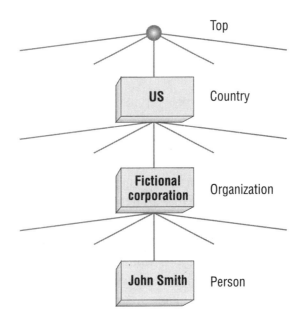

The result is that any leaf node can be identified uniquely by the sum of the values of the entry's attributes. For example, Figure 6.6 (which is an overly simplified representation for the purposes of clarity) shows a leaf node representing the person John Smith, who is affiliated with Fictional Corporation in the United States. This John Smith is differentiated from other John Smiths in the United States because of his connection to Fictional Corp.; within that organization, this particular John Smith would be differentiated from other John Smiths by some additional attribute of his person directory entry. It might be based on telephone number or some local extension to the directory like a hire date or employee number. Of course, an X.500 directory can store more information than is shown in this figure.

Our John Smith's directory entry would look something like this:

```
c: US

o: Fictional Corporation

firstname: John

surname: Smith

...
```

The use of attributes and object classes, along with the distributed hierarchy of directories, supports the use of very powerful queries. Searches can be made on any attribute, in any combination. Rather than having to search the entire directory system, the query would walk down the hierarchical tree, becoming more specific as it checks on each attribute in the query. For example, consider the search for a person named Jane Smith, who lives in the United States and has an e-mail account in the domain `imaginarynetwork.com` and a telephone number that ends in 3456. The search can immediately narrow down to entries under the U.S. hierarchy within the Imaginary Network hierarchy. Querying that directory for all Jane Smiths whose telephone numbers match the search criteria is a relatively simple matter.

Directory Model   The X.500 information model defines how the directory information is structured; the directory model represents the way that users actually store and retrieve information. The functional building block is the Directory System Agent (DSA), which does two things:

- It stores directory information in X.500 format.

- It can exchange information with other DSAs.

Each DSA is responsible for taking care of some part of the global X.500 DIT. A large organization could distribute its directory services across multiple systems, while much smaller organizations might be able to share a DSA system with other small organizations. In either case getting connected with any DSA would allow the user (either human or machine) to reconstruct the entire X.500 directory because each DSA holds its own information, as shown in Figure 6.7. A DSA might hold entries for some or all of the people in an organization or entries for some or all of the organizations within a country, and anything that is not stored locally can be obtained from other DSAs because a DSA can communicate a request for more information from other DSAs.

FIGURE 6.7

Directory System Agents store their own local information and can refer requests for nonlocal information to other DSAs.

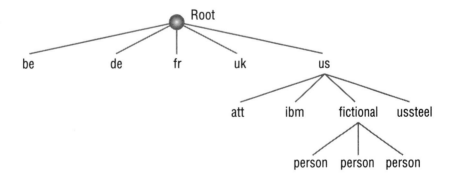

Finally, the Relative Distinguished Name (RDN) is the value of an attribute (or set of attributes) that together distinguish an entry from all other entries with the same subclass. For example, in Figure 6.7, the RDN of each country entry is the two-digit country code; the RDN of each organization entry is the organization name. Similarly, the RDN of a person entry would be the person's complete name.

The Directory Access Protocol (DAP) controls X.500 directory operations and access. DAP provides the structure for all the commands relating to the directory, including things like searching the directory, updating and modifying entries, adding and deleting entries, editing attributes, and modifying objects and subclasses.

X.500 Security   Directory security is an important issue. Some organizations prefer to keep their directories completely private to maintain organizational secrecy, to protect against headhunting by competitors, or just to keep employees out of reach of the general public. More important is the ability to keep outsiders from editing organizational directories, to protect against fraudulent use of organizational facilities, or to keep vandals from deleting or modifying confidential employees' records.

The X.500 standard offers two levels of security:

- Simple passwords (simple security)

- Cryptographic authentication (strong security)

You can make some attributes accessible to the public and others inaccessible by defining access rights to directory attributes. It is the X.500 implementation, not the specification, that implements the security scheme.

LDAP and X.500

The X.500 standard is, like many other OSI-based standards, painstakingly detailed and provides support for every function that the specifiers could envision as being a part of a global directory service. The DAP specifies how all these functions can be accessed and provided. While completeness is a virtue, actually having to implement the complete specification has proved to be daunting, particularly to vendors who need only a subset of the functions specified.

As a result, a Lightweight DAP (LDAP) has been specified to meet the simpler needs of Internet applications. LDAP provides basic read and write access to the X.500 directory for use in simple management applications.

The LDAP Protocol Model

The basic framework in which LDAP operates is that of a client that submits requests to a server, which performs the actual X.500 directory access and then returns the result to the client. These results could be the information requested or an error message of some sort. The server does not pass along any other information about the actual X.500 transaction. For example, when the information requested is stored remotely, the local server does not report any intermediate responses it gets from the X.500 directory. It returns only the result of the request.

LDAP makes no provision for synchronous requests and responses. The only requirement is that all client requests receive a response. Consequently, a client submitting several requests sequentially may receive responses to those requests in an order completely different from the order in which they were submitted. This technique allows both the client and the server to deal gracefully with requests that take much longer to respond to (for example, requests for directory information stored at a very remote DSA).

LDAP uses the TCP transport protocol, which provides a reliable, virtual-circuit link between client and server.

LDAP Protocol Messages

The LDAP protocol consists of two basic units: the LDAP message, which is used to send LDAP operations, and the LDAP result, which is used to send the results of an operation. The details of these messages are provided in RFC 1777, but the basic types of operations and results are summarized here. Figure 6.8 shows the model used for LDAP interactions: the LDAP client sends a request for an X.500 operation to an LDAP server, which interfaces to the X.500 directory and acts on behalf of the client, returning the results to the client through an LDAP result message.

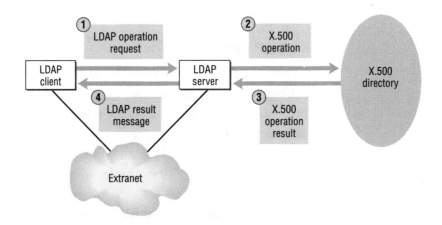

LDAP Operations

LDAP protocol operations initiate and terminate an LDAP session; submit requests for retrieving information from the X.500 directory; and modify, add, and delete directory information. LDAP operations include the following:

- Bind/unbind

- Search

- Modify

- Add

- Delete

- Modify RDN

- Compare

- Abandon

Bind/Unbind   The bind operations initiate a session between a client and server. Authentication parameters may be required. The unbind operation terminates the session.

Search   The search operation allows the client to submit a request to search the X.500 directory. It supports a full set of search operators as well as parameters for specifying how the search results should be handled and how to deal with issues like aliases and scope of the search.

Modify   A client may request the server to modify an object in the X.500 DIB with the modify operation. Changes can be attribute additions, deletions, or replacements, and multiple changes can be included in a single modify operation.

Add   The add operation adds a new directory entry to the X.500 directory.

Delete   The delete operation deletes directory entries from the X.500 directory.

Modify RDN   This operation modifies the Relative Distinguished Name (RDN).

Compare   In the compare operation, the server looks up an entry and compares some attribute of that entry with some asserted value.

Abandon   Outstanding directory requests can be terminated by submitting an abandon operation with a request ID.

LDAP Results

The types of result messages appear in the following list. Most are self-explanatory; they give some idea of the types of operations that you can perform with LDAP and the kinds of responses that the server will generate.

Success

Operations Error

Protocol Error

Time Limit Exceeded

Size Limit Exceeded

Compare True/False

Authentication Method Not Supported

Strong Authentication Required

No Such Attribute

Undefined Attribute Type

Inappropriate Matching

Constraint Violation

Attribute or Value Exists

Invalid Attribute Syntax

No Such Object

Alias Problem

Invalid Distinguished Name Syntax

```
Is Leaf

Alias Dereferencing Problem

Inappropriate Authentication

Invalid Credentials

Insufficient Access Rights

Busy

Unavailable

Unwilling to Perform

Loop Detect

Naming Violation

Object Class Violation

Not Allowed on Non-Leat

Not Allowed on RDN

Entry Already Exists

Object Class Modifications Prohibited

Other
```

Other Open Directory Protocols

LDAP provides a relatively easy way to get into the X.500 directory and is rapidly becoming an important tool for Internet and extranet implementations. However, only in the past year or so have vendors been deploying LDAP solutions in their software products. Up to this point, we have not had a good solution for managing user and group directories over TCP/IP internetworks, but the Internet and the World Wide Web have not been totally without directory services.

The Domain Name System (DNS) has long been used to link host and domain names, which are easy for people to use, with their underlying IP host and IP network addresses, which are easy for computers to use. Likewise, the World Wide Web is built on the URL specification, a method for pointing to network resources that sandwiches a standard file and directory format on top of DNS host names with a standard format for identifying what type of network resource is being referred to. A discussion of URLs and other related uniform resource specifications (URNs, URIs, and URCs) follows.

Domain Name System (DNS)

The Internet was not always as large and complicated a network as it is today. At one time all that was necessary to link host names to host IP addresses was to keep a file on all systems that listed the names and addresses of all the connected hosts. Keeping a host file on every workstation with the names and addresses of all the local hosts sufficed for accessing other local hosts, and the gateway system (they were still called "gateways," not routers, then) to each local network connected to the Internet stored another list of network domain names and addresses.

This state of grace lasted only until the hosts file became a problem rather than a solution. As organizations increased the number of hosts connected to the TCP/IP internetwork, maintaining the host files on each IP node became increasingly difficult. As the number of changes, additions, and deletions increase, the utility of trying to keep track of them in a file copied to all connected systems decreases. Although a host file is still a perfectly acceptable solution in many situations, most organizations and users have found that the DNS is a better way to link host names and network domains to IP addresses.

DNS was designed to provide a system of resolving host and domain names into IP addresses, using a distributed database system. Each organization maintains at least two DNS servers, the primary DNS server and a secondary DNS server to handle overflow and to be available if the primary system fails. As with X.500, a large part of the strength of DNS is in the distribution of database duties locally, to the organization, rather than to some central facility. The benefit is that since each organization is responsible for keeping its own listings current, everyone else can be confident that the DNS information is as current and correct as is possible.

Figure 6.9 shows how DNS servers are deployed. A client may attempt to make a connection with a server, using only a human-readable host name and network domain, also known as a *fully qualified domain name.*

An example of a fully qualified domain name is `fido.dogworld.com`. The domain is `dogworld.com`, and the host name is `fido`.

When a host name appears by itself, the system assumes that the target host is in the same domain as the requesting host. Whether the destination host fido is local or not, the client will send a request to the local DNS server, asking for the target host's IP address. If the client's user does not provide a domain, the client will automatically append its own domain name because it assumes that the destination is local and on the same network.

If the host is on the same network (that is, the domain name matches the local domain name), the DNS server will do a lookup on an address table it maintains and return the IP address to the client. If the host is on a different network, the DNS server will first check its own cache files to see if it has a current address for that domain. If not, it will use the DNS architecture to trace down the correct address for the network.

Domain names are *hierarchical.* That is, all domains branch off from a root. Each first-level domain branches off the unnamed root domain, and each second-level domain branches off one of the first-level domains. Until 1997 all nongeographic domain names belonged to one of seven first-level domains: `com`, `edu`, `gov`, `mil`, `net`, `org`, and `int`. Each

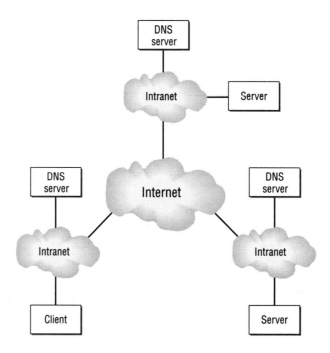

top-level domain is associated with a DNS server that can point other DNS servers to second-level DNS servers. In other words, a DNS server responds to all queries about *.edu domains. Someone attempting to get a network address for the domain stateuniversity.edu would start at the edu DNS server. That domain may contain subdomains, identified with internal internetworks that are part of the organization. As shown in Figure 6.10, a DNS request for the host dev1.research.fictional.com would start at the com DNS server, which would point to a DNS server for the fictional.com. It, in turn, would point to a more local DNS server for the domain research.fictional.com, which would send back an IP address.

DNS provides a directory type service for locating hosts and is an important part of TCP/IP internetworking. It is an integral part of most TCP/IP implementations and is vital to the way resources are now referenced in the World Wide Web, as discussed in the next section.

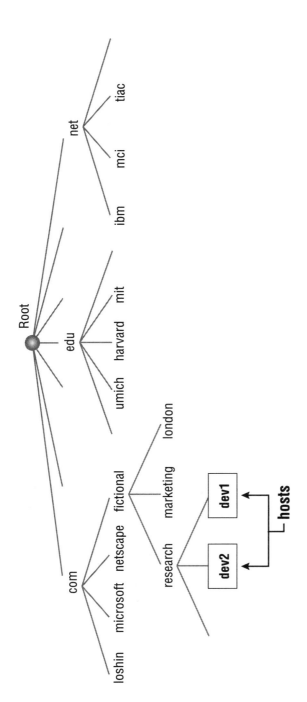

FIGURE 6.10

You can trace a fully qualified domain name through DNS by "walking the tree" and breaking out the domain name one element at a time.

Uniform Resource Specifications

Having cross-platform access to resources across an internetwork is a fine thing, as long as you have some relatively easy way to point to those resources independent of the host platform. In the past users within an organization were expected to know the correct file system syntax to refer to data files stored on a variety of systems. For example, a large organization might have a heterogenous internetwork linking IBM mainframes, DEC VAXes, Wintel personal computers, Apple Macintoshes, and workstations running a rainbow of UNIX flavors, all of which might contain network information. Getting to that information across the internetwork may have required a certain degree of knowledge of operating systems as diverse as MVS, VM, VMS, Unix, DOS (both the PC and the mainframe kind), Macintosh OS, and more.

The advantage of using an interoperable networking architecture, such as the architecture that TCP/IP provides, is that system peculiarities need not be propagated across the network. The client need not be aware of the operating system or file system structure of the remote host for any networking reason, and requiring that knowledge just to reference a resource is counterproductive.

A large part of the success of the World Wide Web is associated with the use of a uniform resource nomenclature, which allows all resources to be referenced with a simple and consistent naming style. The URL is the most widely used type of uniform identifier; it points to a specific network resource and it is considered a subset of the URI. The URI is a more generalized term referring to any of the methods of addressing objects in a standard and concise way. The URN is another type of URI that provides a more permanent pointer to a network resource than the URL does. The Uniform Resource Citation (URC) is a framework for providing information about a uniform resource.

Uniform Resource Identifier(URI)   The URI is more of a concept at this point than a solid specification. The idea behind the URI is that it provides a mechanism for naming objects that belong to a universal set of objects and to include in those names enough information to access that object. Figure 6.11 shows how the various uniform resource mechanisms relate to each other.

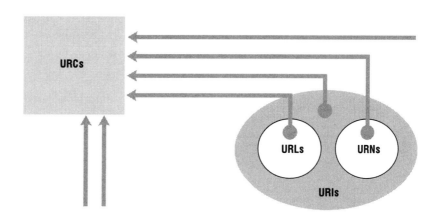

As is apparent, the URI is a generalization of which the URL and the URN are specific examples. The URC can be built out of various parts, some of which are some type of uniform resource and some of which are taken from outside the uniform resource space.

Uniform Resource Locator (URL)   Defined in RFC 1738, the URL is structured with two parts: a *scheme*, which identifies the type of resource, and a *scheme-specific part*, which indicates how to get to that resource. The basic format is

```
<scheme>:<scheme-specific part>
```

The scheme-specific part of the URL provides just enough information to reach the specified resource. Table 6.1 lists some of the schemes commonly encountered on the Internet.

T A B L E 6.1

URL Scheme Identifiers
and the Types of
Network Resource
They Denote

Scheme ID	Network Resource
ftp	File Transfer Protocol (FTP)
http	Hypertext Transport Protocol
gopher	Gopher protocol
mailto	Electronic mail address
news	USENET news
nntp	USENET news using NNTP access
telnet	Reference to interactive sessions
wais	Wide Area Information Servers
file	Host-specific filenames

Each scheme has a unique URL format; Table 6.2 shows most of the common URL formats. In general, these formats can contain host names or IP addresses, port numbers, file paths, e-mail addresses, and network news identifiers, but in all cases the information included in the URL must be sufficient to access the resource. If a user ID and password are required to access a resource, either the URL must contain that information or the user must supply the information interactively when the URL is opened.

T A B L E 6.2

URL Formats for
Different Types of
Schemes

Scheme	URL format
E-mail	`mailto:<rfc822-addr-spec>`
Gopher	`gopher://<host>:<port>/<gopher-path>`
Local HTML file	`file://<host>/<path>`
Network news (by message ID)	`news:<message-id>`

T A B L E 6.2 (cont.)	**Scheme**	**URL format**
URL Formats for Different Types of Schemes	Network news (by news group)	`news:<news group-name>`
	Network news (using direct NNTP access)	`nntp://<host>:<port>/<news group-name>/` `<article-number>`
	Telnet	`telnet://<user>:<password>@<host>:<port>/`
	WWW	`http://<host>:<port>/<path>?<searchpart>`

Uniform Resource Name (URN)   One of the problems of URLs is that they refer to specific resources located on specific systems. Consequently, the location of a URL can often change, which means that any links to that URL must also change or they will point to the wrong resource (or to no resource at all). The URN is intended to be a way to name objects with greater persistence so that the URN points to the same resource whether it is hosted on a UNIX workstation, a DEC VAX, or a Windows NT Server. At this point, standards for defining how to build such URNs are incomplete.

Uniform Resource Citation (URC)   The only information a URI carries about itself is how to get to it. The ability to link attributes to a particular URI would be immensely helpful, particularly when searching for information about a specific topic, by a specific person, or generated from a specific organization. Whereas URIs can usually be characterized as fairly brief pointers to resources, the URC is more similar to a directory object. The URC contains a set of attributes with corresponding values and may be built out of simple information as well as URLs and URNs. For example, a URC might include a URL to point to the particular location of the resource, as well as an author, publishing organization, date of publication, contact information for the author, and summary of the contents.

Proprietary Directory Services

Market forces currently favor directory services that are either linked to de facto standards or are compatible with open standards. Dominate vendors like Novell and Microsoft have managed to make their directory services offerings de facto standards. Novell's Novell Directory Service (NDS) will continue to be important to the many organizations that use NetWare LANs, and Microsoft's Active Directory Services Interface (ADSI) is increasing in importance as more organizations migrate existing networks (and add new networks) to Windows NT Server. Network Information Service (NIS) from Sun has historically been an important directory service for TCP/IP internetworks.

Network Information Service+ (NIS+)

In the 1980s Sun developed a service called yellow pages (YP), a name that it later changed to Network Information Service (NIS). NIS was a centralized system of managing users and groups in a heterogenous network environment. NIS stored account information in a flat ASCII file, and a centralized server provided all directory services for the domain. This approach worked adequately until the size of the internetwork and the pace of change overtook its ability to handle the task. The upgrade to Network Information Service+ (NIS+) solved these problems by migrating toward an architecture better suited to providing network directory services. Rather than being formatted as flat file databases, NIS+ directories are hierarchical.

NIS+ directories can also interoperate with X.500 and other types of directory service. NIS+ can be used as a directory to users as well as to process identifiers, e-mail aliases, user passwords and other objects. Secure authentication and security of information are also features of this service.

Novell Directory Services (NDS)

First distributed with NetWare release 4, Novell Directory Services (NDS) is a global distributed database that contains information on all network resources. NDS includes information on network objects such as individual network users, user groups, server volumes, network printers, and all other devices. NDS, as well as the other directory services discussed here, uses a hierarchical tree structure, and NDS resources are referred to as *objects*.

This description might seem familiar because NDS is based on X.500. NDS provides X.500 functionality, as well as extended functions relating to network management and administration tasks, such as secure authentication and security of information.

Microsoft Active Directory

As with its other Internet-related products, Microsoft is very interested in providing a standard for directory services. Active Directory is Microsoft's directory services offering. It will natively support LDAP and will provide the same kind of hierarchical, distributed directory service typical of X.500 compatible applications. The Active Directory supports the same types of directory service functions as the other directory services support, including management of entries pertaining to individuals, network resources, and distributed components. Active Directory is particularly suited to manage directory entries for COM and DCOM components and can also deal with other types of network resources. Active Directory can interoperate with other types of directory services, including NDS.

Active Directory Services Interface (ADSI)   To simplify developing for the Active Directory, Microsoft also offers a directory services interface. By providing a single set of directory service interfaces, ADSI supports the management of network resources across different types of network operating system directory services. Developing with

ADSI provides a mechanism for administrators to manage network resources across heterogeneous network environments.

ADSI lets the developer provide support for tasks such as

- Adding and modifying users

- Managing printers and other network resources

- Locating network resources in a distributed computing environment

Developers can use ADSI to build applications that can easily interface with the network directory, no matter what type of directory service is in use.

ADSI serves as a directory application interface. The developer writes directory applications that use the standard ADSI interface, and then ADSI handles the actual directory interaction through the appropriate directory service, whether it is NDS, LDAP, or NT. The application itself never needs to be aware of which type of directory server is in use, but will interact appropriately with all of them.

Key Distribution and Kerberos

Although not the only mechanism for managing the secure distribution of keys across an open network, Kerberos is probably the most widely implemented and certainly the most well-know and open method.

Key Distribution

Many issues of authentication were taken up in Chapter 5, but the distribution of session keys over an open network is another issue related to security that is usually implemented as a network service. User passwords are not enough to keep intruders out of data streams transmitted across open networks, and a user is not always able to provide digital signature–level authentication—particularly when the user may use multiple workstations, as, for example, when users log in from network computers or when users connect from public access workstations.

Digital signatures enable clients and servers to authenticate themselves to each other. A public key pair can be assigned to every client workstation as well as to every server. When each system has its own public key pairing, a client can use a digital signature to authenticate itself to the server. However, public keys don't help much when workstations are provided on a public or semipublic basis, as in a university or a corporation with networked workstations for use by transient employees. The workstation may be used by any of dozens, hundreds, or even thousands of people, so assigning a public key to the workstation itself would be pointless.

Therefore, clients and servers need a way to trade a *session key,* or a key that can encrypt the data transmitted between client and server. This requirement faces two problems:

- Authenticating the user

- Exchanging the session key so that an eavesdropper could not intercept the key and use it without authorization

Kerberos solves the problem by the clever application of cryptography to the problem of validating identities through the use of a *shared secret.*

Using Kerberos

Kerberos is a user-authentication mechanism named after the three-headed dog guarding the gates of hell and developed at the Massachusetts Institute of Technology. Users' IDs and passwords can be passed and authenticated across a network without exposing them in plaintext transmitted across the network. In part, the system was developed to allow students, faculty, and staff at MIT to securely use network resources without fear that their passwords, which most protocols allow to be transmitted in the clear, would not be susceptible to interception.

Kerberos uses the Data Encryption Standard (DES) secret key encryption algorithm for all transactions between entities as well as for stream encryption of sessions. Central to the Kerberos service is the security server called a *key distribution center* (KDC) because it distributes keys for each network session mediated through Kerberos. The KDC acts as a central key distribution facility, providing each user with a new session key every time the user log in to the network. Also distributed at that time is a *ticket-granting ticket* (TGT), which is essentially a digital hall pass that enables the user to make a connection to a remote host authenticated through Kerberos.

When the user logs in to the network, the user's workstation sends a request to the KDC for a new session key to be used by the entity owning the transmitted user ID. The KDC begins by looking up the user ID. If the ID is valid and authorized to use Kerberos, the KDC will generate a new session key (to be used only for a limited period), encrypt it using the user's master key (a secret key that it shares with that particular user), and send it to the user's workstation. The TGT, which contains the session key, identification information about the user logging in, and an expiration time for the TGT (after which the TGT becomes invalid), is also encrypted and sent at that time. (See Figure 6.12.)

When the user (which could also be a process running on a networked host) wants to access a network resource (usually a network server), the user encrypts (using the session key generated at login) and sends a request to connect to that resource to the KDC. The KDC creates a new session key to be used only by the requesting user and the requested resource and encrypts that key with the user's master key (not the session key). At the same time the session key, along with the user's ID, is encypted using the resource's master key. This key is the actual session

FIGURE 6.12

The Kerberos KDC
sends a user a session key
and a ticket-granting ticket
when the user logs in.

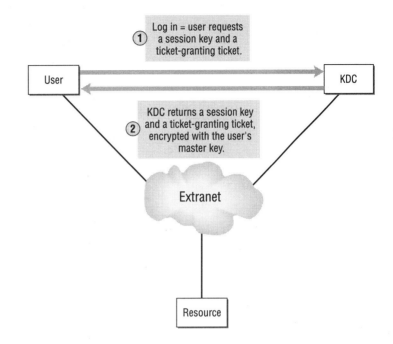

FIGURE 6.12

The Kerberos KDC
sends a user a session key
and a ticket-granting ticket
when the user logs in.

ticket because once the resource decrypts it, it will know the ID of the user wishing to make a connection as well as the session key to use to decrypt that session. This step is illustrated in Figure 6.13.

Both keys are sent to the user; the user's master key is used to decrypt the session key, and the other encrypted version of the session key—the ticket—is forwarded to the target resource. (That ticket can be decrypted only with the resource's master key and identifies the user.) The user and the resource can then continue with their communication, using the new session key to encrypt their transmissions, as shown in Figure 6.14.

Passwords and session keys are never sent in the clear. The result is a reasonably secure mechanism for distributed session keys between hosts using secret key encryption.

When the user is ready to start a session with a network resource, it requests a session key and a ticket from the KDC, which sends them to the requesting system.

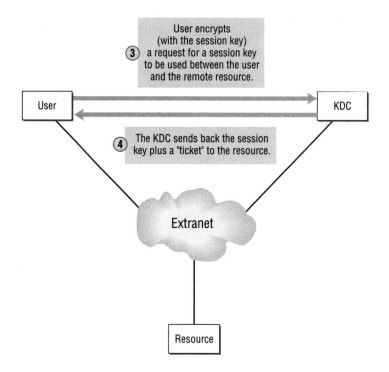

Once the user sends its ticket to the network resource, the user and the resource can start encrypting a data stream using their shared session key.

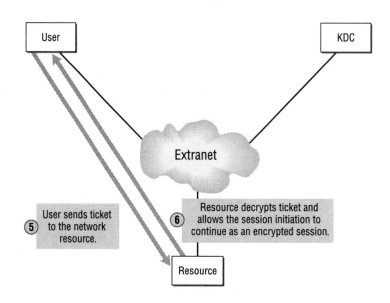

Certification Authorities

The problem with digital signatures in particular, and public key cryptography in general, is that public keys must have a trusted delivery mechanism. Simply publishing a key on an internetwork is not enough security. Evildoers have too many opportunities to intercept the key and replace it with their own, for instance, enabling them to intercept all subsequently encrypted transmissions and to take actions based on a false identity.

Exchange of public keys between trusted individuals is one approach to security. This technique builds a so-called web of trust that includes a pedigree for each key. In other words, one person might start out by exchanging public keys only with people she knows and meets with in person. If each person exchanges public keys with her own colleagues, friends, and relatives, the original group members can interact based on their relationships with their trusted intermediaries.

Figure 6.15 shows how this web of trust works. Person A and Person N want to exchange their public keys to facilitate a business transaction over the Internet. However, each party has been exchanging (and signing) keys with people they trust. The figure shows that they both know, and have exchanged public keys with, the mysterious Person X. Both trust X, and both have had X sign their own keys, which means that they can exchange keys secure in the knowledge that a trusted intermediary was willing to certify that she knew the party whose key she was signing.

FIGURE 6.15

In this simple web of trust, Person X knows and trusts both parties, so those two parties can comfortably exchange keys.

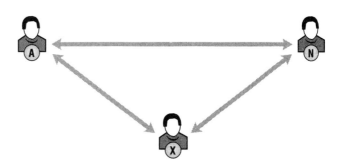

This approach works adequately as long as the web population is small, although the scheme can be scaled to a relatively large population. For example, it can use more than one trusted intermediary to build the web of trust. Several layers of strangers might separate A and N, and some people are willing to trust keys that have been signed by "famous" people they don't know, but whose public keys are widely distributed.

However, a commercialized Internet, or an extranet, cannot afford to rely on what is essentially an informal infrastructure for security. The answer, for a number of reasons, is the certification authority. The *certification authority* (CA) acts as the trusted third party for the type of transactions described above. The CA replaces the individual trusted by both both parties. The CA will sign a public key for any entity that meets the requirements, whether those requirements be submission of some form of proof of identity or payment for the service.

One of the first commercial certification authorities was provided by Verisign, Inc. Other certification authorities include the United States Postal Service and GTE. The most important initial application was to provide certificates to support the Secure Socket Layer (SSL) protocol implemented on secure Web servers. These servers need a public key to exchange with end users' browsers to encrypt an SSL transmission. Although there is no reason why a webmaster could not just generate a public key pair (other than the difficulty of doing so with some server software products), registering the server's key with a trusted third party such as a CA means that potential customers will trust the Web merchant.

Increasingly, individuals are getting and using digital certificates to do two-way authentication. This trend will continue to accelerate as more products support two-way authentication, notably Web browsers and servers, and will be reflected in increased use of certification authorities in extranets.

NOTE Digital certificates have been in general use for some years in Lotus Notes client software, so you should not assume that digital signatures are an entirely new technology.

Why Use a Certification Authority?

As mentioned above, having a trusted third party certify the ownership of a public key is critical to the success of an extranet application that markets goods or services across the Internet. Using a formal certification authority, whether by building one for an extranet or using a CA service from a third party like Verisign, has certain advantages over using the less formal web of trust to maintain digital certificates:

- The primary role of the trusted third party is to make it much more difficult for someone to register a certificate fraudulently in your name. The CA certifies, to a greater or lesser degree, the credentials of the entity applying for a certificate.

- The CA maintains records of certificate revocation. When a revoked certificate is used and certification is requested on it, the CA should notify the requesting entity that the certificate has been revoked.

- A CA has more control over how any individual entry gets into the directory and what its presence means.

- Service availability, reliability, and scope can be specified more completely and easily when using a centralized CA or CA provider.

- Centralized CAs can be monitored more closely to provide even better security. This feature is particularly important because of the importance of digital certificates to commerce.

- Web of trust authentication tends to associate participants, which may be giving away more information than many people care to—the presence of Alice's signature on Bob's key tends to indicate that Alice knows Bob.

Certification Authority Infrastructure

Most certification authorities use the basic X.500 infrastructure, extended with the X.509 specification. Digital certficates are stored as entries in an X.500-based directory. Strong authentication and strong encryption of the data exchanged also provide security.

The CA creates digital certificates by hashing the entry and then encrypting the hash using the CA's private key—in other words, creating a digital signature. Anyone receiving the entry can validate the signature simply by running the same hash against the entry information and encrypting it with the CA's public key. The result should be the same as the CA's digital signature on the certificate. The CA's public key should be available from a public source; for example, some are included with commercial software distributions.

X.509

Based on X.500 directory services, the X.509 is another ITU specification that specifically defines the way directory entries represent digital certificates. As implemented from the current version of the specification, X.509 version 3, certificates include the information shown in Table 6.3 in each entry.

	Field	Meaning
T A B L E 6.3 Valid X.509 v3 Certificates Include These Fields	Version	Identifies the certificate format.
	Serial number	A unique identifier linked with the particular certificate.
	Algorithm identifier	Identifies the algorithm used to sign the certificate, and any necessary parameters.

	Field	Meaning
TABLE 6.3 *(cont.)* Valid X.509 v3 Certificates Include These Fields	Issuer	The certification authority name.
	Period of validity	The start and stop dates of validity for the certificate; the certificate is valid in the period between these two dates.
	Subject	The name identifying the user of the certificate.
	Subject's public key	Includes the name of the certificate user's public key algorithm, all required parameters to use it, and the actual public key.
	Signature	A signature generated by the certification authority on the certificate.

The process of getting an X.509 digital certificate requires some method of authentication of the entity applying for the certificate. One mechanism (used by Verisign) for getting a commercial software publisher certificate (required by Microsoft for its code-signing technology) is the submission of a Dun & Bradstreet rating number.

Data Authentication Strategies

Extranets rely on their own network infrastructure for the distribution of extranet applications as Java applets or ActiveX controls. Using the network saves time, money, and effort but can also cause security problems. To be truly useful, software also needs certain capabilities (like the ability to overwrite files) that could be harmful if not properly applied.

One threat comes from criminals who attempt to replace these distributed network applications with their own doctored versions, perhaps containing viruses or Trojan horse programs to steal information or passwords. Another threat is that users will be desensitized to the use of applets and controls downloaded over the Internet and will allow dangerous ones to be loaded without understanding the risks involved.

As of early 1997 two basic approaches to securing distributed applications are in use:

- **The "sandbox" model** in which network applications have a limited, closely scrutinized set of system resources, literally a sandbox in which the application may play freely under the observation of a system baby-sitter. The Java model was developed to use this model.

- **The code-signing model** that assures the network user that the application he or she downloads from the network actually originated from the organization that claims to have written it. The code is digitally signed by the software developer before it is published on the network, and the network user can then authenticate the signed code. The model was embraced first by Microsoft for its Active Platform.

Although the sandbox approach is associated with Java and the code-signing approach is associated with the Active Platform, they are actually complementary solutions to security problems raised by the use of distributed applications. The Java world is coming to embrace the implementation of code signing, and Microsoft is incorporating the sandbox model in its Java implementations; as time goes on, both approaches are likely to be incorporated into extranet application delivery.

Sandbox Security

The concept of the sandbox has been central to Java from its introduction. The intention of the sandbox is to limit the potential damage that harmful programs can do to a network user's system by restricting the downloaded Java applet's access to files and system services. If the applet cannot read a local password file, write to a local configuration file, or delete disk files, then the potential for harm from a Java applet (whether a virus-carrying applet or simply a buggy applet) can be diminished.

Distributed Application Risks

Downloading software, particularly software that does not require any significant installation or configuration—like Java applets or ActiveX controls, is a much more attractive method of distributing software than the traditional method of shipping diskettes to each user. Unfortunately, downloading also makes it easier to distribute harmful software. The most dangerous threats include viruses, Trojan horse programs, and eavesdropping programs.

Viruses   Any program that reproduces after installing itself on a new host machine, spreading to other host systems, is a virus. It may or may not do any harm to the host machine, although it doesn't do anyone any good: at the very least, it consumes system resources.

Trojan Horse Programs   A Trojan horse program is one that appears to be friendly or benign but actually does something harmful. A Trojan horse may do something useful, or at least appear to do something useful, but has some other purpose. Most common are programs that provide login services but actually steal password and user ID pairs and send them to the program's author. Extranet users can be particularly susceptible to Trojan horse programs because they often download distributed applets or controls with little or no sense of who wrote them and what they do.

Eavesdropping Programs   While threats from Trojan horse and virus programs are relatively well understood, the increased use of ubiquitous internetworking reduces the usefulness (to criminals, not to users or developers) of running "sniffer" programs on many different workstations. These eavesdropping programs can monitor the local area network, perhaps searching for data that looks like user ID/password pairs or credit card numbers (both are usually easily recognizable), and then forward that information to the perpetrator. Again, distributed applets and controls are a prime source of infection for this type of program.

Java Safeguards

Java's design incorporates three levels of security safeguards against harmful applets. The first level of security derives from the structure of the Java language, and two more layers come from the way Java programs are treated before they are executed. In addition to these three levels, you can add more security measures in the form of extensions on top of the client accessing the applet or through code signing, for example.

The Java Language   Designed from the ground up as a network application language, Java excludes various language features that allow unsafe behaviors such as direct access to system memory or system resources.

The Java Virtual Machine   Unlike other languages, Java applets are not run directly by a system but are rather executed by a Java virtual machine (VM). The VM is in effect an abstraction, a simulation of a computer that executes Java code and passes the results on to the actual system running the virtual machine. Java virtual machines add security onto Java applets in two steps.

The first step is a bytecode verifier that checks the actual applet code to make sure that

1. The code actually is a Java program.

2. The code is correct Java code.

3. The code does not contain Java runtime errors (e.g., stack overflow errors that could cause system failures).

Along with these checks, which are performed before the applet is loaded and executed, another security mechanism called a *class loader* segregates Java object classes by their provenance. The classes that are part of the Java runtime implementation have to trust themselves; the classes installed locally have a lower degree of trust, but still more than classes installed from other systems. This separation excludes outsiders from system resources while granting more access to the more trusted Java pieces.

Benefits of Sandbox Security

Researchers, students, engineers, developers, and (presumably) criminal hackers have been hammering the Java specification from its introduction to find weaknesses and security holes. The consensus so far seems to be that Java is more secure than most alternatives, although it is still deficient in some areas. When used with code signing, Java provides a reasonable expectation of security against harmful code, both intentional and unintentional.

Code Signing

One way to avoid installing harmful programs is to install only programs with a known provenance. Before distributed applications, this precaution meant installing only commercial software that had arrived in the office inside a shrink-wrapped package. Applying this type of policy to software would exclude all noncommercial software; however, there have been reports of viruses distributed on commercial program disks.

Code-Signing Mechanisms

Partially as a new feature salvo in the browser wars and partially in response to criticism of the relative lack of security in ActiveX controls (which did not originally have any limitation on access to system resources), Microsoft introduced a framework for ActiveX control (and other distributed code) authentication called Authenticode. *Authenticode* provides a network-aware way to exclude noncommercial distributed software and a mechanism to positively identity the software developer behind the applet or control. Most important, Authenticode provides a way to positively detect any software tampering or corruption, which eliminates the risk of having a legitimate control modified for evil purposes.

Authenticode uses X.509 certificates issued to software developers; the developers digitally sign their distributed code before publishing it. End users downloading the code verify the signature before executing the code. If the signature is verified, the user can be confident that the signer really generated the code. Microsoft Authenticode certificates can be generated by a private certification authority, or they can be purchased from Verisign or GTE.

Java applet code signing works similarly, and applets packaged in conformance to Authenticode specifications can be signed with Authenticode.

Benefits of Code Signing

Code signing is useful only as long as its users understand exactly what it can and cannot do. Very simply, code signing can only guarantee that the signed code was generated by the owner (or under the auspices of the owner) of the certificate associated with the signature and that the code has not been altered in any way from the form in which the owner signed it.

Code signing will not do anything to protect against a harmful program that has been digitally signed, something that could occur, for example, if a disgruntled employee at a software vendor used the corporate keys without authorization or if a criminal obtained a digital certificate from a certification authority under false pretenses. The distinction is important because the presence of a signature guarantees only that the entity generating the signature is the source of the code.

Although the Java sandbox appears to be an alternative to code signing, code signing is in fact complementary to the sandbox approach. In large part, the benefit of code signing is that it allows developers to create much more interesting and useful applications—for example, applications that can read and write to system resources. Of course, at the same time, the accessibility of the system to the Active Platform developer also opens the door to more interesting and dangerous attacks through the network. In the early months of 1997, several such attacks were identified against Microsoft's Internet Explorer, delaying the release of an IE 4.0 beta version and prompting Microsoft to release a security revision to IE 3.0.

CHAPTER

7

Building Extranet Applications

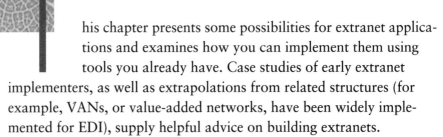

This chapter presents some possibilities for extranet applications and examines how you can implement them using tools you already have. Case studies of early extranet implementers, as well as extrapolations from related structures (for example, VANs, or value-added networks, have been widely implemented for EDI), supply helpful advice on building extranets.

Much of this chapter's hands-on information comes from the work of a few early implementers. As the extranet matures into a mainstream application of internetworking technologies, more of the following types of task-specific tools will become available:

- Application development software for distributed object environments

- Directory services client and server software

- Digital certification services client and server software

- Code signing and authentication services

Likewise, more of the tools currently available for building intranet and Internet applications will be adapted for use in extranets, including

- Intranet/Internet servers that can interface to legacy systems

- Application development tools

- Other client and server products

The Extranet Development Process

The best way to approach any large project, whether building an extranet or building a house, is to break it into manageable component tasks. Traditional project management planning procedures, particularly the techniques specific to developing large systems projects and distributed networking projects, are particularly useful when building an extranet. However, the developer should keep in mind that although building an extranet may be very much like building an intranet, the projects have differences—the most important of which is that extranets provide interorganizational connectivity whereas intranets provide connectivity only within an organization.

The ability to implement interorganizational connectivity is not only the greatest potential benefit of extranets but also *the greatest potential risk.*

You also need to consider the motivation that is driving your extranet project. Attempting to build an extranet simply because it is the hottest new technology is a blueprint for failure (or at least a blueprint for disappointment). That approach fosters unreasonably high expectations as to the potential benefits of the extranet but does not incorporate sufficiently specific criteria for judging the success of the project. A more systematic approach to extranet design and deployment is illustrated in Figure 7.1, as well as in this list:

1. Target a problem

2. Specify the extranet goals

3. Identify the extranet user population

4. Build extranet application requirements

5. Specify the extranet application

6. Build the extranet application

7. Review, oversee, and provide ongoing support

The process, like most system development processes, should be iterative and provide feedback opportunities to allow design goals, project objectives, tools, and techniques to adjust to a constantly changing environment. As new tools, standards, and products become available, parts of the extranet project may become easier (or unnecessary), so careful oversight is a necessity. Although the project team should develop and adhere to a plan regarding the exact nature of the extranet's function, flexibility in terms of how that functionality is implemented is a positive attribute.

FIGURE 7.1

Planning and building an extranet requires careful attention to and constant reevaluation of how well the extranet will solve the organization's problems *throughout* the process.

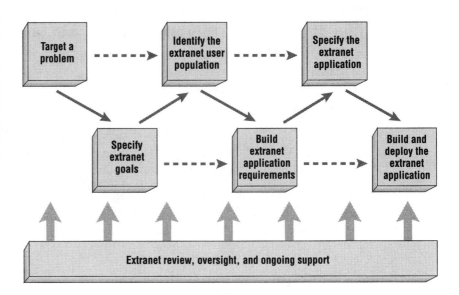

Targeting the Extranet Challenge

To the person with a new saw, every piece of wood may be a little too long. Trying to solve every business problem with the latest cool technology, just for the sake of being able to deploy that cool new technology, is a big mistake. Sometimes this strategy pays off anyway, but more often it backfires. Unfortunately, upper management becomes convinced that the new technology can solve every business problem facing the organization, right away, and for a very small investment. With such a vague mandate and high expectation for success, even a moderate success may be viewed as a failure.

A more successful approach, and one taken by many intranet and Internet presence implementers over the past few years, is to identify the specific business challenge that can most benefit from the new technology. Building a pilot project around such tasks, and including return on investment studies, can help advance the technology most effectively within an organization.

The first problems that many intranet implementers targeted were relatively mundane, such as human resources publishing tasks. Large volumes of information must be made available to all employees, for example, employee and management handbooks, benefits information, job postings, and corporate newsletters. Many human resources publications shared three characteristics that made intranets an excellent mechanism for publishing them:

- They are very big documents, which use a lot of paper and require a lot of delivery resources to distribute them to all employees.

- They change frequently, and every update must be delivered to every employee.

- They are used infrequently by any individual employee, so most of the time the documents are discarded, largely or entirely unread.

Putting these documents on an intranet server means that the cost of duplicating and delivering them (a figure that scales directly with the size of the organization) is replaced by the cost of building and maintaining the intranet web server (a figure that does not increase significantly as the size of the served population increases). For large corporations, the savings from implementing a relatively simple intranet service can be huge—and the end users receive accurate and current human resources information directly, without wasting a lot of time searching for and flipping through out-of-date documents.

The most important points to remember are that when you use a new technology to solve an old problem, the new solution should be an overwhelming and undeniable improvement over the existing solution. It shouldn't just save money; the new solution should make the process better in some significant way, preferably for everyone involved. The more benefits that a new-technology solution generates, the more likely everyone in the organization will support it and help it become a success.

Searching for Extranet Business Problems

Identifying the kinds of business problems that an extranet application can solve in an organization should not be too difficult when you consider the problem in the context of the strengths of extranetworking. If you examine the ways in which organizations currently communicate with other organizations, their customers, and their business partners, some obvious candidates for extranetworking are sure to surface.

You can get some good ideas for extranet projects by looking at the kinds of applications that make successful intranet or Internet implementations. Understanding how intranet or Internet applications succeed (or fail) will help you find good candidates for extranet applications.

Internet and World Wide Web Applications

Pure Web applications—that is, applications that provide no inter-activity—are no longer easy to find. These applications simply publish information to the world. The user connects to the Web site, gets the desired information, and moves on.

The earliest Web sites, set up well before commercial interest in the Internet developed, often published information about the Internet and World Wide Web: what they were, how to use them, and how to find out more. Later, organizations began using their Web sites to publish information about their own products. The resulting sites acted as "brochure servers": serving up copies of the organization's own brochures. Although static Web sites have the potential to offer the most up-to-date information about the organization, in practice they often languish and lose considerable value because they are not updated frequently.

A better model of successful Internet application comes from the use of newsgroups and mailing lists. These mechanisms support the publication and propagation of timely and immediate postings from subscribers through Network News Transport Protocol (NNTP) and e-mail servers. Subscribers can read the most recent postings from other subscribers, and as long as people participate, the content changes and remains timely. News and mailing lists provide an ongoing forum where something new is (in theory) always happening.

Web sites that offer compelling and up-to-date information, therefore, become examples of successful Internet applications. These Web sites are, in effect, digital publications that provide benefit to their end users through their immediacy. Readers don't have to wait for a magazine or newspaper to be printed and delivered, and viewers or listeners don't have to wait for a broadcaster to get in front of a camera or microphone. The content can go online as soon as it is created. News, commentary, weather reports, business and financial market information, product reviews, or reports from international hot spots will draw end users as long as the content is accurate and up-to-the-second.

Advertising or subscriptions might fund this type of site, but in general it does not need to provide any interactivity to succeed.

Intranet Applications

The pure intranet application injects TCP/IP applications into an organizational network without regard to Internet connectivity. External connectivity in such applications is usually a parallel project and usually entails some sort of firewall gatewaying or application filtering.

Like pure Internet applications, as defined above, pure intranet applications can be simple publishing ventures. Or they can evolve to support a considerable degree of interactivity among employees. For example, an intranet application may begin as a pure publishing (noninteractive) endeavor, but as other TCP/IP applications are considered and installed, intranet interactivity invariably increases. E-mail is usually an organization's first interactive application, and network news for groupware applications typically follows.

Within an intranet, even an initially noninteractive application like data publication can become an interactive, participatory one. As use of the intranet increases, creation and maintenance of internal Web content moves outward from the central publishing authorities to a user population that generates Web content during the workday. For example, although an intranet may start as a way of publishing human resources employee guidebooks, a decidedly noninteractive function, the publishing function eventually moves to other departments as they identify areas in which Web publishing would help them solve business problems.

The first wave of intranet applications usually includes other types of information publication, for example, corporate accounting guidelines, marketing schedules, press releases, and corporate newsletters. As shown in Figure 7.2, this type of intranet tends to be a one-way operation, with information flowing only in one direction.

As the intranet matures, it can support more interactivity. An early trend to two-way communications is often seen in corporate bulletin boards on intranet Web sites. Eventually, success tends to force intranet Webmasters to delegate content creation and maintenance functions to departments and the individuals responsible for the information they

FIGURE 7.2

Corporate publishing, an
early intranet application,
is usually a one-way
communication medium.

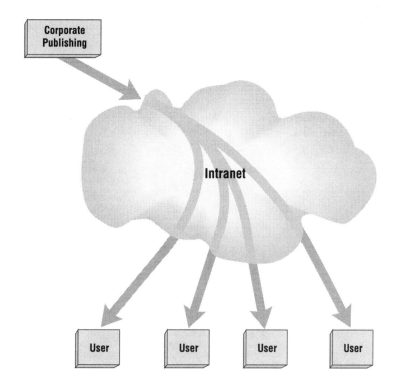

want to publish. The latest generation of Web servers from Microsoft
and Netscape supports content management delegation, with simplified
network administration tools. Figure 7.3 shows what happens when
users can create content as well as browse it.

Decentralization of Web content management is necessary for an
intranet to grow, but it also requires some degree of trust in the content creators—and some degree of control over who has Web content
management authority and how much authority to actually delegate.
Consequently, Web decentralization calls for fairly complex security
infrastructures, usually supported by X.500 or related directory services standards, as well as strong authentication procedures.

FIGURE 7.3

Intranets can support
decentralized content
creation when
Webmasters delegate
some Web management
functions.

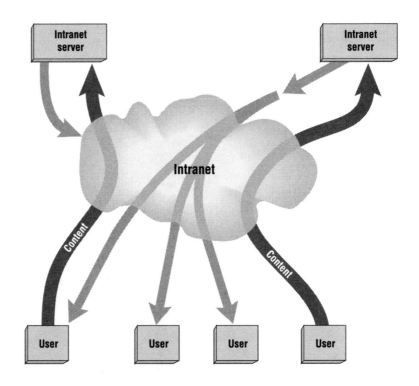

Easy Extranet Targets

One of the perquisites of being an early implementer is having the first
shot at all the easy targets. Building a robust, usable, and useful workgroup application using Web technologies is more difficult than
building a simple Web publishing application—and it may be more difficult to demonstrate a financial benefit from such an application.
Early extranet implementers are finding the same benefit from being
groundbreakers.

The key to finding extranet targets is to identify the areas in which
at least some of the following apply:

- The situation involves a strong interorganizational dimension or
  key customer/vendor interactions.

- The existing solution is expensive or wasteful in some way.

- The existing solution presents a bottleneck to some organizational process.

- The existing solution is unsatisfactory in some way to customers or to the organization.

- The existing solution is already partially automated or could easily be automated.

Obvious candidates for extranet applications are those that can add value to all users through:

- Reduced costs

- Improved product or service delivery

- Improved product or service

- Some other enhancement of the process through automation

Obvious Extranet Applications

Applications that come to mind immediately fall into several different categories, including

- Customer service

- Sales and marketing

- Help desk applications

However, the most obvious extranet application may not always be the best extranet application. You always have to examine the costs and benefits of each application, particularly in light of the intended user population. Will the users be likely to migrate from the existing medium—the telephone, postal mail, or in-person visits—to a networked medium? The other important question, discussed in greater detail later in this chapter, is whether the benefits outweigh the actual and potential costs of implementing the task as an extranet application.

Customer Service   Most organizations that serve large populations must also maintain large customer service departments to handle customer problems and queries. Determining the most common customer service requests may identify customer service applications. If those requests are reasonably simple and require simple database lookups for customers—such as checking the status of a delivery, an account balance, the value of a financial holding, transportation schedules and itineraries, or whether a scheduled payment has been received—the problem may translate into an extranet application.

The most likely candidates for extranet applications will be those whose customer population:

- Has easy access to networked computers

- Is unsatisfied with the existing arrangement (usually a telephone call with lengthy waiting time or confusing voice-mail branches)

- Uses customer service mostly for one particular type of call

Sales and Marketing   Using the extranet to generate sales is a compelling goal, but one that will depend in large part on the acceptance of Internet transaction mechanisms by general users (for consumer transactions) and the cooperation of trading partners in agreeing on an infrastructure for interorganizational transactions (for business-to-business transactions). However, to be successful the commercial transaction extranet application must add some tangible or intangible value to the transaction that is above what the customer would get from some other transaction medium. For example:

- A discount

- Faster order turnaround than available from mail or telephone orders

- Around the clock availability

- Immediate delivery (for data-only products like software or information)

- Up-to-the minute account information available online

- Immediate electronic notification of order fulfillment

Help Desk Applications   Simply publishing a help desk database of questions and answers with a database search button is not enough to satisfy most customers' needs for assistance, although many organizations have attempted just that with their Web sites. Identifying the most common questions, providing the answers, and publishing that information in an efficient and easy-to-understand format will be a more successful application of extranet technology.

Practical Extranet Applications

Extranet applications must be practical. They must meet a current need better than the current solution, or they must meet a new need in an efficient and useful way. They must cost less than the existing solution—or they must provide a significant benefit for a price that customers (and the sponsoring organizations) are willing to pay.

However, an extranet must do more than just provide a service not already offered anywhere else. If consumer demand does not drive that service, then that extranet will fail. On the other hand, an extranet that provides a service to a proven market may be quite successful.

As the case studies section later in this chapter demonstrates, the most practical extranet applications put an organization's clients in more direct contact with the organization's information and services. Cutting costs will likely be a byproduct of the transition to extranet applications, but will not always be the primary motivating factor in building the extranet.

Making the Extranet Pay

Organizations need a detailed and compelling cost justification to agree to try a costly new technology. For example, local area network vendors in the 1980s had to rely on savings through shared printers and hard drives to justify the cost of their cabling, boards, and servers. Once a technology has proven itself, the cost justification is no longer necessary (witness the telephone, the copy machine, the fax machine, the personal computer, and the LAN; Internet connectivity may soon join that club). However, for now the extranet advocate—the person actually doing the selling of the extranet to the organization, whether an internal IT manager or an outside consultant—must clearly demonstrate that the extranet is not yet another technological money pit.

Preparing the cost-justification proposal requires the extranet designer to know, as precisely as possible, about both the extranet and the operations of the prospective extranet organization. Like any business plan, the extranet plan should include information on the following topics:

- Extranet start-up costs

- Ongoing extranet costs

- Value of the benefits to be provided by the extranet

These are discussed in more detail below.

Extranet Start-up Costs

Estimating costs for a project, particularly if the figures are to be used to create a project budget, can be a nerve-wracking experience. Come in with too low a figure, and you may find yourself attempting to build a two-story house with only one story's worth of bricks; come in too high, and you may price yourself out of the market.

Any extranet will have start-up costs, but the costs will differ depending on the degree to which internetworking technologies are already implemented in the organization and its partners. Here are some of the expenses associated with building an extranet:

- **Networking costs** related to linking non-networked users and systems to the extranet. These expenses are usually assumed by the extranet user community, but in some cases they may be the responsibility of an extranet sponsor (for example, a sales organization may mandate use of the extranet by franchisees).

- **Internetworking costs** related to linking LANs and organizations together. These expenses may include the cost of obtaining connectivity from telecommunications vendors, installing routing and switching equipment, and installing client and server software. Be sure to include the cost of any service commitments, for example, when a service provider requires a commitment to use its network for some period following the installation.

- **Acquisition and preparation** of extranet facilities. Only the most rudimentary extranet can be housed in existing unused space; most will require at the least a room that can be secured from casual access and provide some form of disaster protection (a remote backup site or secondary service provider).

- **Building expenses** associated with the network and internetwork infrastructures, for building and maintaining extranet servers and services and for creating and administering extranet applications. Whether all or part of this work is done internally with organizational resources or outsourced to consultants and network service providers, its cost must be quantified and included in any extranet plan.

Other factors to consider when calculating extranet expenses are corporate overhead expenses including the value of benefits packages to employees, the cost of hiring them, the cost of their office space, and the cost of the added systems and network services necessary to bring the extranet online.

Ongoing Extranet Costs

How much the extranet costs to maintain over time provides a baseline for figuring out how much the extranet must contribute to the organization's long-term bottom line to justify its existence. The most important costs include the following:

- **Data communications services,** particularly the cost of extranet and Internet links, high-speed point-to-point links, and related services.

- **Software, hardware, and network maintenance fees.** Where some or all of these tasks are performed by employees, their time must be assigned a value and a cost calculated for the amount of time they spend in support of the extranet.

- **Ongoing facility costs,** including utilities, space rental, and backup services.

Quantifying Extranet Benefits

One way to skip the process of quantifying extranet costs and benefits is to wait until your organization's competitors have already implemented them, and you must implement your own to regain competitiveness. This approach is probably not the most optimal. Although you can save time and money by learning from the mistakes of the early implementers, you stand to lose more by missing out on market opportunities and losing market share. A better choice is to take the trouble to identify and total all the potential sources of savings and, more important, sources of revenue from the extranet. The most compelling argument in favor of implementation is an attractive positive cash flow.

Another option is to piggyback the extranet on top of existing facilities. For example, the extranet may not add significantly to the cost of maintaining an intranet, particularly if it is designed as a lower-cost add-in feature. The same goes for adding an intermediary system between a corporate Web site and a corporate legacy application.

Potential sources of extranet benefits can often be identified through some form of market research, although the research should be truly compelling and be supported by other, more concrete, cost savings. Extranet benefits can come from many different sources. For example:

- Improvement in capturing new customers

- Reduction in the cost of setting up new accounts

- Improvement in retaining existing customers

- Increases in sales per customer

- Reduction in the cost of supporting existing customers

- Savings on publishing costs for brochures and customer support information

- Improvement in order fulfillment turnaround time

- Potential for direct digital sales over the extranet (applicable mostly to software vendors and others whose product can be easily digitized)

Identifying Extranet Users

The extranet user population should be defined early in the planning process; in fact, this step will usually follow logically from the original problem statement and task-specification processes. Determining the user population is important for deciding how to deploy the extranet, rather than for defining the level of the population's technical expertise. The following issues must be resolved very early in the extranet planning process:

- How many people will use the extranet altogether?

- How many simultaneous users should be supported?

- Where are these users located? (This answer is important for internationalization—the preparation of content for international audiences, in different languages, cultures, and currencies—as well as to performance and connectivity issues.)

- What kind of links to the extranet will be typical?

- What is the lowest-common-denominator platform to be supported?

- What platforms will be supported? must be supported?

- What kind of performance should be expected?

- What are the users' expectations for security, reliability, robustness?

- What kind of technical support will be required?

- What kind of population growth should be planned for?

- How will the extranet be paid for, by whom, and how much?

In general, the trend is for end users to expect, and for extranet products vendors to provide (or claim to provide), the best, fastest, easiest to use, most secure, and most scalable solutions. However, there is no such thing as a free lunch, so as the degree of security increases, the ease of use and performance factors tend to degrade. Likewise, systems with more features and better performance tend to cost more to deploy than systems with fewer features and lower performance. The degree to which the underwriting organization (whether it be a corporation or a user group) is willing to pay will often dictate how fast and cool the extranet will be.

Extranet Application Life Cycle

The development life cycle for an extranet application will be very much like any other application development project. It involves the following steps:

1. Stating the objectives of the extranet application

2. Specifying the actual extranet application implementation

3. Implementing the extranet application

4. Ongoing evaluation and monitoring of the extranet application

Stating the Extranet Application Objectives

This process is basically one of identifying, and clearly stating, the exact functions that the extranet application is to perform. In other words, you need to relate the objectives of the extranet to the problem that the extranet is being built to solve.

Identifying Functions

To build an application, simply stating in broad, succinct terms what the extranet is intended to accomplish is not sufficient (although you must be able to provide a broad, defining mission statement). You also need to break out extranet functions by specific tasks. For example, simply stating that the extranet will provide customer services is not enough; the function specification must identify exactly what customer services will be provided and possibly describe how those services will be implemented.

For example, the function specification for a customer support extranet might define the following elements:

- How the customer enters the extranet application (login panel)

- The information the end user must supply to receive support (for example, contact information)

- A separate description for each customer service function (for example, checking account balances, monitoring task progress, or making payments)

- The form in which responses are generated and the delivery method for those responses (for example, e-mail, HTTP, or telephone call)

Two terms used to describe extranet functions are outward-looking and inward-looking. *Outward-looking functions* define how the user interacts with the organization—how the organization collects information from and delivers information to the user. Outward-looking functions can include things like collecting a user's ID and account number and formulating an account request.

The functions that define what happens to the information inside the organization are *inward-looking functions*. Once the user ID and account number are collected, inward-looking functions handle tasks like authenticating the user, retrieving account information, and formatting information for the user.

It is possible to deploy these functions separately, although this benefits no one in the long term. Organizations short on resources could build the outward-looking functions onto their Internet servers first while still fulfilling user requests through more traditional means. For example, a very large computer company (a hardware manufacturer as well as a provider of software and services—we can call them the XYZ Corporation) started offering a digital commerce service in 1996. Information sellers "package" their products using XYZ's service and collect payments through XYZ—all automatically. XYZ provided online registration to information sellers, but had to process the registrations manually behind the scenes because XYZ had not built the infrastructure to automate the registration process.

This approach may sometimes be necessary, especially for organizations with limited resources, but should not be considered as more than stopgap measure. The outward-looking functions providing a user interface to the extranet are necessary, but not sufficient to build an extranet. The inward-looking functions implement the true value of the extranet, but deploying the inward-looking functions before deploying the user interface to those functions provides no benefit to users.

Because the inward-looking functions tend to be more complicated, using distributed object-based solutions is crucial to a successful implementation. Distributed-object solutions will enable your program components to intelligently grab information from the end user, hand that data off to a transaction processor or a legacy system for processing, and then accept the results to turn over to the user. These functions include things like entering orders automatically, processing help desk requests, or modifying customer information securely (that is, with strong authentication).

Specifying the Extranet Application

Actually specifying the extranet application differs from stating the application's objectives. Because this phase is the actual design phase, the result is a set of programming implementation specifications that determine how the extranet will function.

Because of the volatility of the internetworking software and hardware industry, you should specify what the extranet application and infrastructure will look like by functionality, rather than attempt to specify by product or technique. A typical extranet project might run several months or longer from conception to completion. Drastic changes have occurred in similar time periods over the last two years, including the

- Release of one or two major revisions of most important internetworking application client and server packages

- Release of totally new software products based on unique concepts

- Implementation and approval of new Internet standards

- Recognition (and resolution, more or less) of major threats to Internet security and performance

Extranet specifiers should avoid identifying products and vendors and concentrate on defining how the extranet will work. For example, developers looking for Internet servers with specific capabilities (for example, encrypted newsgroup sessions or open-standard calendaring and scheduling functions) must compare the announced feature lists from server vendors and then continue to monitor the actual offerings from candidate vendors.

Internet software vendors have shown themselves more prompt at announcing features than at delivering them over the past year or so.

An extranet could be defined in terms of products, as in example 1 below, but this definition might lock the organization into using an inappropriate product mix for the extranet as it finally appears. Example 2 shows a more broadly functional extranet specification. The extranet application in both cases is an Internet storefront that links consumers to ordering facilities from a dynamic catalog showing current stock and pricing as represented in a legacy database.

Example I

- Secure Web services to be provided through the Netscape Enterprise Server 4.0

- The extranet application will be developed with Oracle Developer/2000 2.0; to draw information from a legacy database

- Internet commerce services to be provided through the Cyber-Cash Internet payment system

- Transactions handled by the Microsoft Transaction Server

In this simple example, products, vendors, and even version numbers are specified at the outset. This technique generates two sets of problems. First, freezing a specification at the current revision of available software means that new products and versions—which may provide significant benefits—may be frozen out of the extranet. Second, looking forward and relying on vendor product announcements for feature lists—which are often revised to remove or modify announced features—can lead to disappointment.

Example 2

- Web services to be provided via a secure Web server product that supports SSL 3.0 and HTTP 1.0

- The extranet application to be developed using development tools capable of interfacing with the organization's legacy database and creating applications accessible to most clients (Microsoft Internet Explorer 2.0 and higher or Netscape Navigator 2.0 and higher) without any additional software (Java applets or ActiveX controls) to download

- Internet commerce services to be provided with a service supporting Secure Electronic Transaction (SET) through a national settlement service

- Transactions to be handled through a robust and reliable transaction monitor or middleware solution

This specification is more general than the specification in example 1; in fact, example 1 is derived from this specification. However, the specification in example 2 identifies the standards and functions that must be supported, rather than trying to identify the products that will support those standards and functions. Building an extranet on the specification in example 2 may require extensive testing of various software solutions but should result in the most appropriate and effective extranet solution.

Building the Extranet Application

To build extranet applications, developers must augment traditional programming techniques. Using object technologies simplifies building the application because extranet logic can be programmed into components or controls that live on the server. Consequently, objects may be portable to other types of servers if a system upgrade is necessary. Writing the application to output standards-based content for transmission to clients eliminates the need to create different versions for each type of client platform, which is a requirement of traditional client/server programming.

However, the extranet developer must be even more aware of changes in the world of open standards. For example, when I began to write this book, the technical community believed that Microsoft wanted to retain total control over its distributed object specifications. Since then, however, Microsoft has decided to make its DCOM and related specifications available to the industry. Although this gesture is far from altruistic (Microsoft stands to profit greatly by having its Active Platform become the de facto standard network application platform, even if other vendors are able to write to it), it has changed the playing field for CORBA supporters who shunned DCOM as a closed specification.

Developers need to be able to guess correctly the best platforms, standards, and tools for their extranets. The following issues are still unresolved:

- The degree to which DCOM and CORBA will be able to interoperate, and the degree to which they will have to interoperate, in the future. Choosing the wrong standard for any particular extranet may cause problems, and some extranets will work better with one than the other (depending on many factors including the exact application, whether it is for a private extranet or a public extranet, the makeup of the extranet user population and what platforms they use).

- The degree to which non-Wintel platforms will affect the market, both for clients and for servers. Any significant move toward total market acceptance of DCOM means that non-Wintel platforms could lose ground to Wintel platforms in terms of function and interoperability.

- The degree to which developers, including Microsoft, will support non-Wintel platforms with extranet-related software.

Moving the Extranet Forward

Building the extranet platform requires what might be called an "aggressive conservatism" or "conservative aggression." In practice, taking this stance means that:

- Extranet sponsors need to provide the most advanced features possible but with the least potential harm in the event of an unforeseen security problem.

- Extranet managers must be very aware of the latest development plans of their competitors so as not be left behind when the competitors implement more advanced features.

- Extranet managers must closely monitor their own extranet's usage to ascertain that it is being used to achieve its stated goals and that it is fulfilling its objectives in terms of cost and functions.

- The extranet must be monitored for security breaches and to keep tabs on any potential security susceptibilities.

Monitoring extranet use means more than just graphing Web site hits or visits. Logging and reporting should cover as much territory as possible, including data such as

- Time of day of visit

- Functions completed

- Each visitor's point of origin

- Time spent at the site

- Time spent completing each function

- Individual usage through login IDs

- Brand and version of user browsers

Using statistical reporting, this data can yield important information about how the extranet can be changed to best serve its users.

Also important is the ability to track network link loads and server loads, as well as link and server performance. Structural architecture changes, such as the addition of a transaction server or even the use of message-queuing technologies, may be indicated as extranet use scales up the number of concurrent users accessing an application.

Extranet Case Studies

These two case studies represent the types of extranets being built in 1997. The first, provided by a member of an internal extranet development team, outlines the basic issues and solutions of building an extranet for a large service organization to enable it to securely, completely, and reliably serve many individual customers with Internet connections. The second, provided by a consulting and network services firm specializing in building extranets and intranets, provides some insight into the creation of an extranet to serve a smaller company selling to a commercial market.

Credit Card Issuer Extranet

Many companies offering financial services, including brokers, banks, credit card issuers, and mortgage companies, are implementing extranet applications to provide some form of customer self-service. Understandably, these organizations are reluctant to supply too many of their implementation details. However, a network professional involved in the development of an extranet for a major credit card issuer has provided some background on that project.

Extranet Application and Implementation

This credit card issuer wanted to provide its current cardholders with access to account information through the Internet. Services available to cardholders include the ability to check the following account information:

- Payments, adjustments, credits, new purchases and other transactions posted to the account since the last statement

- Most recent payment received and current minimum payment due

- Credit limit and amount of credit still available

- Account balance as of last statement

- Current account balance

- Most recent and current statement closing dates

- Any amount past due

Most of this information would otherwise be available to the cardholder through a telephone call or a voice response unit; the cardholder would have to provide account information to a customer service representative (or provide it to the voice response unit), which uses that information to access the corporate database and retrieve the requested information. Functions planned for the future include online statement delivery and online payments.

According to one of the developers of this system, the extranet links cardholders to the card issuer's account management system, running internally on the company's private network. The extranet allows current cardholders and prospective cardholders to communicate with the issuer as if they were interfacing through a voice response unit or talking directly with a customer service representative. The extranet uses a store-and-forward messaging approach to deliver secure, authenticated transactions from the Web server to the source of data and back.

Challenges and Lessons

The most technically challenging tasks encountered while implementing this extranet were

- Building a mechanism for user authentication that satisfied a range of security requirements

- Building a system that provided sufficient reliability to satisfy the needs of the cardholders and the card issuer

- Optimizing the system to perform responsively, particularly in light of the need to use an SSL-encrypted link for security purposes

The developer who provided this information believed that one of the most important lessons learned in the development process was: "The technical architecture will obsolete itself over time as the business model matures and awareness of this capability becomes more prevalent in the business. The technical architecture will need to be reviewed over time, and the tools to create and support new business functionality will be state-of-the-art at each new phase."

He went on to say that it was crucial for the developer to always "continue to define, specify, and understand the business model for which the extranet will be the solution. Be specific in your requirements and focus on increasing customer value."

Commercial Printer Extranet

The preceding case outlines the typical large-scale extranet implementation, where a large organization provides extranet services to a large customer base. The underlying model for that type of extranet is well grounded in the World Wide Web publication approach to customer services in which one organization controls the extranet infrastructure, builds the extranet application—and pays for the extranet. The user population consists of many individuals who are customers and who use the extranet to access information about themselves and their accounts through whatever browser or client software they have available.

Offering customer self-service in a business-to-business selling environment poses many of the same challenges as encountered in consumer extranets. The differences in the details will become apparent as you read the following case study.

DS Graphics in Lowell, Massachusetts, contracted with Wing.Net of Woburn, Massachusetts, to build an extranet, which was delivered in early 1997. Wing.Net's approach is to build an infrastructure for the extranet and deliver with it all the tools needed to allow the end users to access information in a database warehoused at the Wing.Net facilities. The end user accesses the data through intuitive GUI interfaces while Wing.Net maintains the infrastructure for the client.

WOLFNet

The network described here is called WOLFNet (Work Order On-Line Fulfillment Network) and was built for DS Graphics, a commercial printer. The goal of the extranet was to simplify—and speed up—the process of dealing with customer requests. According to Dick Woodbury, Wing.Net vice president of marketing and business development, WOLFNet achieves this goal by offering DS Graphics customers a seamless and efficient communications medium, over which they can perform tasks like print-job ordering, reordering of existing standard inventory materials, and checking on the status of complex fulfillment tasks. Automating these processes speeds them up because the customer can perform them directly, interacting with their vendor's own database instead of using a customer service representative as an intermediary to that database system.

Woodbury explains that the result has been an impressive increase in the ease with which DS Graphics clients are able to order; the system has been instrumental in both capturing new clients and retaining existing clients. According to Woodbury, "New clients are beating down their doors because [the extranet] is easy, saves time and money, and becomes a hook for DS Graphics for their next print job. A real win-win situation."

WOLFNet Infrastructure

The WOLFNet infrastructure is hosted through Wing.Net, which has five distinct redundant paths to the Internet for high availability. This arrangement, shown in Figure 7.4, allows Wing.Net to do load balancing and least-congested-route routing for high performance on the extranet's Internet links.

Security for the extranet is provided with a combination of the mechanisms discussed in Chapter 5. Wing.Net uses Netscape servers to provide 128-bit SSL channel encryption to compliant browsers, as well as firewall gateways, packet filtering, IP address gateways, and other techniques. Network monitoring software notifies the technical staff directly whenever it senses potential problems.

Access to corporate information is provided through the Netscape Enterprise Server with LiveWire, connecting to an Informix database (other Wing.Net extranets use the same basic infrastructure to access Oracle or Progress databases). The use of relational databases behind a simple browser-based GUI front end allows the extranet user to use the extranet to retrieve precise information without mediation of the extranet sponsor's customer support staff.

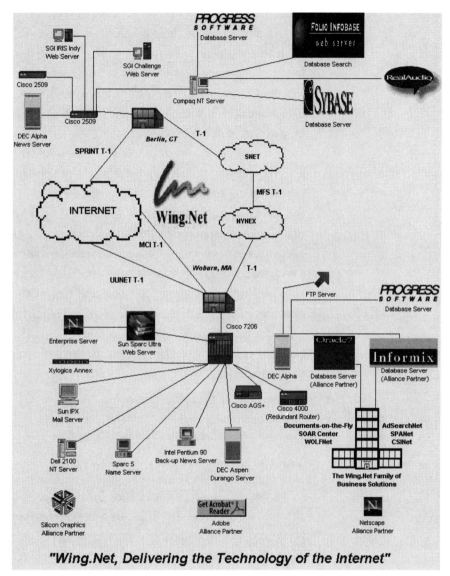

FIGURE 7.4

WOLFNet extranet topology

WOLFNet Applications and Services

According to Mark MacAuley, Wing.Net sales manager, the primary WOLFNet application was an advanced order-entry solution.

MacAuley said, "DS Graphics clients were requesting a way to submit orders and monitor their own accounts remotely without human intervention each time. They were using file transfer protocol as a solution but it was cumbersome, archaic, and required a lot of time for the sender and recipient to configure a proprietary software-generated file into a workable standard, like Excel, so that it could be manipulated by anyone at the receiving end."

The order-entry system then ties into the Intranet running on a TCP/IP network with a browser as a graphical front end. DS Graphics clients are permitted limited access to temporary libraries of the DS Graphics database. The result is that the client can track an order, make changes to the bill of materials, and submit other account requests through a standard browser connected to the extranet through the user's own Internet access account.

Woodbury described the basic features of the first phase of the extranet application as including an external Internet order form: an online form accessed by DS Graphics clients through which various account tasks can be completed, in particular work orders for various tasks, such as

- Initiation of print or fulfillment jobs

- Initiation of media replication jobs

- Use of a "pick list" to generate work orders

The extranet work order form allows the client to attach spreadsheets, word processing files, or any other supporting file to a request for quote (RFQ) order. Also available is bill of materials (BOM) viewing and editing, inventory control by reorder point, materials requirement planning (MRP), and access to work-flow information about fulfillment jobs (that is, printing jobs that include producing brochures, marketing letters, or other promotional materials; stuffing and addressing envelopes; and preparing the materials for delivery to a mailing list).

The forms themselves are the interface to the DS Graphics intranet; the end user has no direct access to any legacy systems. The extranet acts as an intermediary between DS Graphics and its customers.

WOLFNet Accomplishment Objectives

The initial function of this extranet was to provide direct real-time access to transaction tracking, job pricing, and inventory levels to the clients of DS Graphics. According to Woodbury, the following objectives were of paramount importance when Wing.Net was building the DS Graphics extranet:

- Establishing a communication mindset for the client and modeling the extranet to meet the business requirements of DS Graphics clients

- Providing electronic links to DS Graphics clients to make doing business easier

- Reducing transaction costs to make DS Graphics a more attractive vendor in the very competitive commercial printing industry

- Providing an experience that draws in new customers and keeps them

These objectives identify the most important issue when implementing an extranet: How will the investment in the new technology add to the bottom line of the business? In this case the result is drawing in new clients, keeping them as repeat customers, and keeping the costs down for all participants.

Lessons Learned

According to the Wing.Net sales manager, MacAuley, the most important lessons for extranet implementers relate to understanding the difference between a project such as building an extranet and purchasing a piece of hardware or software. MacAuley said that "implementing an extranet is a process, NOT an event"; as such, it has to be handled as an ongoing, organic entity.

More specifically, MacAuley suggests that extranet implementers keep these lessons in mind:

- Wherever possible, use open and interoperable platforms (for example, TCP/IP for networking applications and ODBC-compliant database systems for managing extranet application data).

- Find baseline standards and use them (for example, file formats for data transmission and client browser software).

- Keep project management focused and team oriented. Project management by committee can be a disaster without some firm leadership to build consensus.

Building a partnership between the extranet design and implementation team and the extranet sponsor organization means the project has a better chance for success—and makes the experience more rewarding for all the participants.

CHAPTER

8

Detailed Examples of Extranet Software

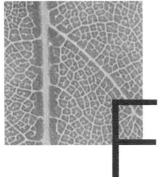

Extranets call for the use of many relatively familiar types of internetworking software, including:

- Web servers

- Internet network application servers

- Web browsers

- E-mail clients

- Content-generation tools

- Java and other language application development tools

- Firewalls

- Transaction processors and transaction monitors

However, of particular interest to the extranet implementer are these three new categories of internetworking software:

- Web application servers

- "Webtop" client software

- Message queuing

This chapter introduces a sampling of some of the products available or about to become available in 1997, and how they fit into the modern extranet. The products chosen here are not necessarily the only ones in their product category, nor should inclusion here be construed as an endorsement: these products may be representative of their category, category-leaders, or some combination of both.

For categories with more than one product in the sections below, products are listed in alphabetical order by vendor name.

Web Application Servers

The basic Web server is a fairly simple machine: all that is necessary is a computer that can store data files, runs TCP/IP, and can respond to HTTP (Hypertext Transport Protocol) requests from hosts wishing to retrieve those data files. There are no technical reasons why such a server could not run on a personal computer, on a Unix workstation, or even on an IBM mainframe system. HTTP is a relatively simple application protocol, mostly providing a means for browsers to request specific network resources and for servers to respond with those resources (or an error message stating why the resource is unavailable).

However, the straightforward type of Web server is rapidly being replaced by a new kind of product: the Web application server. Basic Web servers are excellent tools for the publication of information, but are limited in the type of interaction they can support between client and network resources hosted on the server. In other words, simple Web servers can be very useful for publishing a static product catalog or organizational directory, but these simple servers don't easily support interactive functions like customer queries or commercial transactions. Simple Web servers handle functions that go beyond simple publishing with mechanisms like the Common Gateway Interface (CGI), a specification that provides programmers with an interface between HTML and other network resources like databases.

The Web application server, however, provides a mechanism by which the extranet developer can more tightly integrate application-oriented functions like database queries and consumer transactions with the Web server. This means that the actual application, which might be a consumer catalog, can operate more quickly than with a traditional Web server interfacing through CGI to a separate database, and it can operate more intelligently. For example, a Web application server hosting a catalog can keep track of customers and present them with specials appropriate to their previous purchases. Web application servers can do all this customization with far less programming labor than the traditional approach.

This section highlights three leading Web application servers, those from Lotus, Microsoft, and Netscape. There are others, and upgrades to some or all of these will likely have been released before the end of 1997.

Lotus Domino

Based on the Lotus Notes groupware application, Lotus Domino is a server that provides a set of integrated services for building, deploying, and maintaining interactive applications for extranets. Domino services include:

- Object Store
- Directory
- Security
- Replication
- Messaging
- Enterprise Integration
- Workflow

In addition to providing basic Web services through Domino, the services listed above and described below help the extranet developer to produce a richer distributed Web application.

Object Store

Central to Domino is its object store: a database structure that can contain any number of objects and any kind of data types, ranging from simple ASCII text to multimedia files to Java applets and ActiveX controls. The object store integrates with directory information, making it possible to dynamically tailor the content presented to each user.

Directory

As with most extranet software, X.500 support is central to managing resource directory information for the server and for tasks including network configuration, application management, and security. Domino 4.5 synchronizes its directory information with Microsoft's Windows NT server directory services.

Security

The Domino server uses a full range of security features, including user authentication, encryption, and digital signatures. Access control can be maintained at the level of data fields, so extranet users can be provided with some database fields but not with all. This is particularly useful for permitting outside access to the public portions of databases that may contain proprietary information.

Replication

Domino supports replication of information and applications across organizational boundaries and among widely separated servers. As with Lotus Notes, Domino provides a means for individuals and organizations to work with replicated data rather than having to reconnect to a single network server.

Messaging

Domino provides e-mail services, again similar to Lotus Notes. It supports Lotus Notes clients as well as other POP3, MAPI, and SMTP clients.

Enterprise Integration

Domino provides integration with existing corporate legacy systems, including relational databases, mainframe applications, and transactional systems through programmable real-time and batch-level mechanisms.

Workflow

As with Lotus Notes, Domino provides a workflow engine that can distribute, track, and route documents defined in a workflow application. Since its debut in the early 1990s, the Notes workflow engine continues to be the most successful product in this market area, and Domino makes it possible to coordinate organizational activities inside and outside the organization.

How Domino Works in an Extranet

Domino is a Web application server that integrates e-mail as well as many other basic extranet specifications, including:

- Public key encryption for maintaining privacy

- An object approach to distributed applications, supporting CORBA and DCOM

- X.500 compliant directory services

- Open standards for accessing information through HTTP and SMTP

Domino provides a flexible and extensible platform for building extranet applications. Its replication and workflow features make it particularly attractive for implementing extranet applications that solve complicated business problems.

Microsoft Internet Information Server

More than any other vendor, Microsoft offers a complete, top to bottom, set of extranet solutions. Building on the networking services provided in the Windows NT Server platform, Microsoft adds:

- Internet Information Server (IIS) for publishing information and applications over TCP/IP internetworks

- SQL Server for database services

- Transaction Server for robustly handling network transactions

If you want to use Microsoft's Internet Information Server, you've got to use Windows NT Server. Unlike other vendors, Microsoft's offerings are tightly integrated with a single operating system: there are no Unix versions of Microsoft's servers. The stated reason is that providing a highly integrated suite of network services requires a high degree of integration with the underlying operating system, not only for performance but also for robustness, reliability and an impressive feature set. Such integration also tends to force organizations, users, and developers to commit to using Microsoft products and standards like DCOM.

Microsoft's Internet Information Server includes extranet-friendly features like:

- Support for X.500 compatible directory services

- Support for distributed object architecture (DCOM)

- Support for database and transaction services through SQL Server and Transaction Server

As a Web application server, Internet Information Server includes one very special feature: Active Server Pages. By taking advantage of the vertical integration among Microsoft server platform products, Active Server Pages make it easy to create Web pages combining HTML, scripts and ActiveX controls. Very simply, Active Server Pages allows the developer to produce pages based on the dynamic results of a program rather than on statically maintained output.

Active Server Pages

Extranet developers can use Active Server Pages to create content that is dynamically linked to the end-user, as well as dynamically linked to a database or application inside the organization. As shown in Figure 8.1, when a client requests an Active Server Page from the Internet Information Server, the associated control (or other program or script) is executed. That control, program, or script may also pass parameters taken from the user, for example, a user ID. In the illustration, the ActiveX control queries a SQL Server database and returns the database server response to the Internet Information Server—which processes the results of the query into HTML format and sends that result to the end-user. Active Server Pages can be used to pass information from the user to the server, as well as to allow dynamic interaction between user and network resources.

FIGURE 8.1

With Active Server Pages, Microsoft's Internet Information Server acts as an intermediary between extranet resources and extranet users.

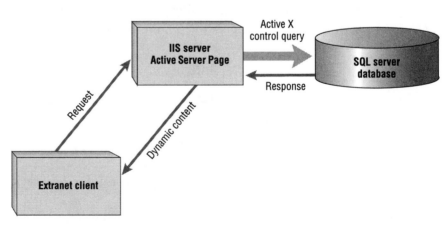

How Internet Information Server Works in an Extranet

Active Server Pages provide a simple yet powerful interface to legacy systems through a Web server. Access to this information may be provided to the public or to a more limited audience. For example, a typical public extranet application is the retail catalog. In this example, when consumers request information on a particular product category, for instance, hiking shoes, the Active Server Page queries the retailer's database for products that fall within that category and that are currently available (in stock). The result appears to be a standard catalog page (which could also include ordering options), but that shows only those products in stock and that shows all current retail prices (and any saleprices or special offers). Proprietary information like the retailer's costs and stocking levels are, of course, not displayed.

Netscape Enterprise Server

While Microsoft's Internet Information Server is part of a complete server solution, all built on a single operating system, Netscape's Enterprise Server is part of a suite of internetwork application servers that can run on several different operating systems, including Windows NT and various Unix platforms. Special features include:

- Advanced Web publishing and management features

- Intelligent agents

- Support for open network-oriented applications (including support for open network standards like CORBA, IIOP, X.500, and LDAP)

Advanced Web Publishing and Management

Netscape incorporated various advanced Web publishing and administration features in Enterprise Server. These include functions that allow publication and management of dynamic content to the Internet, intranets, and extranets. Some of these features include:

- Web publishing from the desktop, allowing individuals to publish Web information from any desktop to an extranet server

- Version control functions for tracking and controlling how versions are updated and how links are administered to dynamic content

- Flexible access and update controls, allowing individuals to control who has read and write access to the content they publish

- Access to information stored in a wide variety of data formats, including Microsoft Word, Adobe PDF, and others in addition to standard HTML

Intelligent Agents

Users have access to intelligent agents that are able to notify the user when some event occurs, in particular, some change in data in the server's content store. Users can create agents simply by following a link or filling in a form, specifying the task to be performed by the agent.

Open Network-Oriented Application Support

Enterprise Server supports deployment of Web applications through the Netscape ONE platform: a set of services available to any applications hosted on Enterprise Server, built with JavaScript, Java, C and C++, among others. Enterprise Server also includes native support for CORBA, making it possible for applications to interoperate across platform and network boundaries.

Netscape's LiveWire database service also provides simple access to Informix, Oracle, and Sybase legacy databases. LiveWire also supports ODBC for connectivity to information stored in other data formats.

How Enterprise Server Works in an Extranet

Like the other Web application servers discussed in this section, Netscape's Enterprise Server provides a platform for running applications across an extranet. Enterprise Server supports dynamic content presentation, through software integration with applications and resources stored elsewhere in the extranet. It also supports the collection, management, administration, and publication of content from individuals. Central to Enterprise Server is support for a wide range of open standards, ranging from HTML and HTTP to CGI, CORBA, and IIOP.

"Webtop" Client Software

By the end of 1996, over a dozen different companies were offering push technologies: software mechanisms that proactively move information from the content provider to the content consumers based on preferences indicated by the consumer. Users subscribe to various information streams, which are delivered to them—the users no longer have to surf by the information provider's site, rather the provider sends new information to the user when it is ready and available.

By the spring of 1997, *Wired* was proclaiming the death of the browser and the birth of a new era of push technologies. Browser developers Microsoft and Netscape were hardly unprepared for this eventuality, however. In the fall of 1996, Netscape announced a new techology code named Constellation. It integrated the computer desktop with the corporate intranet as well as the Internet and provided an interface to which push technologies could deliver information, while retaining browsing capabilities. The technology was demonstrated as early as November, 1996, at the fall Comdex show in Las Vegas, and Constellation was incorporated into a public beta of Netcaster, a component of Netscape's Communicator suite, in the spring of 1997.

At about the same time, Microsoft was also busily readying its next salvo in the browser war, Internet Explorer 4.0. With early betas available in February 1997, Microsoft rolled out an extranet interface that turned the operating system (Windows 95) into an extension of the extranet. All resources, whether remote or local, can be accessed through the Internet Explorer browser, and network resources can be subscribed, so the user need not explicitly pull new data down but have it pushed to the desktop.

Referring to these new products as new versions of old browsers misses the point: the browsers are actually evolving into a new type of software, sometimes called "Webtop" software (to differentiate it from the desktop). These products can help simplify the approach to the desktop, but at the same time continue to call on consumers and organizations to make a very specific choice: Opt for the Microsoft desktop, which works only where Microsoft Windows does; or choose Netscape's desktop, which works on almost any platform.

The result of this struggle could greatly influence the future of networked computing as well as the future development of internetworking technology. If Microsoft wins this struggle, it means that virtually all networked devices will ultimately have to run Microsoft operating system software in order to interoperate with the rest of the world. If Microsoft fails to dominate the market completely, there will still be room for other operating systems for networked devices. In any case, there is little doubt that Microsoft will continue to dominate the world of personal computing software and operating systems.

Microsoft Internet Explorer 4.0

Rather than approach the problem of building an integrated Webtop with open standards, Microsoft is leveraging its huge share of the operating system market to build a Webtop into the operating system itself. If you want to use Microsoft's Webtop solution, you need Windows and you need Internet Explorer 4.0. Internet Explorer 4.0 users can subscribe to specific Web sites: this means that a Webcrawler agent runs at scheduled times and checks the subscribed Web sites for changes. Results can be cached locally on the user's personal computer for quick response when the Web site is accessed, or the changes can be delivered to the user through the Outlook Express e-mail client that ships with Internet Explorer.

Data Channels

Internet Explorer 4.0 supports data channels, which deliver broadcast content through a single user interface. Microsoft is opening the channel architecture, but this simply means that the specifications for delivery of data through the channel are open—it does not mean that the client side of the specification is being opened up. This means that the specification is open to the extent that any push technology vendor can use the channel architecture specification to deliver information directly to any Internet Explorer 4.0 desktop, but it is not open to the extent that any browser vendor could write an interface to receive these channels.

Web and Desktop Integration

New with Internet Explorer and the upgrade to Windows 95 (code named Memphis, due out later in 1997) is far greater integration of the desktop with the Web. A large part of this integration is the extension of the Web interface to the desktop. The familiar File Manager interface can now be replaced with an Internet Explorer 4.0 interface, complete with the familiar browser control icons across the top of the window and single-click file and folder activation.

Beyond File Manager, the Web navigation paradigm extends to the actual desktop, which can now include HTML content as well as ActiveX controls and Java applets. Anything that can appear within the Web browser can now be dragged and dropped directly onto the Windows desktop, including display windows showing live data channel broadcasts.

How Internet Explorer Works in an Extranet

The concept of desktop integration is important to the extranet, and integrating extranet applications in the form of ActiveX controls "built-in" to the desktop through the Internet Explorer interface helps achieve the goal of integration. Likewise, the ability to subscribe to particular Web sites will help users to gather information from external sources: Web servers that are outside the organizational and extranet boundaries. At the same time, use of data channels for directed delivery of information from within the organization and the extranet helps to increase the immediacy of data distribution.

Netscape Constellation Technology

Constellation, as shown in Las Vegas at Fall Comdex 1996, appeared to be a replacement for the desktop, offering users a seamless integration between extranet and desktop: network and desktop resources were equally accessible to the user, and network resources could be updated in real time. Even more interesting was the ability to maintain a virtual desktop that persists from one session to the next: no longer is the user bound to a single physical computer as a "home" workstation. Documents, folders, e-mail, and other session-oriented resources could be accessed from any network-connected workstation. Access was controlled by password and user ID, so one user could use any workstation, laptop, terminal or any other type of network computing device to access the exact same working area. Likewise, many different users could share the same workstation to access their work areas.

Netcaster

Netscape Netcaster is distributed as a component of Netscape Communicator, and it incorporates many of the functions demonstrated at Constellation's debut. Netcaster enables push delivery of information and offline browsing, seamlessly integrating with Netscape's Channel Finder, a source for Internet data delivery channels. Users can subscribe to the information they want and have it delivered automatically, or can use offline browsing to retrieve extranet or Internet resources and use them when not connected. Netcaster was developed with open Internet standards of HTML, Java, and JavaScript.

Netcaster Features List

Netcaster includes many of the impressive features shown in the original demonstrations of Constellation, including:

- Seamless push delivery of information (using Marimba Castanet for access to data channels)

- Offline browsing

- Centralized browser administration and control

- Anchoring of channels to desktop in "webtop" mode for persistent view of current information in the channel

- Background Web site downloading and user-scheduled updates

- Flexible preferences to specify how often to update, maximum cache size, and the number of pages to download

How Netcaster Works in an Extranet

By providing an open interface to Web-based resources, Netcaster offers a suitable client platform for extranets. With access to push delivery, persistent views of current information extracted from the extranet, and Webtop integration, Netcaster provides extranet implementers and extranet users with a mechanism for seamless and simple access to extranet resources.

Message Queuing

One big problem with using a big internetwork spread over a wide geographical area, like the Internet, is that connections are almost always replaced by virtual connections. Separating any two hosts can be many other hosts, networks, and data communication links. It is very difficult to guarantee graceful and robust recovery from intermediate failures using standard TCP/IP protocols because that would require tracking the transmission and acknowledged receipt of each and every datagram sent between two hosts.

Some internetworking protocols can provide relative reliability. For example, Transmission Control Protocol (TCP) virtual circuits make use of four different timers which keep track of data flowing between hosts. These timers help the protocol stack to sense, and in some cases recover gracefully from, intermediate network failures.

This level of reliability is costly because it requires lots of processing just to keep track of all the data being passed between a server and clients using the server. This level of reliability is also unnecessary for most simple Internet applications, since errors in transmitting a file can be recovered by re-requesting or resending the file. However, the applications where absolute reliability is most important are also the applications that are of greatest interest to extranet developers building commercial transactional applications.

The necessity of tracking the status of each and every datagram gains importance when each datagram may contain a request for a financial transaction from a consumer, or the response of a merchant, bank or financial institution to that request. If a consumer submits a payment request to a bank, the consumer needs to be certain that the actual request has been received and not dropped on the floor by some over-worked router in between the consumer and the bank. The consequence of a failure is likely to be a late payment fee or worse. Likewise, if the consumer's system crashes before receiving a confirmation of receipt of such a request from the bank, the consumer needs some assurance that the request was processed (or not) before attempting to resubmit the request—which could result in double-payments of bills.

Message queuing systems can provide this functionality for commercial transactional systems. These are systems that require robustness that goes beyond what is necessary for the delivery of free information: banking and commercial applications, for example. The cost of delivering simple information must be close to zero, and thus standard TCP/IP protocols can be used; these are sufficient to guarantee that most of the time the data is delivered, and when there are problems they provide a simple means of recovering reasonably gracefully. Even infrequent failures in banking and commercial applications, on the other hand, could cost a lot to fix. Thus, the additional expense of implementing message queuing is justified.

IBM MQ Series

With support for many different platforms ranging from Microsoft Windows, IBM's OS/2 to various Unix flavors as well as IBM and Digital mainframe operating systems like MVS and VMS, IBM's MQ Series is designed to guarantee the asynchronous flow of information between processes and between hosts.

The term "asynchronous data transfer" refers to transfers of data between hosts that have not created a synchronized connection. Synchronous connections are not always possible, particularly when a host may be unavailable because it is busy or unreachable. Asynchronous communication is more commonly implemented on mainframe systems, and allows them to accept data from other systems and put it into a queue to be processed as soon as it has the time and resources.

How MQ Series Works

As shown in Figure 8.2, applications can either PUT a message into a queue or GET a message from a queue. MQ Series provides the infrastructure to support delivery of messages by queues on different systems—whether or not there is a current live connection available to a destination host. In other words, the messaging systems on each host will hold onto queued messages until a destination host comes back on line, rather than simply timing out the message and discarding it when the destination host is unavailable.

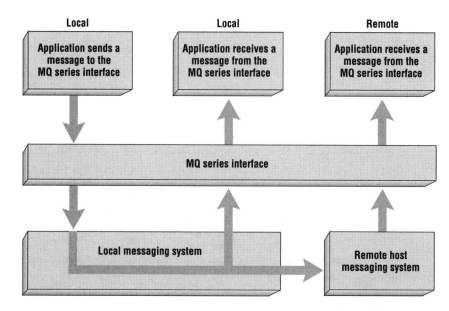

Each application written or adapted for MQ Series can write messages to the MQ interface—in other words, they can create messages in a standard format that can be understood across all MQ Series platforms. Each application is also able to understand such messages when they are delivered. Each system maintains a local messaging system that handles queues for local applications: when a local application posts a message for another local application, the messaging system adds that message to the queue for the destination application and delivers it as soon as possible. When the message is directed at an application running remotely, the messaging system is responsible for transmitting that message to the messaging system running on the same host as the destination application. When the messaging system receives a message, it puts the message into a queue for the destination application and delivers the message as soon as possible.

How MQ Series Works in an Extranet

The key to message queuing is that it supports asynchronous data transfers. This means that systems can interoperate no matter whether they are connected or not; in a sense, message queuing is a form of batch processing. Messages can be submitted to queues as they are generated, and applications that need those messages can retrieve them as soon as it is possible to do so—but without the need for a continuous network connection.

Another important aspect of message queuing is that it can support the use of the same message by different applications. For example, this means that in a financial environment, traders can execute securities transactions and generate messages pertaining to each trade. While the traders' organizations need to process the trades internally, a securities settlement firm may also have to process the settlement of the trades (the transfer of funds and securities between buyers and sellers). With message queuing, messages about each trade can be received both by the traders' firms and by the securities settlement firm—an important time saver as securities exchanges increasingly support fully-digital trading and trading volumes increase.

Thus, message queuing with IBM's MQ Series of products is appropriate for extranet environments requiring a very high degree of reliability while at the same time more than one application requires access to the same information—and wherever asynchronous processing is a requirement.

CHAPTER

9

Managing and Administering Extranets

anaging and administering an organizational network is already a heavy task; so taking control of an interorganizational network like an extranet may seem impossible—which doesn't mean that implementing extranets necessarily leads to anarchy. This chapter surveys some of the techniques you can use to handle extranet network management, configuration, and administration tasks. Most of the tasks that must be accomplished to keep an extranet running are the same as those required to keep any network running. However, with extranets the tasks tend to be more complicated because they have to accommodate more users representing more organizations, each with a stake in the extranet.

The following tasks are discussed in this chapter:

- Administering the infrastucture

- Administering user accounts

- Managing extranet devices

- Managing security issues

- Special, extranet-only issues

This chapter provides an overview of the most important issues related to each task and explains how managing each task for an extranet may be different (or the same as) managing it for an intranet.

Introduction to Extranet Management and Administration

The best networks are totally transparent, and the best network management teams are invisible. When applications are so well integrated into the network; when the network is so well integrated into the desktop; and when the network is so reliable, responsive, and robust, users will be totally unaware of the huge effort involved in making it all work. Network management becomes visible only when things go wrong—and it is a sad fact of life for network managers that the only kind of recognition they are likely to get is of the negative sort.

Network managers have three primary objectives:

- To keep the network up and running reliably and at 100 percent availability at all required times. Any authorized user should be able to use the network whenever the network is supposed to be up and running.

- To keep the network running efficiently. The network manager strives to keep the network itself from being the limiting factor in application performance.

- To keep the network running securely. The network manager is usually responsible for making certain that all authorized users can use the resources for which they have authorization—and to keep network resources secure from unauthorized use.

These goals are achievable for any extranet, particularly when the extranet has been properly planned and implemented. For example:

- Building the extranet infrastructure according to a well-thought-out plan will help achieve the goals of reliability and availability.

- Keeping tabs on performance and network loads will help achieve the goals of efficiency and performance.

■ Implementing the security and other extranet services discussed in this book (like directory services, distributed code verification, key distribution, and certification authorities) will help achieve the goal of extranet security and prevention of unauthorized access.

Administration of Extranet Infrastructure

The infrastructure—of anything—is the foundation upon which every dependent application runs. If you were to build the world's most beautiful skyscraper in a remote area and forgot to build an access road to it, no one would be able to use or enjoy it. The same goes for any network, and particularly for any extranet. As Figure 9.1 shows, extranets depend largely on the following pieces of infrastructure:

■ **Extranet connections**—the actual physical wires, cables, and devices that allow one computer to communicate with another

■ **Extranet servers**—the systems that provide both the platforms on which distributed applications are stored and executed and the extranet services

■ **A transmission medium for extranet information distribution**—defined by the sets of networking and application protocols that support the extranet applications

■ **A framework for authorization and authentication**—defined by the security and directory services protocols used by the extranet applications

Some of the decisions inherent in building an extranet are easy to make; for example, most extranets will use the TCP/IP internetwork protocols for transporting data between systems. Directory services

FIGURE 9.1

The extranet infrastructure provides a foundation for all extranet functions; early planning and design work will pay off with smoother operation.

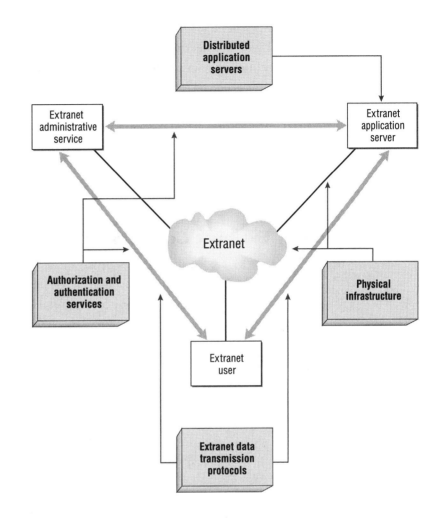

will usually be provided through some form or flavor of directory service application that complies with or is compatible with the X.500 standard.

Other decisions inherent in building the extranet will be out of the hands of the designer. For example, in most cases the individuals and groups connecting to the extranet will have significant control over what hardware and operating system platforms they use, what type of network client software they use, and what type of local area network (or dial-up connection) they use to link to the extranet.

Although the actual devices and products that implement the chosen protocols and applications can be viewed as part of the infrastructure, they are not necessarily an inherent part of it. When implementing a virtual private network, choosing the correct protocol for your needs is a more permanent decision than choosing the hardware platform to run it on—the hardware may be replaced for upgrades, repairs, or budget considerations, but the protocol will very likely remain the same.

Administering Extranet Connections

If networks are information highways, then it is vital to keep the roads clear so that traffic can get through. Extranets, far more than intranets, live or die by their connections to the outside world. Organizations cannot interoperate without routes over which to carry messages. Whether the extranet uses virtual private networks to connect organizations through the Internet or dedicated network links to connect organizations over a private backbone, if those connections (to the Internet or to the extranet backbone) fail, the extranet will fail.

Administering extranet connections means keeping those connections up and running with acceptable availability, performance, and reliability. Some of the tasks the extranet manager must do to accomplish this goal include

- Managing actual extranet links

- Monitoring extranet traffic

- Monitoring extranet service vendors

Managing Extranet Links

Any data communications link that can support an extranet connection for a remote user is an extranet link. For facilities supporting extranet access for large numbers of users, these links may be expensive, high-speed data communication channels. Individuals may also be able to connect to the extranet through a dial-up link. In both cases the theory of the connection is the same; the big differences are in the equipment. The extranet link itself requires the following components:

- **A transmission medium** (for example ISDN, T1, Ethernet, satellite, FDDI, and ATM) through which the extranet sends and receives data. This medium can also be a link over the publicly switched telephone network (PSTN) connection—in other words, plain old telephone service (POTS).

- **The equipment linking the local facility to the transmission medium,** including customer premises equipment (CPE), channel service unit (CSU), and data service unit (DSU). These components enable the extranet to connect to the transmission medium. For PSTN links, this link would be a modem.

- **The device that connects the facility to the CPE.** This device may be a firewall system with a network interface connected to the CPE and another network interface that leads back to the facility. For individual modem connections to the extranet, this device is the workstation or terminal from which the dial-up connection is being made.

Management tasks related to the actual links include providing reliability, performance, and security. For example:

- **Providing reliability** through the following preventive measures:

  - Arranging for redundant service in the event of one vendor's network failure

- Arranging for backup power supplies to protect against power surges and outages

- Providing sufficient bandwidth to cover peak usage

- **Providing performance** through link monitoring (see next section) and analysis of extranet traffic.

- **Providing security** by physically protecting the data communications equipment (keeping it in a securely locked room, for example). Dial-up links require different security arrangements, including strong authentication methods (discussed in Chapter 5).

Monitoring Extranet Traffic

Network congestion can threaten network availability as much as any external factor, and lack of traffic on expensive, dedicated data communications links can waste valuable bandwidth. Keeping tabs on how much data is (or is not) flowing through each extranet link is as important for keeping the extranet available as it is for minimizing extranet costs.

You can arrive at an average transmission for any given link by totaling the amount of data transmitted over the link and dividing by the time of the measurement. For example, consider a basic rate ISDN link capable of supporting up to 128Kbps. If that link averages a total of 3.6Gb worth of data every day, you might think you are using only one-third of its total capacity; after all, 3.6Gb divided by 24 hours divided by 36,000 seconds (in an hour) gives an average load of about 42Kbps.

This calculation is correct, but it may not be very useful; reporting on network traffic loads requires a greater degree of granularity. In practice, this example more likely shows a highly stressed link, particularly if it is used primarily during normal office hours. With minimal traffic before 8:00 a.m. or after 6:00 p.m., that link would be running at or near its absolute maximum capacity.

Network traffic analysis is a fairly well-understood discipline that can help extranet managers determine the type and quantity of links necessary to provide any required level of service. You can find a more detailed discussion of traffic engineering issues in texts like Darren Spohn's *Data Network Design 2nd edition,* (McGraw-Hill, 1997).

Monitoring Extranet Services Vendors

Keeping tabs on extranet links and the traffic that flows over them is an important adjunct to the task of watching your extranet services vendors. Tracking network performance and network traffic over time is useful when evaluating how well your vendors did at recommending the proper data communication services and configurations. It will also help you negotiate the right rates and services from your providers as your extranet grows and matures.

Administering Extranet Servers

Because extranets provide interorganizational connectivity, proper administration of the servers hosting the extranet's distributed applications is necessary to avoid security breaches and other types of system failure. Issues of user and account administration, which are so important to extranet servers, are discussed later in this chapter, but you also need to be aware of other management tasks, including

- Tracking and controlling application revisions

- Scheduling extranet server downtime and performing routine server maintenance tasks

- Ensuring extranet server availability

- Planning for changes in the extranet applications

- Providing full server interoperability and compatibility

Some of the issues involved in these tasks are discussed below.

Extranet Application Revisions

As noted in Chapter 3, one of the biggest benefits of building applications based on distributed objects is that (in theory) you can update or replace one part of the application without having to recompile or reprogram any other part of the application. In practice, the situation is not quite so simple, but certainly simpler than more traditional programming methods—and becoming even simpler as distributed technologies continue to spread. This feature is particularly helpful when different parts of an application are hosted on different servers or even within different organizations.

Updating extranet applications that use traditional programming models requires substantially more effort than updating applications that use distributed technologies. For example, you may have to take the traditional system offline to implement the upgrade, and the extranet manager might have to schedule additional server maintenance (described next).

Scheduling Extranet Server Maintenance

Extranet servers, like any network servers, must undergo a variety of routine maintenance procedures along with the usual unscheduled emergencies (system crashes) and nonroutine procedures (system updates).

Some Routine Procedures That Shut Down Servers

- Disk backup

- Disk defragmentation

- System diagnostics

- Security checks for viruses and destructive programs

Some Nonroutine, Nonemergency Procedures That Shut Down Servers

- System software upgrades

- Hardware upgrades (for example larger hard drive, increased RAM)

- Installation of additional software (for example server tools or monitoring programs)

Some Emergencies That Shut Down Servers

- System crashes

- Hardware failures

- Power failures

- Suspicion of a security breach

- Discovery of a software bug

To the extent possible, the extranet system manager will attempt to schedule maintenance and service to coincide with the periods of least use of the system. For example, many organizations experience a significant drop in network usage sometime around late Friday afternoon that continues until the next Monday morning. Friday nights are thus a traditional choice for performing network server maintenance; Friday nights of a three-day weekend are popular for tasks suspected to be particularly problematic.

Unfortunately, as extranets can span time zones and continents, there may never be a very good time to take down the system. Use of redundant systems can help alleviate the problem, as can the use of middleware and message-queuing solutions.

Extranet Server Availability

The extranet manager's goal is to provide 100 percent system availability, or at least as close to 100 percent as possible. Extranet server availability can be impaired by any situation that can cause the server to crash or be brought down for maintenance, as described in the previous section. Some of the approaches to providing 100 percent availability include

- Server clustering.

- Middleware solutions (transaction monitors and transaction servers) that support load balancing.

- Use of "failover" backup servers that come online when the primary server fails. (They cut over automatically on failure; hence the term *failover*.)

- Fault tolerance, using two processors and two storage facilities that operate in lockstep, allowing transactions to continue despite failure of one system.

All of these approaches require a modification to the basic structure of the extranet; most typical servers don't scale up as gracefully as might be preferred as the number of concurrent users increases. Handling dozens or possibly even hundreds of processes running simultaneously may be within the capacity of most Web servers, but thousands of concurrent users will bring most of them to their knees.

Just as important an issue for server availability is the amount of bandwidth available to serve all users. The most powerful server in the world will have trouble serving even a handful of concurrent users in any meaningful way if it is connected to the extranet with a slow serial connection (for example, 9600Kbps or even 28.8Kbps). The links over which the server is connected to the extranet are very important. If the local network is linked with the extranet over a fat pipe like a T3 line (45Mbps), but the server is connected through a slower link like a 10BaseT Ethernet LAN (maximum 10Mbps), then both the server and the T3 link have the potential to be underutilized while still not meeting all the demand. This scenario is illustrated in Figure 9.2.

FIGURE 9.2

Intermediary links between the extranet and the extranet server may prove to be bottlenecks to server availability.

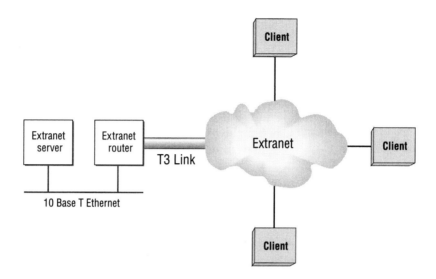

Coping with Changing Extranet Applications

Many types of changes can affect how an extranet application works. For example:

- **Changes in user population**—Usage increases can stress the application and server; they may require upgrades to the server hardware, server software, extranet link, or some combination of the three to handle the increase. Decreases in loads may require a reevaluation of extranet resource allocations.

- **Changes in the size or scope of the underlying application data-bases**—Rapid increases, particularly if the original application uses a relatively lightweight database management system, can cause increases in response time and may require upgrading the application. Use of distributed object architectures for the original extranet application design can help ease changes like these.

■ **Changes in the program logic and application functions offered by the extranet application**—These changes usually require some form of reprogramming, depending on how the application was originally designed. Again, using a distributed object architecture can simplify this type of modification.

■ **Changes in the way the application is actually used**—End users may find new ways to use the application that the developer did not anticipate or plan for. These changes may result in wide variations between anticipated network resource usage and actual usage.

Managing Extranet Protocols

Extranet protocols are not so much managed or administered as they are studied and implemented by extranet managers. During the 1980s a network joke made the rounds: Networking standards are great because there are so many choices—and if you don't like the current crop just wait until next year's models come out. You can still choose from many standards, but the velocity of change is much greater now. Some of the extranet-related protocols that need to be monitored and evaluated follow.

■ **All Web-related protocols** including HTML and all its extensions and flavors, HTTP, CGI and uniform resource specifications

■ **All network application programming protocols and specifications** including Java, JavaScript, ActiveX control programming, and all related tools

■ **Internet commerce protocols** such as the Secure Electronic Transaction (SET) specification as well as other transaction-oriented protocols and services

■ **Internet security protocols** including channel encryption protocols like SSL and IPsec, general encryption tools like S/MIME and PGP, authentication specifications like Authenticode and X.509, and key distribution protocols like Kerberos

- **The underlying TCP/IP protocols** including the Internet Protocol (especially version 6) and transport layer protocols like TCP and UDP

- **The underlying distributed object architectures** including DCOM and CORBA, as well as supporting specifications like Active Platform and IIOP

- **Emerging Internet and networking technologies** including push protocols (for example, Pointcast and Marimba's Castanet) and gigabit Ethernet

Keeping up with all these specifications can be a huge task. In fact, this task is probably impossible for anyone who has responsibilities beyond tracking the specifications. The best approach may be to choose the areas of greatest importance and interest to follow closely and to try to keep up-to-date on the rest. Members of extranet development teams may be able to divide up the task to make it more manageable. Here are a few ways to keep up with the latest information:

- Subscribe to Internet newsgroups and mailing lists.

- Monitor industry news through online news services and industry Web sites.

- Join professional organizations for the Internet, distributed objects, and related technologies.

- Attend trade shows to see new products from leading vendors (as well as leading-edge start-ups).

- Participate in professional meetings and technical conferences.

Administering Extranet Services

Extranet services include all the typical services provided in a TCP/IP intranet or the Internet, as well as some others (see Chapter 6). Determining which services to provide and how to implement and support them are matters best left to TCP/IP and intranet management texts. Administering X.500 and compatible directory services, a vital extranet service, is discussed briefly in the next section.

Administering Extranet User Accounts

As discussed in Chapter 6, managing extranet user accounts is a critical service that is increasingly being standardized with X.500 and compatible directory services. Anyone who has ever set up a network service or multiuser system should be familiar with the actual administration of users and groups:

- Defining individual accounts with access rights to network resources

- Defining user groups with default access rights to network resources

- Assigning users to groups

The basic account administration functions include the following tasks:

- Adding new users and groups

- Modifying users and groups

- Keeping track of users and groups

The two dominant intranet/extranet server vendors, Microsoft and Netscape, take different approaches to administering user accounts. Microsoft's servers are built to run on top of the Windows NT Server platform, which provides the basic security framework. All resources are controlled through that basic structure. A user who has permission to access resources such as files or directories on the NT Server through a direct login session will also be able to access those resources through the Microsoft Internet Information Server, since it uses the NT directory service to authenticate logins. On the other hand, Netscape has deployed an X.500 directory structure for its SuiteSpot server offerings that can be shared by the separate server applications even if they are not installed on the same host.

Managing Extranet Devices

Extranet devices are, by and large, very much the same devices used in intranets and the Internet to provide connectivity between networks. Extranet network devices include

- Extranet routers and gateways

- Firewalls

- Virtual private network devices

One of the challenges when dealing with extranet devices is to manage them properly, particularly when an extranet has multiple sponsors. Even for single-sponsor extranets, though, maintaining these devices properly is vital.

Extranet routers, like all internetwork routers, must be configured correctly and monitored periodically to be sure they are performing adequately and are able to handle all the traffic they receive. Protocol gateways should also be monitored and segregated to avoid traffic problems as well as denial of service attacks.

Firewalls, as discussed in Chapter 5, are crucial to protecting intranet assets and have their own administration issues including the need to configure them so that

- Packet filters do not provide unnoticed security holes for intruders to exploit.

- Application gateways provide just enough connectivity to permit normal work while prohibiting potential dangerous applications.

- Firewall operating systems do not provide toeholds for criminals to exploit, like insecure passwords or weak authentication or unnecessary system services that can be subverted.

- The actual devices operate in a physically secure location that affords reasonable protection against tampering.

Virtual private network devices, many of which double as firewalls, should receive the same kind of attention as firewalls. In fact, virtual private networks are at least as important to the security of the extranet as firewalls are.

The rest of this chapter examines some other issues related to extranet device management, starting with these topics:

- Remote administration

- SNMP and network management tools

- Audit trails and system logs

Remote Administration

Administering a system that may be "sensitive" (that controls sensitive information or that controls strategic organizational resources) presents a problem. If you have to respond to a potential problem with a sensitive system, which approach is more important?

- Managing the system remotely to allow much faster response by system managers to speed problem resolution.

  or

- Managing the system locally through a system console or a terminal directly connected to the device to avoid potential attacks by criminals electronically impersonating the system manager.

Vendors are increasingly offering remote administration as an option even for sensitive systems like firewalls, as they already do for most internetwork server products. Provided a strong authentication scheme is in use (as described in Chapter 5), remote administration should be considered an acceptable solution. Responsiveness to potential problems, particularly when extranet security is being threatened, is an important tool to use against attackers. When remote administration is paired with automatic system manager notification (by e-mail, pager, or even digitized voice messaging through a direct phone call), network administrators can more quickly respond to threats than they would be able to if they had to report to the physical location of the device. Remote administration is also a boon to extranet managers responsible for devices spread over a wide geographic area.

SNMP and Extranet Management

The Simple Network Management Protocol (SNMP) is a framework for keeping tabs on network devices using the internetwork itself to allow that information to be gathered by network management workstations. Though industry acceptance came slowly at first because of some deficiencies in the specification (see sidebar), the latest revisions in the standards have addressed many of these.

Using SNMP to manage extranet devices expands the tool kit for network administrators. Managed devices can be powered down and rebooted, have routing tables reconfigured, be queried for traffic since the last reboot, and provide information about traffic including data such as the protocols being passed and protocol errors.

However, running SNMP across the Internet may pose potential security risks because network management information is incredibly sensitive. If it were to fall into the wrong hands, control over network management could allow a criminal to destroy a network. The use of proper security is, therefore, vital. Care also should be taken to avoid some of the network traffic problems that improperly configured and deployed network management tools can cause—usually in the form of too much traffic generated by network management workstations set to gather status information from all network devices every five minutes.

> **SNMP at a Glance**
>
> Until 1996 when strong authentication was added to an updated SNMP specification, SNMP provided no real protection to keep unauthorized users from reading and modifying configuration parameters of network devices. Because some of these parameters are crucial to the device operation (for example, SNMP uses the contents of data registers to determine whether to take actions such as rebooting the system), the lack of any real security was a major impediment to SNMP's implementation. Until 1996 access to SNMP-managed devices was controlled by a value called the *community*. SNMP management workstations send this value in the clear over the network to the device so anyone monitoring the network with a protocol analyzer could search for SNMP messages and quickly detect the password. However, snooping was often unnecessary because many network devices were manufactured with the exact same value hardcoded in. (This situation was convenient for network managers.)

Audit Trails and System Logs

As with other network management information, audit trails and system logs are useful only when they are comprehensible as well as comprehensive. Attempting to log every action on every extranet device may require investing in extra network servers to store all the logs. As long as you record the potentially sensitive actions, you can often safely ignore more benign actions.

Managing Extranet Security Issues

The essence of a bank's business is the transfer and handling of money, and as a result, banks are well-known for the care they take to protect their customers' money with armed guards, yard-thick steel-walled vaults, 24-hour surveillance cameras, and other security measures. Companies whose business is based on information, a category whose ranks are expanding every day with new software vendors, consulting firms, designers, publishers, and financial institutions, must take comparable measures to protect their information.

It is difficult to overstress the importance of security to any internetwork, and particularly to an extranet; security issues are pervasive in these networks. As a result, rather than repeating what has been discussed at length elsewhere in this chapter as well as throughout the book, particularly in Chapters 5 and 6, this chapter ends with a summary of two of the most important security-related tasks for the extranet manager:

- Firewall maintenance

- Security auditing

Firewall Maintenance

Even the most securely locked door should be jiggled every now and then—and occasionally opened up and inspected. The same goes for firewalls. Security audits should address firewall security from several directions by including the following techniques:

- Use of attack simulations to test integrity of the firewall

- Tracking of firewall software vendor updates

- Monitoring of firewall operating system updates

- Tracking reports of system and software security issues released by security organizations like reports issued by the Computer Emergency Response Team (CERT)

Security Auditing

Waiting for a security breach to happen before taking action on security is probably a mistake. Auditing security of a network should be an ongoing task and requires network managers to take a highly security-conscious stance. Every aspect of the network that has any impact on its security should be identified and periodically reviewed. Here are some safety measures you can take:

- Run Internet-cracking software against the extranet from the outside to find security holes

- Urge users to select difficult-to-guess passwords and to change them frequently

- Run password-guessing software against exposed systems frequently

- Perform a physical audit of network resources to reduce threats from intruders wishing to place unwanted protocol analyzers or other software or hardware mechanisms on your network

- Review access controls and authentication systems

- Review organizational human resources security procedures.

Special Extranet Issues

The most important issues unique to managing an extranet derive from the fact that it is a mechanism by which organizations share information across their borders. The two really fundamental issues involve the management of the extranet infrastructure and the management of the extranet data. How these issues are resolved in large part depends on determining ownership of the structures in question.

Extranets with a single sponsor are managed by the sponsor. In that respect, they are little different from other networking projects within the organization. However, extranets with multiple sponsors require special treatment; each sponsoring organization may be expected to contribute in some way to the management effort. The form of the contribution—be it money, personnel, equipment, or all three—will vary from extranet to extranet. Extranet advisory boards and oversight committees may also be required.

Managing the data in the extranet raises further questions for all extranets. Whether the extranet links organizations to other organizations or links individuals to a single organization, the extranet itself will eventually generate information related to itself. For example, mass market extranets will eventually aggregate consumer information, whereas purely organizational extranets will generate information about how those organizations interact.

Extranet managers need to be aware of this type of information byproduct and identify the risks and rewards associated with it. The manager of a public extranet may not collect and store data that might pose a potential liability; for example, chat room traffic should probably not be archived through the extranet to avoid having to reproduce conversations held among private users. Likewise, extranets providing access to published materials (including books, periodicals, music, and video recordings) should consider whether their databases receive the same protections as libraries and video rental stores.

The extranet manager should also be aware that the system will generate a flood of data, some of it valuable to the extranet sponsors or to others. Public extranets are sure to generate information of value to the extranet sponsor's marketing and sales departments, and work-flow information can help private extranet sponsor organizations work more efficiently together.

Building an extranet is only partially a technological task. The most important aspect of any extranet is how well it fulfills its purpose—how well it satisfies the needs of the individual people who use it and rely on it to achieve their business goals. Without the technology, an extranet cannot exist; but without satisfied users, companies will not allocate resources to sustain the technology.

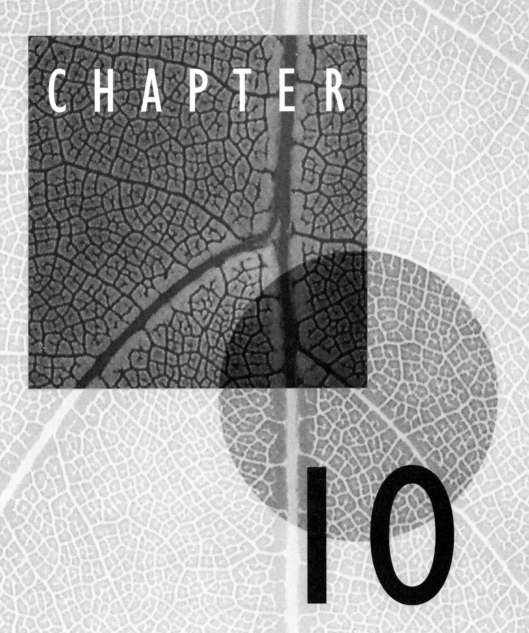

CHAPTER

10

Combining the Future and the Past

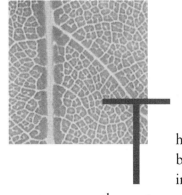

his chapter summarizes the concepts presented in this book and also suggests how extranets will affect the ways in which we implement internetworking technologies as the next waves in internetworking overtake extranetworking.

The Extranet Wave

The extranet wave, as described in Chapter 1, integrates the technologies developed in the Internet wave and the intranet wave—and adds some new twists with cryptographically enabled secure channels for virtual private networks and implementation of distributed applications. Previous waves, as shown in Figure 10.1, fuel the waves that follow them by upping the technological ante. The rest of this section recapitulates the basic extranet concepts introduced in this book.

FIGURE 10.1

Technology waves, like those related to inter- networking, tend to build on their predecessors.

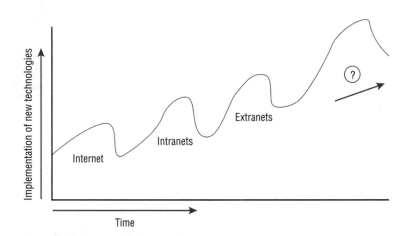

Summing Up the Extranet

Very simply, the extranet wave introduced internetworks that permit their users to do things that previous types of internetworks, like the Internet and intranets, did not always support. Extranet users are able to

- Cross organizational boundaries

- Use distributed applications

- Interact directly with organizations and their systems

- Use cryptography for interorganizational security and authentication

- Use internetworking services to make the extranet appear transparent

Extranet Benefits

The only reason to build an organizational system is to provide some benefit to the organization. Extranets, like intranets and the Internet, provide significant benefits to organizations that implement them. Extranets allow organizations to achieve goals that include

- Implementation of customer self-service

- Acceleration of commerce

- Submergence of distribution applications

- Easing pressure on IT/IS departments

- Enhanced productivity

- Improved use of existing systems

Implementation of Customer Self-Service

Customer service is usually nothing more than providing the customer with some information, either about the customer or about a product available for purchase by a customer, that is stored on some system within the organization's network. Extranets enable the customer to interface directly with those resources, eliminating the go-between from the transaction. With extranet access to account information and product information, more customers can be served better, faster, and more satisfactorily.

Customer service in this form helps reduce the cost of each marginal sale, which keeps management happy. Customers able to get immediate answers to their questions at any time of the day or night are also happy. The extranet itself can provide new opportunities to generate additional sales from existing customers by making them aware of special offers tailored specifically to them, satisfying customers by meeting their precise needs while satisfying management by generating new revenues.

Acceleration of Commerce

Improvement in the way that customers and potential customers interact with a selling organization means acceleration of online commerce. Extranets provide a direct link between buyer and seller and allow the seller to simplify and speed up the purchasing process. Direct access to the seller's internal systems means that the customer can determine exactly what products are available, how much they cost, and how quickly they can be delivered; the extranet enables the fastest and simplest types of commercial transaction. Using extranet client software that manages user payment and shipping information means that a sale can be completely transacted with nothing more than a click of the buyer's mouse.

This direct access between seller and buyer, as provided through extranets, will only continue to accelerate the velocity of commerce, bringing products to market more quickly and providing consumers with more differentiated and more customized products.

Submerging Distributed Applications

The distribution of software and the increased use of software components in extranet applications help to submerge the actual application mechanisms. End users accessing the applications from standard client software are usually not even aware they are using specialized application software; they are merely interacting with an information resource through a Web browser window. The extranet sponsor also benefits from the use of distributed applications through reduced costs of maintenance and development.

Reducing Pressure on IS/IT Departments

Information systems (IS) and information technologies (IT) departments in most organizations have been hard pressed to deliver all the applications for all the platforms requested by other parts of their organizations. User populations tend to view most computer problems as much easier to solve than they actually are; support organizations tend to become quickly overburdened with urgent tasks. However, the use of distributed applications and object technologies implemented in an extranet environment promise to reduce some of this pressure. The ability to interface legacy systems to distributed applications through one or two basic object interfaces means that formerly "urgent" upgrade tasks such as migrating legacy systems to GUI client/server or even Internet applications are eased considerably. Writing the interface to the legacy system means that the costly existing infrastructure does not have to be replaced to provide enhanced services to users.

Productivity Enhancement

The widespread installation of computing equipment has not always produced the anticipated enhancement of productivity. Although the actual costs of hardware and software have been relatively low, significant yet less obvious costs remain in the areas of user support and system maintenance. Many of these costs are directly attributable to the difficulty of configuring and troubleshooting custom systems.

These systems are often orphaned by their developers (who are frequently either independent consultants or employees whose primary job is not system development and who lack the time or patience to document their work). These systems very often work on a single platform and sometimes perpetuate the use of obsolete operating systems simply to preserve the application.

Using distributed applications over extranets addresses many of these problems. End-user support can be simplified, and the benefits of this approach are being touted both by Microsoft, which is using the network as the platform for an initiative to reduce support and maintenance costs of Active Platform systems, and by vendors who are developing OS-neutral network computers (NCs) that draw their configuration from centralized application servers. Use of standardized network platforms of either type can help reduce the costs associated with developing (and supporting) client/server front ends for multiple computing platforms.

Existing applications can benefit as well. Large organizations may find quite a few different solutions to the same problem implemented in different departments and operating units, and the use of object technology can help them standardize on a single approach while still providing access to all users—simply by building a single distributed object application interface for use by networked systems.

Improved Use of Resources

As extranets help organizations move beyond issues of compatibility and interoperability and toward solving real business problems, organizational resources from bandwidth to personal computers to skilled programmers and developers can be used to further the goals of the organization.

The Next Waves

The actual cresting of any of the internetworking waves, the point at which that wave commands attention, is preceded by much preliminary activity. The Internet had been around for quite a few years before it attracted very much attention from the business community, and intranets had been implemented in academic, research, and computer industry organizations well before the word was coined. Likewise, the defined concept of an extranet came well after the first organizations deployed their own versions of internetworking bridges to their internal resources.

In the same way, we can anticipate the future of internetworking by looking at the present. The coming waves of internetworking will build on the previous waves. In all likelihood, the next waves will include

- Ubiquitous high-speed network access

- Mass acceptance of digital commerce

- HomeNet and BodyNet

High-speed network access is with us now, but it is not ubiquitous. Rather, it is relatively rare, expensive, and difficult to use. Likewise, digital commerce has been accepted to some degree, but it cannot yet be counted on as a mechanism to buy and sell products directly through extranets. Once that type of digital commerce is universally deployed and supports commercial transactions quickly, easily, and completely, then the digital commerce wave will be able to crest. Finally, other possibilities, including the extension of internetworking technologies beyond the desktop and office, will develop once internetworks carrying digital commerce at high speeds for home and office computing are commonplace.

Ubiquitous High-Speed Network Access

At the moment, the vast majority of individuals connected to the Internet are connected through "thin pipes": modems connecting them to an Internet service provider at transmission rates of up to 56Kbps, but usually less. Even organizations, which usually have larger Internet pipes, find those pipes filling up easily with the mass of new information services their employees subscribe to. The situation will continue to get worse as long as demand for information increases. Although some existing methods can help allocate the bandwidth we have more efficiently, including improvements in routing and smarter use of push and multicast technologies, the most obvious solution for the long term (and for individual users) is to increase the amount of bandwidth available to all.

The increase in demand for bandwidth is being fueled by the previous waves. As the Internet and the extranet become increasingly indispensable tools for businesses and individuals and as the volume of information that users require from internetworks increases, so does the need for speed. As high-speed modem communication specifications continue to gel in 1997, more users and commercial Internet service providers will be able to get 56Kbps out of regular telephone lines. Other potential sources of high-speed network access include

- High-speed modems, currently widely supporting speeds of 28.8Kbps and 33.6Kbps, can now support up to 56Kbps with the proper equipment. However, modems over telephone lines are unlikely to provide any more than 56Kbps transmission speeds because of the physical limitations of the telecommunication medium—it simply cannot carry much more information.

- Basic rate ISDN can provide individuals with as much as 128Kbps (in two channels of 56Kpbs or 64Kbps each) in total bandwidth, although installation and monthly charges tend to be somewhat higher than standard telephone service. Furthermore, many users prefer to use only one channel for data and to reserve the other channel for voice or other services. The result is not appreciably greater than that provided by the latest generation of modems.

- Asymmetric Digital Subscriber Line (ADSL) is a new modem technology that can convert existing twisted-pair telephone lines into links capable of handling three channels:

  - A standard POTS service, which is in place in the event of a failure of the other channels

  - A medium-speed duplex channel (capable of carrying traffic in both directions) providing up to 640Kbps service

  - A high-speed one-way channel that can handle as much as 6Mbps

This technology depends on the use of ADSL modems at either end to create a circuit capable of carrying much more data than standard modem circuits previously supported.

- Satellite access is currently being rolled out in various forms and from several providers. Transmission rates of anywhere from 400Kbps to as high as 6Mbps (for inbound traffic; up to 2Mbps for outbound) have been reported. The advantage of these services is that they do not require any infrastructure (for example, a cable network or a telephone network) for delivery.

- Cable modems are now available in markets across the country in various configurations. Transmission speeds range from 500Kbps (in both directions) to as high as 10Mbps for inbound services (with outbound service available as high as 768Kbps). Significant problems are associated with the use of cable television networks to carry computer network traffic, most of them deriving from the fact that the cable networks were designed to delivery high rates of data with virtually no outbound data transmission (from the user to the cable head end or from the connector to the cable operator).

Other possible solutions for high-speed network access are probably under development at this moment, but whatever technology or technologies succeed must provide a sufficient increase in bandwidth to fuel new services. Relatively small increases in bandwidth such as those provided by traditional modems over the past three years (moving from an industry standard rate of about 14.4Kbps to an industry standard rate of 33.6Kbps and increasingly 56Kbps) are enough to improve performance of current tasks like downloading text and graphics files, but are sufficient to propel new services such as delivery of

- **Customized content,** such as that already seen in use of personalized information services, subscription to Web pages, and push technologies. Higher bandwidth means that more content, of higher quality, can be delivered; for example, video-on-demand becomes practical at megabit rates.

- **Software via extranet,** such as that already seen in components like Java applets, controls, and plug-ins. Retail delivery of more complete applications is already common on the Internet, but not yet particularly practical. For example, Web and Internet client software packages for sale by Netscape (or distributed free by Microsoft) are on the order of several megabytes—a 10Mb package could easily take an hour or more to download at typical modem connection rates of around 28.8Kbps. The same file, at 10Mbps, can be downloaded in seconds.

- **High-bandwidth services,** such as those already seen in services like audio and video conferencing and broadcasting. Higher bandwidth supports this specialized form of content delivery and also provides more options for the delivery of high-quality images, sound, and multiparty conferencing.

Mass Acceptance of Digital Commerce

Again, the next wave will be driven by the previous wave. Because the volume of data that can be delivered becomes larger, the type of service available also becomes more interesting as a profit-making enterprise. This wave will also be driven partially by the issue of making digital commerce palatable to the public as well as to the other parties involved: the banks issuing credit, the merchants using the extranet for sales, the companies producing new methods of doing digital commerce, and the regulatory bodies concerned with policing the way commerce is carried on and currencies are issued.

The following issues of security, privacy, reliability, and governability must be resolved:

- **Security** is key to all parties. The financial institutions that will underwrite much of the online commerce must be comfortable with the risks they take while the merchants, who directly bear the brunt of financial risk of credit card fraud, must also be happy with the security of the system. Consumers, who in the end wind up paying for any such service, will very likely find that increased convenience more than compensates them for the marginal cost they incur.

- **Privacy** of transactions and transaction information may be an issue for consumers who do not wish to have their buying habits correlated in any way with their Web-surfing habits, or even simply connected with their name and address. The solution to this issue will likely be a combination of technologies that allow aliased or anonymous transactions and sociopolitical solutions that include rules and regulations concerning how organizations can handle and use data they collect through the Internet.

- **Transaction reliability** is one problem that will likely be solved through mechanisms like transaction monitors and other technologies discussed in Chapter 3 well before online commerce attains mass acceptance.

- **Governability,** or the ability of governments and regulatory bodies to control and oversee digital commerce, is an issue that has little to do with the technologies involved. Many legal issues arise from digital commerce, not the least of which are collection of taxes and detecting and prosecuting illegal transactions. Other transactions of interest to governments may include copyright violations, transfers of trade secrets, and trade in child pornography—all likely targets in democratic nations. Dissemination of political and religious unorthodoxies may be prosecuted in other societies.

Once digital commerce is accepted widely and the infrastructure for its use is in place for consumers and merchants, it will enable many new services for fee through the extranet. Here are some possibilities:

- Interactive communication services like voice and video conferencing

- Software rentals and sales that provide immediacy for the consumer while reducing the sales cost for vendors and eliminating wasteful paper and plastic packaging

- Media rental and sales, including delivery of movies, television programs, news, sporting, and other entertainment events, as well as music and other audio content

- New delivery methods for text products like books and periodicals

- Personal services like programmed gift buying; online shopping for practically anything from groceries to clothing; entertainment and gaming opportunities

HomeNet and BodyNet

Integration of internetworking infrastructures can move beyond linking just computers and computer devices to linking just about any modern device. Again, the previous waves will drive the growth of these new waves; high-speed networking and the acceptance of digital commerce will create demand for networking that goes beyond the computer and the workplace, moving it into users' homes and personal lives.

HomeNet

Some time in the future, the home will become an increasingly wired environment (even though it may use some sort of wireless networking medium). HomeNet is a vision of this networked home. With HomeNet, all home appliances, environment control systems, and other "smart" devices can be connected through a network. The devices themselves can be controlled and queried for current status through the network. Using internetworking technologies means that all these devices will be accessible from, potentially, anywhere in the world (as long as the home is connected to some public network and the person controlling the home can connect to that network too).

No more worry about whether you forgot to turn off the stove—you will be able to control all your household appliances remotely. Of course, protecting access to the HomeNet is critical to its success, but the advantages are huge. Types of functions possible include

- **Controlling appliances**—lights on and off, start/stop cooking or coffee, program washing machine or dishwasher to take advantage of off-peak utility rates, control over thermostats and air conditioners, and so on

- **Managing personal communications through smart answering machines**—paging the owner for emergencies, forwarding calls, etc.; monitoring or recording radio or TV shows for time-shifting; control over access to TV (for example, to enforce punishments of "no cartoons for a month")

- **Managing utilities**—monitoring use to help improve efficiency and reduce waste

Of course, many of these functions are not yet available, but others already are—the difference is that HomeNet makes them accessible to anyone from anywhere. HomeNet enables you to not only check the system's status remotely but also manage your home system from anywhere. Finally, future home management functions can become much more complex than those currently available. If home system management protocols are based on a model similar to that used by SNMP, which maintains system status through simple switches and registers, then a wide range of interesting activities becomes possible.

Simple Remote Network Device Management

Simple Network Management Protocol (SNMP) may provide a glimpse of how household appliances and systems can be managed from a management console. The Management Information Base (MIB), which defines how the information is stored, is a framework for the network management information that SNMP needs to manage a device remotely. All devices store their information in the same format so that the network management console can access this information from any device on the network without having to know in advance what type of device it is.

How does this technology apply to HomeNet? SNMP-managed devices use a very limited selection of data types to store control information. For example, devices may store figures relating to the number of network datagrams they have passed since their last reboot (the time of which is also stored in a management register). More important, these devices can be controlled by changing the values in other management registers—one field might contain a value that is either on or off. Such a field might control the status of a network interface, whether a network service is being offered, or simply control whether the device is actually turned on or off.

HomeNet devices could use the same type of management structure, storing their status as well as their operating statistics in a manner accessible to any authorized management console. Instead of turning on a network interface, you could turn lights on or off; open or close a garage door; or even activate devices and services like call forwarding, voice mail, or household alarm systems.

HomeNet relates to extranets because they provide more opportunities for organizations to interact with individuals and their families. For example, customer service calls for refrigerator repair can be simplified; authorizing an agent to probe the refrigerator's diagnostic registers could result in much faster (and more convenient) service. The diagnostic probe could determine the cause of the problem (and in some cases fix it); at the least, it should be able to identify the part or parts that need replacement or repair and speed up repair calls.

BodyNet

Perhaps less frightening than the name implies, the concept of BodyNet is to intelligently link the things we carry around with us every day, and allow us to manage and use them in ways not possible up to now. For example, consider the following items:

- Wallet

- Address book

- Memo pad

- Date book

- Pager

- Cellular telephone

- Business card case

As the use of personal digital assistants (PDAs), for example, the U.S. Robotics Pilot and the various devices running Microsoft's Windows CE operating system, increases, more of these functions are moving from physical constructs to digital constructs. Address book, date book, and memo pad functions are already being transferred to these devices; paging and cellular telecommunications are ready to migrate to these devices when the right accessory/service package is introduced.

Portable Electronic Devices

Portable electronic devices have been common for years. They range from the simplest portable calculator to digital appointment books to full-blown, pocket-sized microcomputers. Referred to variously as personal digital assistants (PDAs) or "wallets" (more common in Europe), these devices have generally lacked a high degree of communications capabilities. Many include modem support through a proprietary modem add-in option, built-in modem, or a PCMCIA card (PC card) slot, but so far the devices have tended to offer only partial (or no) network connectivity. However, the story is changing. By the middle of 1997, these devices were increasingly supporting networking protocols and applications:

- U.S. Robotics Pilot, a popular PDA, provides support for synchronization with a desktop system using TCP/IP networks as well as support for reading and sending e-mail.

- Apple Newton, granddaddy of all PDAs, provides Internet support, with TCP/IP support and Web browser and e-mail software.

- Microsoft Windows CE devices equipped with PC card slots are available from various vendors and support a significant subset of the Windows operating system.

The digitization of these devices is a necessary, but not sufficient, prerequisite for BodyNet. Development of some mechanism linking these devices (and others) will enable BodyNet. For example, people would be able to exchange business card information simply through the act of shaking hands—each person enabling a transmission of that information while being receptive to such transmissions from the other. The personal digital wallet will support digital currencies as well as handle transactions through your credit cards and checking accounts, all potentially more safely than existing payment methods.

Extranets will fuel much of the movement of commerce to Body-Nets; the ability to support complex transactions means that entities can complete complicated interactions much more simply. Now, if two strangers want to conduct a commercial transaction—for example, Bob wants to sell a used television to Alice—they have limited options. Although most sellers prefer to transact a cash sale, some people are willing to accept checks from strangers. With BodyNet, the two entities participating in a transfer can involve other intermediaries in the transactions. Alice might use a credit card to transfer funds from her credit account to Bob's checking account, involving not just Bob and Alice but also Bob's bank, Alice's credit card issuer, and at least one company to settle the transfer.

Looking Forward, Looking Back

One comforting facet of internetworking is that it evolves over time. The insight and knowledge you gain from understanding computing help you when you start networking. Similarly, the insight you gain from understanding networking helps you to understand internetworking. Unlike many other technologies deployed over the past 25 years for computing, both in hardware and software, internetworking so far has been built on a foundation laid by researchers and experimenters who wrote specifications based on what worked and what made sense when implementing interoperable and networked systems. Unlike software vendors whose agenda calls for building proprietary systems to build and keep market share, internetworking software helps establish a base of compatibility upon which vendors can build products that compete on the basis of superior performance and superior functions.

As we move into the next century, internetworking based on open standards should prove more beneficial to more computing and networking vendors than proprietary standards ever were. As long as consumers continue to demand products that support open standards, profitability will increase for both vendors and consumers. With the ability to interoperate with other systems as a minimum requirement for vendors, all vendors of compatible products will be able to eliminate incompatibility with existing systems as an obstacle to sales. With all products interoperating, consumers will no longer have to invest in proprietary systems that are certain to become obsolete in just a few months.

Following on the heels of the widespread use of the Internet for business and the installation of organizational intranets, extranets will continue to reinforce the benefits of open standards and will help foster an environment in which internetworking permeates our modern world.

APPENDICES

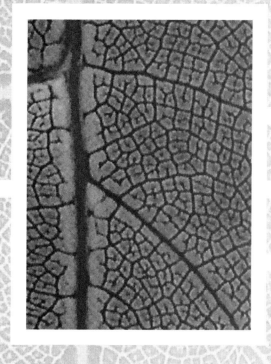

APPENDIX

A

Extranet Resources

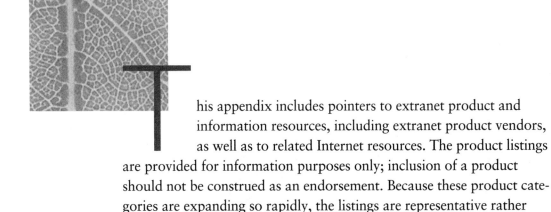

This appendix includes pointers to extranet product and information resources, including extranet product vendors, as well as to related Internet resources. The product listings are provided for information purposes only; inclusion of a product should not be construed as an endorsement. Because these product categories are expanding so rapidly, the listings are representative rather than comprehensive. The interested reader is urged to use Internet resources to gather the most up-to-date information.

Extranet Resources on the Internet

Interest in extranets has been exploding. Whereas an Internet search on the term in November 1996 may have returned as few as 100 hits, just two months later the same search returned about 3,000 hits. Any major Web search site is a good starting point for getting the latest news on extranet developments and products. This section provides pointers to extranet resources on the Web that may not always show up in Web searches, including links to associations, working groups, and standards bodies.

Associations and Working Groups

The organizations that have the most direct impact on extranets deal with object technologies and with internetworking technologies. As of early 1997, however, no organizations or groups are devoted explicitly and strictly to the extranet.

- **Object Management Group**—A consortium of software developers, publishers, and end users devoted to promoting the use of object technologies for developing and deploying distributed applications and systems. As of early 1997, the OMG had more than 700 members.

  `http://www.omg.org/`

- **Internet Society**—A nonprofit, international organization dedicated to global coordination of the Internet and to cooperative development of the Internet and its underlying internetworking technologies. The Internet Society is the umbrella organization under which the Internet Engineering Task Force (IETF), as well as many other Internet-related groups, are coordinated.

  `http://www.isoc.org/`

- **Internet Engineering Task Force (IETF)**—The body responsible for developing and engineering Internet protocols. It publishes Requests for Comment (RFCs), usually descriptions of Internet protocols.

  `http://www.ietf.org/`

Protocols and Specifications

The most important specifications for extranets are generated by the open standards bodies: the IETF, the OMG, and the ITU. Copies of standards are available for free download from the IETF and the OMG; standards can be ordered online from the ITU for digital or hard-copy delivery.

- **IETF RFCs**—One of the services provided by the InterNIC is to publish the IETF RFCs. These are available and searchable online at the following URL:

  `http://ds.internic.net/ds/dspg1intdoc.html`

- **IETF Working Groups**—The IETF sets up working groups to meet needs as they arise. A number of groups are currently in existence. Their names, along with pointers to the drafts and RFCs each group has drafted, are listed in the following URL:

  `http://www.ietf.org/html.charters/wg-dir.html`

- **IP Security Protocol (IPsec) Working Group**—Working group drafts, as well as more information about the working group, can be found at this address. Of particular note is the IPSec working group's work on Internet key distribution and certification authorities.

  `http://www.ietf.org/html.charters/ipsec-charter.html`

- **OMG Specifications**—Pointers to all OMG specifications can be found at

  `http://www.omg.org/library/library.htm`

- The CORBA/IIOP specification is available online from the OMG at this Web page; you can also order printed and bound copies here.

  `http://www.omg.org/library/specindx.htm`

- **International Telecommunications Union (ITU)**—This international standards and coordination organization is based in Switzerland. It is responsible for development and publication of the X.500 and X.509 standards (among many others). You can order the standards, either for download or in bound form, through the ITU Web site.

  `http://www.itu.ch/`

Extranet Vendors and Products

As of early 1997, I have found no products marketed specifically as extranet solutions. However, virtually any product that can be used to build an intranet or that can be used to provide Internet connectivity can also be used to build an extranet. This section provides pointers to some of the leading providers of IP server and client software, although it is by no means a comprehensive listing. Many other fine products are available.

Extranet Software

Like virtually all internetworking applications, extranet applications operate on a client/server model. Consequently, the implementer needs to set up server software to provide extranet services, and the end user needs to use some kind of client software to access extranet services. Most often the server software is a general-purpose TCP/IP standard-supporting network server with custom applications and perhaps some optional modules. The clients are also standard TCP/IP clients, also with options or custom-built modules added.

Extranet Servers

These Web application servers are just a selection of the more popular products in use on corporate intranets and extranets. Many other servers are available from software companies publishing networking, Internet, workgroup, and groupware software.

Microsoft Servers   Microsoft Corporation

http://www.microsoft.com

One Microsoft Way
Redmond, WA 98052
Tel: 206-882-8080
Fax: 206-936-7329

Microsoft's Internet services are sold as part of the BackOffice family, which includes the servers described in the table below. Microsoft's Windows NT Server package includes the Internet Information Server, Microsoft's Web server, as well as the following Back-Office products:

BackOffice Product	Purpose
Merchant Server	To help businesses build and administer full-service, secure Web stores
Proxy Server	A proxy server, providing proxy access to the Internet
Transaction Server	Middleware that simplifies the deployment of components-based applications over intranets, the Internet, or extranets
Systems Management Server	For deployment of network applications and distribution of software over the network
Exchange Server	An e-mail/messaging server

Netscape Servers   Netscape Communications Corporation

http://home.netscape.com

501 East Middlefield Road
Mountain View, CA 94043
Tel: 415-937-2555 Corporate sales
Tel: 415-937-3777 Individual sales
Tel: 415-254-1900 Executive offices
Fax: 415-528-4124

Netscape's SuiteSpot server family includes nine products, all of which can be combined as desired to provide the services needed for an organizational intranet or extranet.

SuiteSpot Server	Purpose
Calendar Server 1.0	Workgroup and Internet calendaring and scheduling, using open standards
Catalog Server	To manage online document catalog
Certificate Server	To manage, issue, sign, and certify public key certificates
Collabra Server	To support group discussions
Directory Server	To manage directories of names, addresses, and certificates
Enterprise Server	To provide Web services for content publication and for network applications
LiveWire Pro	To support network application development; includes Informix database
Media Server	To provide audio-streaming services over Web sites
Messaging Server	To implement Internet–standards-based e-mail services
Proxy Server	A proxy server for replication and filtering of Web content

Lotus Domino Servers   Lotus Development Corporation

http://www.lotus.com/

55 Cambridge Parkway
Cambridge, MA 02142
Tel: 617-577-8500

Lotus's collaborative computing product, Notes, has evolved into a family of open-networking products. The Domino family of servers provides a platform suitable for extranet development.

Product	Description
Domino	Transforms Notes into an Internet/intranet/extranet applications server product
Domino.SPA	Service Provider Applications: allows the organization running the server to rent out user applications and allows the user to download applications for pay-as-you-go pricing
Domino.Action	Web-building toolkit
Domino.Merchant	A storefront-building toolkit for Domino server
Domino.Broadcast	A PointCast-enabling technology, allowing Domino server to broadcast Web channels

Extranet Clients

The commercial market is now dominated by two browser vendors: Microsoft and Netscape. Although other vendors sell Web browsers, including Lotus's Weblicator, their impact on the market is dwarfed by the top two products. Microsoft and Netscape have both announced new technologies, expected to be released sometime around mid-1997, to integrate information services (including those specific to extranet applications) into the browser and the desktop. Netscape's Constellation technology and Microsoft's Internet Explorer 4.0 should change the way Web browsers are used for extranets.

The newer push technologies listed in the following section add a new piece of client software that is increasingly being used by the general public and is of great importance to extranet users.

Netscape Communicator/Constellation   Netscape
Communications Corporation

http://home.netscape.com

501 East Middlefield Road
Mountain View, CA 94043
Tel: 415-937-2555 Corporate sales
Tel: 415-937-3777 Individual sales
Tel: 415-254-1900 Executive offices
Fax: 415-528-4124

Microsoft Internet Explorer   Microsoft Corporation

http://www.microsoft.com

One Microsoft Way
Redmond, WA 98052
Tel: 206-882-8080
Fax: 206-936-7329

Lotus Weblicator (for use with Notes clients)   Lotus
Development Corporation

http://www.lotus.com/

55 Cambridge Parkway
Cambridge, MA 02142
Tel: 617-577-8500

Push Technologies

As early as 1995 it was becoming clear that the World Wide Web was
becoming too big a search space for the "pull paradigm"—where the
end user searches for and explicitly pulls down the information
desired—to work very much longer. Push technologies provide client
software that works with netcasters to allow data that meets the user's
criteria to be pushed down the pipe as it arrives. By early 1997, there

were easily a dozen or more serious products in the push market. Here are pointers to some of the more serious contenders.

AirMedia   AirMedia

http://www.airmedia.com/

3501 Jamboree Road, Suite 400, South Tower
Newport Beach, CA 92660
Tel: 714-737-5410
Fax: 714-737-5434

ArrIve   IFusion Com Corporation

http://www.ifusion.com/

79 Fifth Avenue, 7th Floor
New York, NY 10003
Tel: 212-352-4500
Fax: 212-352-4645

BackWeb   BackWeb Technologies

http://www.backweb.com/

2077 Gateway Place, Suite 500
San Jose, CA 95110
Tel: 408-437-0200
Fax: 408-437-0214

Castanet   Marimba, Inc.

http://www.marimba.com/

445 Sherman Ave.
Palo Alto, CA 94306
Tel: 415-328-JAVA
Fax: 415-328-5295

DataChannel DataChannel

`http://www.datachannel.com/`

10020 Main Street #205
Bellevue, WA 98004
Tel: 206-462-1999
Fax: 206-637-1192

Downtown inCommon

`http://www.incommon.com/`

411 Borel Avenue, Suite 512
San Mateo, CA 94402
Tel: 415-345-5432
Fax: 415-345-6986

INCISA Wayfarer Communications, Inc.

`http://www.wayfarer.com/`

2041 Landings Drive
Mountain View, CA 94043
Tel: 800-300-8559
     415-903-1720
Fax: 415-903-1730

Intermind Connect `http://www.intermind.com/`

Intermind Corporation
217 Pine Street
Seattle, WA 98101-1500
Fax: 206-812-6377

NETdelivery   NETdelivery Corporation

http://www.netdelivery.com/

1901 East Horsetooth Road, Suite 100
Fort Collins, CO 80525
Tel: 970-223-1110
Fax: 970-204-1240

PointCast   PointCast Inc.

http://www.pointcast.com/

10101 North De Anza Boulevard
Cupertino, CA 95014
Tel: 408-253-0894

Rapid Application and Object Development Tools

Building extranet applications requires the use of rapid application
development (RAD) tools and object or component development tools.
Developers will find some of the componentware and objectware
included with application servers, particularly in the form of basic
components or objects for basic tasks like ODBC database queries.

Borland   Borland International Inc.

http://www.borland.com/

100 Borland Way
Scotts Valley, CA 95066
Tel: 408-431-1000

Product	Description
Delphi	A Windows development tool with optimizing compiler supporting reusable components and with a scalable database architecture
IntraBuilder series	A visual JavaScript tool kit
J Builder	A Java application development tool

Computer Associates   Computer Associates

`http://www.cai.com/`

One Computer Associates Plaza
Islandia, NY 11788-7000
Tel: 516-342-5224
      800-225-5224

Product	Description
Jasmine	An intranet/Internet/extranet-enabled application development system for object-oriented database development
CA-Visual Objects	A fully object-oriented 32-bit development system for Windows 95/NT

Microsoft   Microsoft Corporation

`http://www.microsoft.com`

One Microsoft Way
Redmond, WA 98052
Tel: 206-882-8080
Fax: 206-936-7329

Product	Description
Visual Basic	Programming environment for ActiveX controls, among other applications
JScript	An interpreted scripting language for the Internet for use in World Wide Web browsers and other applications that use ActiveX Controls, OLE Automation servers, and Java applets
Visual J++	A visual Java applet/application development environment
Visual SourceSafe	A version-control product for Web content (including applet/application) development
FrontPage	A Web development tool kit

Firewall Gateways

The theory underlying firewall gateways is discussed in Chapter 5. In practice, firewalls can be implemented in software only, as turnkey software and hardware packages, or even provided as a service that can include network management and security functions performed by the supplier. This listing should not be considered exhaustive, and any firewall purchaser should check the trade press for current product roundups. Because the firewall is such a central part of your network security strategy, you must have confidence in your firewall vendor. Before you allow any consultant to install a firewall, you should get plenty of references and investigate all of them.

For more details about these products, contact the vendors directly. This listing should not be construed as an endorsement for any of these products; it is provided merely as a source of information for the reader.

AltaVista Firewall   AltaVista Internet Software

```
http://altavista.software.digital.com/
```

30 Porter Road
Littleton, MA
Fax: 508-486-2017

BorderWare   Secure Computing Corporation

```
http://www.sctc.com/
```

2675 Long Lake Road
Roseville, MN 55113
Tel: 612-628-2700

ComNet Solutions Mediator One V2.0 Firewall   ComNet
Solutions Pty Ltd

```
http://www.comnet.com.au/
```

Unit 4/12 Old Castle Hill Road
Castle Hill NSW 2154 Australia
Tel: (02) 899 5700
Fax: (02) 634 1432
E-mail: enquiry@comnet.com.au

CONNECT:Firewall 2.2   Sterling Commerce Communications
Software Group

```
http://www.csg.stercomm.com/
```

5215 North O'Connor Boulevard, Suite 1500
Irving, TX 75039-3771
Tel: 972-868-5000
      800-700-5599
Fax: 972-868-5100

CryptoSystem CryptoWall   RADGUARD LTD.

http://www.radguard.com

24 Raoul Wallenberg Street
Tel Aviv 69719
ISRAEL
Tel: 972-3-645 5444
Fax: 972-3-648 0859

U.S. Headquarters
ISI West Passaic Street
Rochelle Park, NJ 07662
Tel: 201-909-3745
Fax: 201-368-2102

CyberGuard Firewall   CyberGuard Corporation

http://www.cyberguardcorp.com/

2101 W. Cypress Creek Road
Ft. Lauderdale, FL 33309-1892
Tel: 800-666-4544 x5513
       954-973-5513

Firewall-1   Checkpoint Software Technologies Inc.

http://www.checkpoint.com

400 Seaport Court, Suite 105
Redwood City, CA 94063
Tel: 415-562-0400
       800-429-4391
Fax: 415-562-0410

Guantlet   Trusted Information Systems

`http://www.tis.com`

Trusted Information Systems, Inc.
3060 Washington Road (Rt. 97)
Glenwood, MD 21738
Tel: 301-854-6889
       410-442-1673
Fax: 301-854-5363
E-mail: `tis@tis.com`

Gemini Trusted Security Firewalls   Gemini Computers, Inc.

`http://www.geminisecure.com`

P.O. Box 222417
Carmel, CA 93922
Tel: 408-373-8500
Fax: 408-373-5792
E-mail: `tft@geminisecure.com`

GFX Internet Firewall System   Global Technology Associates, Inc.

`http://www.gta.com/`

`http://www.gnatbox.com/`

3504 Lake Lynda Drive, Suite 160
Orlando, FL 32817
Tel: 800-775-4GTA (domestic only)
        407-380-0220 (domestic and international)
Fax: 407-380-6080
E-mail: `info@gta.com`

Guardian Firewall   NetGuard, Inc.

`http://www.netguard.com/`

2445 Midway Road
Carrollton, TX 75006
Tel: 214-738-6900
Fax: 214-738-6999

NetSeer Firewall   enterWorks.com

`http://www.enterworks.com/`

19886 Ashburn Road
Ashburn, VA 20147
Tel: 800-505-5144

PrivateNet   NEC Technologies, Inc.
Internet Business Unit

`Internet: http://www.privatenet.nec.com`

110 Rio Robles Drive
San Jose, CA 94134-1899
Tel: 800-668-4869
      408-433-1549
Fax: 408-433-1230

Raptor Systems Eagle Firewall   Raptor Systems, Inc.

`http://www.raptor.com/`

69 Hickory Drive
Waltham, MA 02154
Tel: 800-9-EAGLE6
      617-487-7700
Fax: 617-487-6755
E-mail: `info@raptor.com`

SmallWorks NetGate Firewall   SmallWorks, Inc.

http://www.smallworks.com/

4501 Spicewood Springs Road, Suite 1001
Austin, TX 78759
Tel: 512-338-0619
Fax: 512-338-0625
E-mail: info@SmallWorks.com

Virtual Private Networks

Increasingly important to organizations wishing to expand their intranets to encompass remote offices as well as to organizations building
extranets of all kinds, virtual private networks can be built with relatively straightforward software and sometimes hardware installations.
These products are stand-alone VPN solutions. Firewall gateway vendors are increasingly implementing some form of VPN within their
gateway products as an optional module or as a standard feature—any
firewall gateway capable of encrypting network traffic based on
source/destination addresses can be configured to create a VPN.

AltaVista Tunnel   AltaVista Internet Software

http://www.altavista.software.com

30 Porter Road
Littleton, MA
Fax: 508-486-2017

Virtual IP Network (VIP Network) Architecture   FTP Software, Inc.

http://www.ftp.com/

100 Brickstone Square
Andover, MA 01810
Tel: 508-685-4000
        800-282-4387
Fax: 508-794-4488

APPENDIX

B

TCP/IP Internetworking

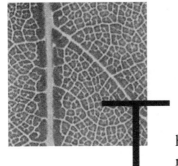

This appendix is intended as a brief overview of the technology that underlies all internetworking (Internet, intranet, and extranet) as we know it. It covers the following basic concepts:

- The Internet Protocol (IP) and Open Systems Interconnection (OSI) network reference models

- TCP/IP network layers (link, internetwork, transport, and application layers)

- IP encapsulation

- Routing

- Application protocols

The material serves as a brief introduction for the novice, as a refresher for the network veteran, or as a pointer to other materials for the reader who wants to know more. Readers interested in a more complete and in-depth introduction to the subject are directed to another book by the author, *TCP/IP Clearly Explained* (Academic Press Professional 1997).

Extranets and TCP/IP

TCP/IP stands for Transmission Control Protocol/Internet Protocol and is, in effect, the global standard for network data transport.

This protocol suite, which is often referred to as just IP, or the Internet Protocol, includes various *protocols*—sets of rules for communicating—that operate at different levels of abstraction to facilitate the exchange of information across large networks of networks. IP is concerned with all aspects of data communication except for the actual protocols governing the physical transmission of data from a computer to the network medium. These protocols may change as new technologies are developed, but IP is concerned with all the other rules for moving data between disparate systems across all types of physical network media.

All systems directly connected to the Internet run TCP/IP, which is often referred to as the *Internet Protocol suite.* The TCP/IP communication protocols are the only mechanisms that Internet-connected systems have in common. Regardless of whether they are connected to Ethernet or token-ring LANs; to X.25 WANs; or to ATM, FDDI, or just plain POTS serial line links, the systems are all capable of sending and receiving IP packets. *Seamless interoperability* between disparate systems and networks is the feature that gives the Internet its strength.

Intranets, on the other hand, do not necessarily require that all connected systems run TCP/IP. Although intranets generally do require that Internet application protocols, like those of the World Wide Web, be supported, no technical barrier prevents these applications from being transported across the organizational networks using some other network protocols. Because the Internet protocol suite is modular, Internet applications can interact with standard IP protocols, which handle transmission of data between computers on a network.

As extranets gain in popularity, the move to TCP/IP will be inexorable. As with intranets, private extranets do not necessarily have to use all the TCP/IP protocols. However, those that do not support TCP/IP will restrict themselves unnecessarily—and take on additional financial burdens as the cost of deployment and support rise. An increasing number of open extranets will support TCP/IP by definition, particularly those linking individuals and organizations over the Internet.

Anyone involved in the design, deployment, configuration, administration, or support of an extranet must understand the fundamentals of TCP/IP internetworking.

Internetworking Reference Models

The problem of internetworking is how to build a set of protocols that can handle communications between any two (or more) computers, using any type of operating system, and connected using any kind of physical medium. To complicate matters, we can assume that no connected system has any knowledge about the other systems: there is no way of knowing where the remote system is, what kind of software it uses, or what kind of hardware platform it runs on.

In an attempt to simplify matters, the researchers working on this problem created models of data communication, the purpose of which is to break down all the functions performed in the course of internetworking. Two of the most important of these models are the OSI reference model and the Internet model. Both break internetworking functions into several different layers. At each layer some entity can be imagined residing in a system that communicates with its counterpart on the remote system. At the same time, each layer entity must communicate with the layer entities above and below it on the same system. Each layer entity takes information from layers above or below, adds or removes layer specific information, and passes it on to the next layer. This process, called *encapsulation*, is central to internetworking and is discussed at greater length in the section "Encapsulation."

Because layered models are often represented as stacks of modules, internetworking protocol suites are often referred to as *stacks*. The two most important reference models, the formally derived OSI model and the more empirically derived Internet model, are discussed next.

The OSI Reference Model

The *OSI seven-layer reference model* is based on work done on the OSI project; it is illustrated in Figure B.1. The goal of this model was to partition each level of network activity into its own layer so that inter-action between systems could also be partitioned. The result would be systems capable of seamless interoperability, independent of any underlying network variables.

FIGURE B.1

The OSI internetworking reference model has seven layers.

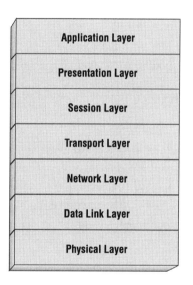

The OSI layers, with practical examples of layer protocols, are described in the following paragraphs.

Physical Layer   The physical layer is the most basic, or physical, level at which data is turned into impulses to be transmitted as actual bits. For example, the actual signal characteristics that are to be interpreted as either zeroes or ones when transmitted and received across an Ethernet are part of a physical layer protocol. The only units that operate at this layer are bits.

Data Link Layer   Systems connected to a physical network need some way to handle electronic bit streams that flow across the wires (or light waves that flow through fiberglass cables or electromagnetic pulses transmitted by radio). These systems generally require a method of identifying the bits' source and target destination, as well as a method of clumping groups of bits together into protocol data units. They also need rules about how the source and destination hosts can determine that a protocol data unit has been successfully received. The data link layer defines the exchange of data between two computers connected to the same physical network.

Network Layer   Dissimilar networks can be connected to each other in many ways, and systems connected to different types of networks need a way to interoperate that functions above any physical specification of the locally connected network media. Communication between systems may require routing of data across these dissimilar networks and may require the repackaging of the data being transmitted. Network layer protocols define how data is to be transmitted between two hosts without reference to the physical networks to which the hosts are connected.

Transport Layer   Communication systems that run only one program at a time would not need any more specificity of addressing than that provided at the network layer. Data originating from a client host could come only from a single process and could be intended only for the single process running on the server. Multitasking systems are now more the rule than the exception, and the need to run multiple concurrent sessions between two systems is long-standing (for many years most networked users were connected via mainframe systems). The transport layer protocols define how processes on two systems can communicate with each other.

Session Layer   The flow and timing of a connection is handled at the session layer, as is determining whether data is being sent and received by the communicating processes.

Presentation Layer   With some computer manufacturers choosing to do data representation their own way, notably IBM using the EBCDIC representation and most other vendors using some flavor of ASCII, interoperable networks require that data be converted to some globally accepted representation before being sent out over the network. The alternative, requiring applications to determine what system is at the other end of the line and then converting data received, is unacceptable, as it would require implementers to develop much more complicated software and to constantly update it and monitor it for completeness. Protocols for the presentation layer were intended to handle this problem.

Application Layer   At the top of the stack is the application layer, where protocols define the way applications that use the network behave and interoperate. For example, file transfer protocols define the way that a client requests files from a remote server, and terminal emulation protocols define how a server handles input from the client.

Desktop applications such as Microsoft Word, Lotus 1-2-3, or Adobe Illustrator operate above the application layer. Networked applications, however, will operate in whole or in part at the applications layer.

The Internet Reference Model

The OSI model rigorously separates all possible network functions into separate layers. However, implementations based on this model have not gained the kind of acceptance enjoyed by TCP/IP implementations. Some experts have argued that the OSI model is overly complex and that the TCP/IP model, based on actual experimentation, solves the more important internetworking problems while ignoring the issues not relevant to internetworking.

The TCP/IP, or Internet, model uses only four layers, as shown in Figure B.2. The physical layer, as defined in the OSI model, is still acknowledged but is ignored as being beyond the scope of an internetworking protocol stack. The Internet model layers are described in the following paragraphs.

Network Interface or Data Link Layer   Similar to the data link layer defined in the OSI model, at this layer the IP protocols define methods for moving data between computers connected to the same physical network medium. Data communication at this level can occur only between systems on the same physical network, which means that you cannot use data link layer protocols alone to pass data over an internetwork. You must use the data link layer protocols to handle the local delivery of data that is being transmitted by the next layer up. Data link layer protocols hand data down to the physical network medium layer for delivery and also receive data for processing from the next layer up.

Network Layer   Comparable to the network layer of the OSI model, this is where the Internet Protocol (IP) operates. IP defines how data is moved between computers without regard to whether the computers are connected to the same physical network. Data passing between distant systems is routed by intermediate systems called *routers* that examine the IP protocol headers, but the data itself is not interpreted in any way. The data is, however, passed down to the network interface layer in order to move it from the originating system to a router, between routers, or from a router to a destination system. IP allows systems to interoperate whether or not they are on the same physical network. Network layer protocols pass data down to the data link layer for local processing; network layer protocols receive data for processing from the next layer up.

Transport Layer Protocols at this layer define the way that data is passed between any two processes. The TCP/IP transport layer protocols allow a system to run more than one process without concern that incoming data will be passed along to the wrong process. The transport layer allows interoperation between processes running on widely separated hosts, but does not require that the source and destination hosts be widely separate. In fact, both processes could be running on the same computer. Transport layer protocols hand data down to the network layer protocol for distribution to a destination host and receive data for processing from the next layer up.

Application Layer Implementers have determined that a single layer can fulfill all the functions defined in the top three OSI layers, namely, the presentation, session, and application layers. The Internet model uses a single layer, the application layer, to handle connection management and data representation issues in addition to the standard issues of how client and server applications themselves are to behave.

FIGURE B.2

The Internet reference model uses only four layers.

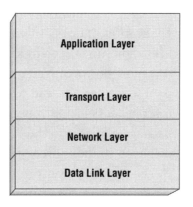

The rest of this appendix describes many protocols of the Internet suite, using this reference model as a framework. The protocols appear in a bottom-up chronology.

Encapsulation

The concept of *encapsulation* is vital to understanding many networking concepts—but it is of paramount importance when discussing the TCP/IP protocol suite. Encapsulation can best be explained by walking through the process.

The network application generates some data to be sent out to a remote system. The application takes the raw data (which may be keyboard input from a human or data generated by some other process running on the same system or from some other source) and wraps it up with its own headers that tell the application at the other end what is inside.

This process is somewhat similar to the process of putting something inside an envelope and writing a direction, destination, or description of what's inside on the outside of the envelope. The application then takes this package, or protocol data unit, which includes a destination application, and passes it down the protocol stack to the transport layer protocol.

The transport layer protocol is concerned with making sure that processes are able to communicate. When it receives a package from an application, it does not worry about what kind of data is contained inside, but just needs to know what process to send the data to. The transport protocol wraps the application protocol package inside its own set of headers and passes it down the protocol stack. Transport layer headers include enough information to make sure that the data package makes it to the destination process and that replies can be delivered to the source process.

The network layer protocol is concerned with delivering the package it receives from the transport protocol to some host. It is not concerned with the contents of the data package. The network layer wraps the package with its own set of headers that identify the source and destination hosts and then passes that data package on down to the data link layer protocol. At this layer the protocol determines whether the data package is destined for a locally connected host, in which case the data link layer is used to deliver the package to its final destination, or whether the data is destined for a host connected to some other network, in which case the Internet Protocol uses the data link layer to deliver the package to a router that can move the package closer to its final destination.

Figure B.3 shows how the process of encapsulation adds addressing and delivery information to each protocol data unit as the data moves down the protocol stack. When the package is finally delivered to the network interface card, the system receiving it goes through the reverse process. First, the data link layer looks at its headers to determine if the data is intended for its interface. If it is, then the data link layer protocol headers are removed and the data packet is passed to the network layer protocol. The network layer protocol headers are examined, and if the data is intended for that computer, the packet is again stripped of that set of headers and passed up the stack.

At this point, however, the network layer protocol may determine that the final destination system for the packet is another computer, in which case the system processing the packet might be required (if it is a router) to determine the correct system to send that packet to, reencapsulate it with a new set of data link layer headers, and resend it.

The transport layer protocol at the final destination receives the data package from the network layer protocol and examines its own set of headers to determine which process is being addressed. It strips out the existing set of protocol headers and passes the data package on up to the application layer—which, in turn, examines the headers to determine the contents of the package and to act accordingly.

Encapsulation allows the protocol software at each layer to communicate directly with its counterpart software on a destination system while allowing protocol software at each layer to cooperate with the layers above and/or below it to deliver data to its destination.

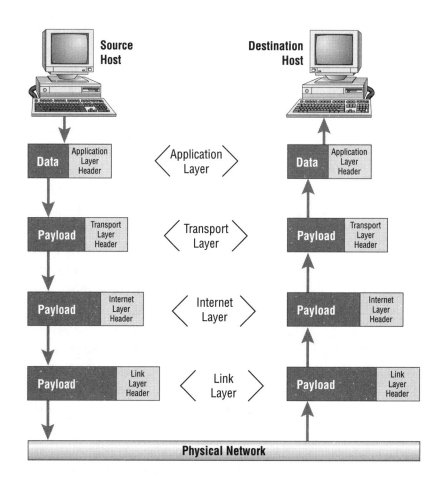

Encapsulation allows different internetwork layers to interoperate appropriately and seamlessly.

Link Layer Protocols

In general, data link layer protocols are not specific to internetworking, but define the way that network interface cards (for example) send and receive data across an Ethernet LAN. Although a thorough understanding of these protocols is not necessary to understand TCP/IP, knowing roughly how these work and what they do is useful.

Most simply, link layer protocols define the way in which data is passed between two network connection devices across a single network medium. For example, protocols at this layer specify how data is transmitted from a network interface card across a coaxial or twisted-pair cable and received by a network interface card connected to the same cable. In other words, the link layer is about communication between physical network interfaces.

Address resolution protocols help simplify the problem of determining the destination address of a previously unknown host. The key to these protocols is the use of a standard format by which a host can broadcast a request for the hardware (data link layer) address of a system whose higher-protocol address is already known. TCP/IP makes extensive use of Address Resolution Protocol (ARP) to provide connectivity between hosts on all types of networks.

Network Media Protocols

With one major exception, what goes on at the link layer of the internetwork is of no concern to the TCP/IP protocols. Whether the target or destination hosts are connected to thin-wire Ethernet, token-ring, fiber, satellite, or carrier pigeon links is irrelevant to the upper-layer protocols. The one exception is that the network layer IP needs to have some way to link an IP network address (which is assigned independent of any system, network, or hardware considerations) with the address of the host on its local link.

Link layer protocols, which include specifications for how data is delivered across physical links group individual bits into a protocol data unit called a *frame*. Frames have headers that include source and destination addresses, as well as some information about the contents of the frame, for example, the next higher protocol encapsulated within and the number of bytes included in the frame. Frames often contain a preamble that signals the start of the frame, as well as some form of check sum on the contents as part of a trailer.

Readers unfamiliar with link layer protocols can find out more about them in practically any good book about networking and in many books about TCP/IP. Examples of link layer protocols include Ethernet; IEEE 802 media protocols, used by many LAN products; and Point-to-Point Protocol (PPP); and the Serial Line Internet Protocol (SLIP), used by most serial connections to the Internet. These protocols are discussed at greater length in my book *TCP/IP Clearly Explained* (Academic Press Professional 1997).

Address Resolution Protocols (ARP and RARP)

When IP hosts transmit data across an internetwork, they must at some point physically transmit the data across a local link. Since the originating host has no knowledge of the platform or network on which the destination host operates, it has no way to specify any local addresses—only the IP address can be used. Furthermore, since data may be passed across an undetermined number of intermediate networks and links, the originating host couldn't specify link layer addresses for those networks. Hosts running IP (as well as other network protocols) use ARP to determine the physical network addresses connected with IP addresses on the local link.

ARP requests are sent out as broadcast messages on the local link (messages intended to be received by all connected hosts). Very simply, the ARP request includes the IP address and the physical address of the requesting host, as well as the IP address of the host for which a physical address is being requested. Although all connected hosts on the local network listen to these requests, only the host whose IP address is specified in the request responds. That response includes the IP address and physical address of both the responding host and the requesting host.

Simply put, the requesting host yells out to every other host on the local network, "Who has this IP address?" If that IP address is local, the host with it will respond, "That's me." The requesting host can then address data directly to the responding host over the local network.

A slightly different but related problem occurs for hosts that know their physical address, but not their IP address. Network terminals and diskless workstations may use a Reverse ARP, or RARP, request to find out how to configure themselves. RARP requests use the same format as ARP requests, but leave their own IP address blank and specify a RARP server address as the destination of the request. The RARP server maintains a table of physical and IP addresses, which it consults before responding to a RARP request with the requesting host's IP address.

The structure of the ARP message, as well as finer points of how ARP and RARP are implemented, and issues like RARP storms, are beyond the scope of this appendix. See *TCP/IP Clearly Explained* (Academic Press Professional 1997) for more detailed discussion of these topics.

BOOTP and DHCP

Another issue in TCP/IP networks is how to configure hosts remotely. Initially, this problem began with diskless workstations that could boot themselves from network servers, but which needed some way to discover their own IP configuration information in order to boot themselves to the network. The solution was the Boot Protocol, or BOOTP. The workstation could be programmed to implement a very minimal IP stack able to discover a boot server over the network and send a request to that server (typically, notifying the server of everything the client knows about itself).

As diskless workstations became less common, and personal computers more common, BOOTP became less useful. It provided only the most minimal configuration information and was often not implemented for personal computer platforms. However, as the number of internetworked personal computers grew, the problem of remotely configuring TCP/IP stacks became more complicated. When changes in network segments occur, or when many different PCs must share a limited number of IP addresses, some automatic mechanism is necessary to track the addresses.

The answer is the Dynamic Host Configuration Protocol (DHCP). Based on BOOTP, DHCP adds more configuration options and provides for vendor-specific configuration information. DHCP clients request IP configuration information from DHCP servers; IP addresses may be supplied on a per session basis, expiring after some set amount of time, or they may be supplied more permanently.

DHCP can simplify TCP/IP system configuration management, reducing both the resources necessary to keep systems configured properly as well as easing some of the pressure on IP version 4 address space issues by allowing an organization to share a limited number of addresses among any number of clients. With DHCP the number of IP addresses available limits the number of concurrent IP hosts rather than the absolute number of IP hosts.

Network Layer Protocols

Network abstraction can occur at the internetwork layer. The IP uses a universal addressing scheme, which transcends local network and platform issues, to create the abstraction of a global Internet. All connected networks are assigned their own, unique, network addresses. Hosts connected to each network are assigned their own, unique, host addresses within the network. The result is that any host connected to the internetwork can direct data to any other host connected to the internetwork with the assurance that as long as both hosts have connectivity through some path, the data will be delivered to the correct system.

Just as link layer protocols define the way data is passed between network interfaces, the network layer protocols define the way data is passed between hosts, with the physical aspects of the network abstracted out of the equation. Whereas link layer protocols are concerned with the address of a network interface, IP is concerned with network host addresses.

This appendix discusses IP version 4 (IPv4) only. Implementation and deployment of IP version 6 (IPv6) is still underway as of 1997. Although there are substantial changes, the underlying principles are mostly the same. A more complete discussion of IP versions 4 and 6 appears in *TCP/IP Clearly Explained* (Academic Press Professional 1997), and an excellent source for information about how IP addressing works is Buck Graham's *TCP/IP Addressing*, also published by Academic Press Professional.

IP Addressing

All networks must have some form of network addressing to work: they must have some way to direct data to uniquely addressed hosts connected to the network. Addressing is at the root of one of the basic problems of internetworking. Each local network or link must use some method of uniquely addressing each node, but those addressing methods cannot be used between different networks without a huge amount of administrative effort. If one administrator numbers hosts on her network consecutively, starting from one, then no one else may use that numbering scheme. Likewise, if another administrator assigned addresses at random, he would have to confirm the uniqueness of each address with all other network administrators.

In fact, this type of problem is the least of the internetworker's worries. It assumes that hosts connected to any type of network will be able to recognize the size and format of addresses for all other types of networks. The reality is that different network media use different address formats and lengths, and it becomes clear that devising a new, global, addressing scheme is more efficient than using existing addressing schemes.

IP addresses are 32 bits, or four bytes, long. This address space, originally specified in the late 1970s and early 1980s, can support no more than about 4 billion hosts—a number that was then considered to be much more than adequate for the immediate and future needs of an experimental network, even if it were to ultimately see general use. In practice, far fewer hosts can actually be accommodated because of the way the address space is partitioned. By dividing each 32-bit IP address into two parts, a network address and a host address, routing is simplified.

The network is specified in the most significant bits of the IP address, while the host address on each network is specified in the least significant bits of the address. As long as the originating host knows its own address, it can also tell whether or not the destination is local or distant. IP routers (which sort traffic between networks) can also determine where to send messages based on network addresses. Data intended for directly connected networks can be sent directly, whereas data intended for remote networks is forwarded again to another router.

Five classes of addresses were originally specified, as shown in Table B.1. Class A addresses were intended for truly huge organizations. Because the network part of these addresses is only one byte long (the first bit identifies it as a Class A network, the other seven bits are available for addresses), only a few (no more than 126) of these networks can exist, but each network can be truly huge, supporting an absolute maximum of over 16 million hosts. The IP architects originally thought that only countries would be able to support Class A networks, particularly because ubiquitous and inexpensively networked personal computers were unknown during the late 1970s and early 1980s. At that time, almost all networked computers were large and quite expensive.

T A B L E B.I IP version 4 addresses fall into five classes.		Class A	Class B	Class C	Class D	Class E
	Used for	Very large networks	Large networks	Small/medium-sized networks	Multicasting addresses	Not assigned
	Maximum network available	126	16,384	2,097,152	N/A	N/A
	Maximum nodes in network	16,777,214	65,534	254	N/A	N/A
	Lowest address in class	0.0.0.0	128.0.0.0	192.0.0.0	224.0.0.0	240.0.0.0
	Highest address in class	127.0.0.0	191.255.0.0	223.255.255.0	239.255.255.255	247.255.255.255

Class B addresses use the first two bytes for the network portion of the address and two bytes for the host portion. The first two bits identify the address as Class B, and the next 14 bits are available for network addresses, meaning that as many as 16,000 Class B networks can exist, each with no more than about 65,000 hosts. These networks were originally intended for large organizations with many branches and many large computers. Class C networks, which use the first three bytes for network address, can support no more than 254 hosts each, but more than 2 million Class C networks can exist. (The first three bits identify the address as a Class C; the next 21 bits are available for addresses.) Class C networks were intended for smaller and medium-sized organizations with fewer hosts to connect.

Class D, or multicast, addresses are used to distribute data to groups of hosts that subscribe to a particular address. Multicasting was seen as a more efficient alternative to flooding networks with broadcast data for certain types of applications. Although multicasting is still not yet widely supported, multicasts have entirely replaced broadcasts in IPv6. Class E addresses were reserved for future use when the address architecture was adopted and have not been assigned for any use at this time.

Just as the entire IP address space is assigned hierarchically, each individual IP network can also be partitioned. Instead of using the entire three bytes of host address for host addresses in a Class A network, most larger networks steal part of the host address to create subnetworks. In other words, if the first byte of the IP address is between 001 and 126, the address is on a Class A network. The next three bytes could be used entirely to sequentially address up to 2 million separate hosts; however, it is much more efficient to segment this large address space further. For example, the next byte might be used to partition a single Class A network so that it functions like as many as 255 Class B networks. Further, each of those Class B networks could steal the third byte of the address to partition themselves into as many as 255 Class C networks. Subnets can be used with any class IP address and can use any number of the available host address bits, as long as at least a couple of bits remain to assign to actual hosts.

The Internet Protocol

The Internet Protocol defines how data contained in IP datagrams is delivered from the source host to the destination host. IP is an unreliable protocol, meaning that it does not include any mechanisms that can guarantee end-to-end delivery. It is also a best-effort protocol, which means that it does not have any mechanisms to gracefully notify the sender when an intermediate or destination system is unable to process datagrams. Implementers have long considered these functions to be the proper domain of higher-layer protocols because if they were performed at the IP layer, meaning at every intermediate router, reliability checks would be a major drain on routing resources.

Figure B.4 shows how a source host connected to an Ethernet LAN can cross several networks to reach a destination host connected to a token-ring LAN. Connected to each LAN is an IP router, a host dedicated to forwarding packets to remote networks from local hosts and from remote networks to local hosts. When a host is sending an IP datagram to a remote host, it checks the destination address against its own address.

- If the destination host is on the same network (or subnetwork), the originating host will use ARP to determine the local network address of the destination host and send the datagram directly.

- If the destination host is on a remote network (any network not directly connected to the source host), the originating host will send the IP datagram to a router on its own network.

FIGURE B.4

IP routers allow widely separated hosts to communicate with each other.

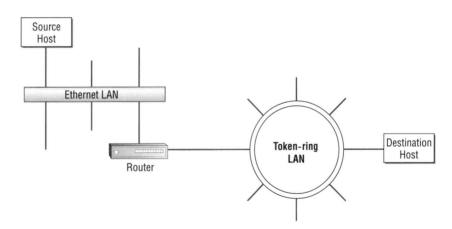

IP routers (which are increasingly infrequently referred to as *gateways*) are always connected to more than one physical network. They are multi-homed (hosts that have "homes"—network interface connections—on more than one network) hosts that can forward packets. As shown in Figure B.5, a router can take a datagram from one network to which it is connected and pass it directly to a destination host on another network to which it is also connected. More important, a router can take a datagram from a directly connected network and pass it to another router so that it can be forwarded to a remotely connected network.

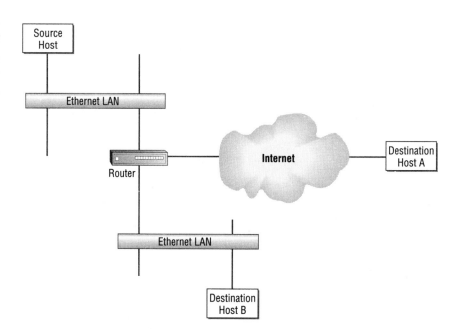

The IP Datagram Header

The IP datagram header defines the information necessary to move data across a TCP/IP internetwork. Nearly 20 years of implementation experience has shown that some of the data fields required by IPv4 are less important than originally thought (these have been modified or replaced in IPv6), but the protocol overall has been remarkably successful.

All IPv4 headers are between 20 and 60 bytes long; data within is normally handled in four-byte words. Figure B.6 shows the datagram fields, which are explained in Table B.2.

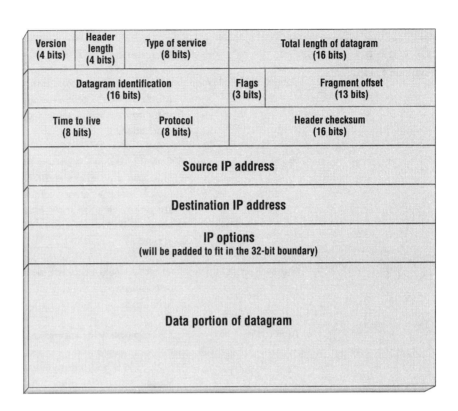

FIGURE B.6

IP headers align on 32-bit boundaries, with fields grouped into four-byte words.

TABLE B.2	Field	Description
IP version 4 header fields	Version	A four-bit field indicating the version of IP being used. Current values are either 4 (for IPv4) or 6 (for IPv6).
	Header length	A four-bit field indicating the number of four-byte words in the header; valid values range from 5 (20 bytes) to 15 (60 bytes).
	Type of service (TOS)	Only three bits of the eight reserved for this field are used to make TOS requests of IP routers. Only one of the three can be set for on delay, throughput, or reliability. The TOS bits did not make the IPv6 upgrade.
	Datagram length	A 16-bit field indicating the length, including header, of the entire datagram.

T A B L E B.2 (cont.)	Field	Description
IP version 4 header fields	Datagram identification	A unique 16-bit identifier assigned to a datagram by the originating host, intended as an aid to reassembling datagrams that may have been fragmented en route to their final destination.
	Flags	Only the second and third of these flags are used. The second bit indicates whether the datagram may be fragmented; the third indicates whether additional fragments to the datagram are yet to come. The More Fragments flag works with the datagram ID field to assist hosts in reassembling fragmented datagrams.
	Fragment offset	This 13-bit field indicates how many units from the start of the original datagram the current datagram is, measured in eight-byte words.
	Time to live	This eight-bit field indicates the length of time the datagram may exist after entering the internetwork. The maximum value is 255, and although this value was originally intended to appear as a number of seconds, in practice it has become a hop count. In other words, this value is decremented by one each time it is forwarded by a router.
	Protocol	This eight-bit field indicates what protocol is used by the encapsulated data in the IP payload. In other words, it specifies which transport protocol is in use.
	Header Checksum	This 16-bit field contains a checksum on the IP header only. It is not intended as a method of adding reliability so much as a way to quickly identify datagrams that have become corrupt so they may be discarded.
	Source/destination	These fields are the actual 32-bit (four octet) IP addresses of the originating host and the destination host.
	IP options	These fields set the handful of options that can be added to an IP datagram that allow additional control over how routing is performed.

Transport Layer Protocols

While the data link layer is concerned with communication between physical network interfaces and the network layer is concerned with communication between hosts, the transport layer protocols are concerned with communication between programs running on those hosts. The transport layer is also where reliability becomes effective because the applications communicating can include guarantees of service. The data communicated at this layer is not processed or interpreted by any intermediate systems, so it is easier for the source and destination systems to agree on how to provide reliability. For example, TCP is a reliable protocol, meaning that the protocol handles issues like guaranteed delivery of data, flow control, and retransmission of data not received.

The TCP/IP protocol suite has two widely used transport protocols: the Transmission Control Protocol (TCP), which makes up 60 percent of the Internet protocol suite acronym, and the User Datagram Protocol (UDP). TCP provides a virtual circuit between two processes and offers a reliable service for applications that require it. UDP is a connectionless packet service that offers a more efficient transport service for applications that require less reliability.

Transmission Control Protocol (TCP)

The Transmission Control Protocol provides a mechanism for processes to communicate reliably across an internetwork. TCP is a connection-oriented protocol, meaning that two processes initiate a two-way communication circuit, also known as a *virtual circuit*, from which TCP's reliability features derive.

The TCP virtual circuit service between two processes acts as if it were a direct link between them. Each process is associated with a port, so every virtual circuit can be described by

- The IP address of the client host and the port associated with the client process running on that system

- The IP address of the server host and the port associated with the server process running on that system

- The protocol being carried between the two hosts

Each of these pairings, a port and an IP address, are referred to as *sockets*.

Server processes usually use "well known" port numbers, allowing client processes to connect to server processes knowing nothing more than the service and the server IP address. The server process listens for client requests on the port through a *daemon process* (a program running on a server whose only purpose is to listen for requests and make sure that they are handled by the server) that handles the creation of new TCP circuits.

To establish a virtual circuit, the client and server processes engage in a three-step handshake. The process initiating the circuit sends a request to open a circuit; the responding process sends back an acknowledgment of that request, along with a request for an acknowledgment that the circuit has been opened. When the initiating process returns the acknowledgment, both ends of the circuit are "in synchronization," and the circuit can be used to send and receive data.

Each TCP transmission must be acknowledged as received; when an acknowledgment is not received in reasonable time, the sender must retransmit that data. The use of acknowledgments on all data transmissions is what makes TCP a reliable protocol. TCP is a complex protocol, compared to datagram protocols like IP and UDP (see the following section). TCP must use several mechanisms to ensure that data is being transmitted fast enough to perform adequately while avoiding going too fast (and having to retransmit data) or too slow (negatively affecting performance).

Most applications requiring reliability, like file transfer–based protocols (including FTP and HTTP), use TCP to guarantee that data is transmitted accurately. Most applications offering high levels of interaction, like terminal emulation protocols, use TCP to ensure responsiveness and performance.

User Datagram Protocol (UDP)

Reliability is expensive. Setting up TCP connections (and taking them down), as well as keeping track of every byte of TCP data streams involves significant overhead. In situations where reliability is less important than performance, the User Datagram Protocol (UDP) offers a simple best-effort datagram service at the transport layer.

Whereas TCP is well suited to applications that require continuous interaction, UDP is well suited to applications that use simple queries and responses. Network management protocols generally use UDP, as does the Network File System (NFS) protocol. Network management protocols use UDP to keep unnecessary network traffic to a minimum; NFS uses UDP for its high performance and implements reliability, necessary for any file system service, at the application layer.

UDP uses sockets to identify client and server processes, as does TCP, but because it allows broadcasts (for example, sending out a query to all systems connected to a network), UDP is not a connection-oriented protocol. UDP is a fairly simple protocol, requiring minimal information in the protocol headers. (By comparison, TCP headers are complicated by data sequencing, acknowledgment, and flow-control information.)

Application Layer Protocols

Application clients and servers exchange information by encapsulating it into transport layer protocols and sending it on down the network stack for processing. When applications send data to remote hosts, the applications insert various commands in their own headers, and the receiving host interprets those commands and responds appropriately to them. Typically, a client application might send a request to a server to send some piece of data, and the server would respond by sending the data.

Successful IP applications are simple enough to be generalized across all user groups and end-user applications. For example, e-mail has always been an immensely popular network application. The power of FTP is not in its ease of use, but its extensibility and ease of integration within other applications. Terminal emulation with telnet meets a basic need for a standard interface between dissimilar systems across IP networks.

FTP and Telnet

In the early days of internetworking research, the two most important applications were terminal emulation and file transfer. After all, in the 1970s almost all computing was done through a terminal, and the ability to use a single interface to access any connected computer (rather than an assortment of hardware terminals running proprietary communications protocols) was a worthy goal. Of roughly equal importance was the ability to move data files from one computer to another—once you used your terminal session to create, modify, or gather data, you had to move that data either on or off the remote host. Data might be processed on one host and stored on another, or code might be edited on a local host and compiled and executed on a remote host.

Telnet

The problem with doing terminal emulations has always been that computer manufacturers insist on differentiating their products. Whether they use proprietary protocols, as IBM does with SNA, or unique character representations, as IBM does with EBCDIC, making a universal terminal client has always been difficult. Most computer manufacturers at one time or another attempt to add special features to their products in an effort to attract new customers. This approach may provide a short-term benefit for customers, but it tends to cause problems in the long term as increasingly incompatible systems are deployed in an organization.

Telnet provides interoperability across most of these system incompatibilities through the use of a logical construct: the network virtual terminal (NVT). NVT is an idealized and generalized version of a terminal, with a generalized display and input (keyboard and mouse). All Telnet clients map actual mouse and keyboard input to the NVT, and telnet servers map the NVT input appropriately. Likewise, all Telnet servers convert their actual display data into the NVT display format, which telnet clients accept and map onto their real-world displays.

Telnet uses TCP to ensure that terminal sessions are maintained reliably. Telnet protocol commands cover functions like opening, closing, and managing a terminal session. The parts of the telnet protocol relating to the NVT are implemented within the client and server software.

FTP

Using a very basic set of primitive file transfer commands coupled with reply codes, FTP provides a straightforward application that can be submerged within other applications and interfaces. For years, FTP implementations simply reproduced the same basic set of commands, like get (to retrieve a remote file), send (to send a file to a remote system), and dir or ls (to list a directory). The FTP client software sends these commands, with parameters such as file names where applicable, to the FTP server on a remote host. The server responds to all client commands with a three-digit reply code that gives some indication of the result. For example, a reply code might indicate that the request failed, succeeded, or required some additional information or action on the part of the client program.

Because the set of FTP commands is small and all implementations must support the same basic set of commands, developers began creating GUI versions of FTP clients for use in graphical operating systems. These implementations use the same commands and reply codes but offer users a friendlier interface.

FTP connections use TCP for reliability of file transfers. Unlike many other application protocols, FTP uses two TCP circuits for all transfers. A client request to open a session with a server initiates a control session. This circuit is used to pass commands from the client to the server. When a file transfer is requested, the server requests the client to open a second TCP circuit over which the file is transferred.

World Wide Web

As the "killer app" of the Internet, the World Wide Web has enjoyed unprecedented success since its creation in the early 1990s. It provides a framework by which multimedia documents can be published and accessed over the Internet.

Although the Web uses the Hypertext Transport Protocol (HTTP) as its application protocol, two important supplementary specifications are, to some extent, more important than HTTP:

- The Hypertext Markup Language (HTML) is a platform-independent specification for creating multimedia documents.

- The Universal Resource Locator (URL) specification defines a simple way to uniquely and simply point to these multimedia documents and other internetwork resources.

Hypertext Transport Protocol

HTTP clients, also known as Web browsers, use this protocol to request documents from HTTP servers, also known as Web servers. Interactions between Web clients and servers are similar to interactions between FTP clients and servers. That is, the client requests multimedia files, and servers respond appropriately (and also use reply codes to indicate the status of requests).

The greatest difference between FTP and HTTP is what happens to files after the browser retrieves them. Rather than simply storing the files locally, the browser displays the file in an appropriate format: text files are displayed as text, and graphics files are displayed as images. Properly equipped browsers can play sound and video files or display 3-D or virtual reality files.

Hypertext Markup Language

The Hypertext Markup Language (HTML) is the glue that creates hypertext documents. Based on an earlier specification, the Standardized General Markup Language (SGML), HTML uses tags to indicate the functional purpose of each part of a document. For example, a heading is set off from the rest of the document with the tags <h1> (at the start of the heading) and </h1> (at the end of the heading). The result is a document that can be interpreted and displayed as appropriate by the system through which it is retrieved. For example, a text-only system would display the text of an HTML document with text messages in place of any graphical or multimedia files. The same document, when displayed on a graphical workstation, would include all images.

Universal Resource Locator

File system naming conventions vary sufficiently from system to system. Transparent interoperability requires that clients never have to know any of the operating system details of servers, so a method of identifying files, resources, and multimedia documents is needed. The URL specification provides the solution. URLs consist of three sections by which any internetwork resource can be uniquely and reliably identified.

The first portion of the URL is the *scheme,* identifying the application protocol by which the resource should be retrieved. Table B.3 shows some common schemes. The scheme is set off by a colon and is followed by the other two sections of the URL, the host and domain name of the server, and the resource itself. The host name is set off by a slash and is followed by the directory and file name of the resource.

Scheme	Protocol
http:	Hypertext Transport Protocol, multimedia file
shttp:	Secure HTTP
https:	HTTP using Secure Socket Layer (SSL)
ftp:	File Transfer Protocol
gopher:	Gopher menuing protocol

APPENDIX

C

Extranet Glossary

Active Platform　An integrated set of client and server development technologies developed by Microsoft Corporation to support object interoperability across internetworks.

ActiveX　The set of core technologies for Microsoft's Active Platform, including COM and DCOM, that enable communication between components running locally or across a network.

ADSI　Active Directory Interfaces. Microsoft's directory services interface, based on and compatible with X.500 but with proprietary extensions.

API　An application programming interface that provides programmers with a uniform interface to write programs to without having to recode important functions.

applet　A miniapplication usually written in Java that has limited functionality, including restrictions on what system resources it may use (for example, it may have limited or no file-writing access), as well as on how the application is displayed (e.g., usually the applet runs within a Web browser).

application layer　The application layer is part of an internetwork reference model and represents that level at which applications running on systems connected to a network interoperate.

ATM　Asynchronous transfer mode is a high-performance, cell-switching data communications protocol that can be used for voice, data, and video.

backbone　A backbone provides reliable and fast network services specifically to link two or more separated internetworks.

BOOTP The Boot Protocol specifies a mechanism for managing IP network-connected host configurations remotely. It provides a framework for transmitting requests from workstations booting to the network and returning IP address and other configuration information.

bridge A device linking two networks at the data link layer. A bridge receives data from one network and reprocesses and retransmits the data on another network. Bridges usually retransmit data only on the network segment for which they are intended and can reduce local traffic across segments.

browser The client software used to access data published on the World Wide Web. A browser uses HTTP to send requests for data and receive data from servers. It also interprets data formatted with HTML.

CCITT The acronym stands for Comite Consultatif International de Telegraphie et Telephonie. The function of this international standards body is to ensure international communication interoperability. This body is now known as the International Telecommunications Union, or ITU.

certification authority An entity that, using public key cryptography and digital signatures, provides a means of checking and certifying the authenticity of a digital certificate.

collaborative groupware Software specifically designed to allow its users to interact within the workgroup, usually supporting task flows or other group interactions.

COM Microsoft's Component Object Model; also sometimes referred to as Common Object Model. COM grew out of the OLE standard developed at Microsoft in support of object interoperability and portability across applications.

CORBA   Common Object Request Broker Architecture. An open standard for distributed object computing developed by the Object Management Group (OMG).

DARPA   Defense Advanced Research Projects Agency.

data link layer   An internetworking reference model layer, referring to the level of network interaction where connected hosts interact with other hosts connected to the same network medium. For example, Ethernet is a data link layer protocol, as is ATM.

datagram   A protocol data unit, usually associated with the Internet Protocol or other network layer protocols.

DCE   Distributed Computing Environment; developed by Open Software Foundation.

DCOM   Distributed COM. A distributed object architecture introduced by Microsoft and proposed as an industry standard.

DES   Data Encryption Standard. A standard for symmetric encryption, approved for use by the government. DES uses 56-bit keys; triple-DES (DES encryption repeated three times on the same plaintext) is considered stronger. DES is widely implemented internationally for financial and other types of secure applications.

DHCP   Dynamic Host Configuration Protocol. A protocol that permits dynamic host configuration with parameters like IP host address, network address, and subnet mask, as well as other configuration parameters. It is an extension of the BOOTP protocol and supports vendor-specific configuration items.

digest function   A cryptographic function that takes as its input a data file of any size and generates a unique, fixed-length result. Also known as a *hash functions,* digest functions are often used for digital signature applications.

digital signature   A string that is generated when a user runs a message digest function on the data to be signed and then encrypts the results of the digest function using the secret key of a public/secret key pair. The result is the digital signature, and it allows anyone wishing to certify a piece of signed data as being generated by the owner of the public key to do so. To certify the data, it is run through the same digest function, and the result is encrypted with the originator's public key. The result should be the same as the digital signature string.

directory service   A service that provides a method of linking a name with a resource or some other entity. Directory services provide a method of linking a person's login ID to their network permissions or to link a system resource name to the resource.

DNS   Domain Name System (also known as Domain Name Service). A distributed database system long used within the Internet and other TCP/IP internetworks to link numerical host IP addresses to fully qualified domain names that are more easily remembered and manipulated by humans.

EDI   Electronic Data Interchange. A method of providing interorganizational data communication used for business-to-business electronic commerce in the 1980s and 1990s. Each organization maps the data in its proprietary and legacy databases to generic data types. (For example, it might map a part number in its inventory system to a more generalized "part number" data item.) EDI allows the exchange of data between organizations to support transactions like electronic submission of purchase orders.

encapsulation The process of wrapping data inside a header or some other logical construct in such a way that the encapsulated data is transmitted or manipulated based on the directive of the encapsulating header. For example, network data is usually encapsulated with a header that indicates the destination of the data. Objects can also encapsulate information to protect it from unauthorized manipulation.

extranet An internetwork, usually based on the TCP/IP protocol suite, that connects organizations (or an organization with individual customers or partners), often using the Internet as a communications medium.

fat client Client software that includes much or most of the business logic and presentation infrastructure. Usually differentiated from the thin client, which provides a simple interface and permits the server side to provide most or all of the business logic and processing tasks.

firewall gateway A system, device, or grouping of devices that acts as a gatekeeper to an organizational internetwork, permitting some packets or streams of data to pass through to or from the internetwork, and denying access to other packets or streams of data.

frame A protocol data unit, usually applied to data transmitted at the data link layer.

FTP File Transfer Protocol. One of the first Internet applications, it provides a reliable and efficient means of transferring files from one host to another.

gateway Usually, a system that links other systems or networks across a protocol boundary. For example, e-mail gateways allow the movement of proprietary e-mail messages (e.g., Lotus cc:Mail or CE Software QuickMail) to Internet protocol-compliant e-mail (SMTP, IMAP, POP).

groupware   Software that fosters interaction among members of a group. Lotus Notes was the premier groupware product of the 1990s; CollabraShare offered a less-structured, easier-to-use, but less adaptable product. Netscape purchased Collabra in 1996 and incorporated news/collaboration software products into the Communicator product.

handshake   A protocol-level interaction often used to initiate a circuit. TCP uses a three-way handshake to open a virtual circuit between two processes.

hash function   See *digest function*.

HTML   Hypertext Markup Language. A markup language based on Standard Generalized Markup Language (SGML) and used to create content whose format can depend on the client displaying it. For example, a nongraphical browser does not display an HTML page that includes graphics, but rather displays a character-based marker to indicate the presence of a graphic.

HTTP   Hypertext Transport Protocol. The application protocol of the World Wide Web. HTTP defines a series of requests that can be submitted by a browser to a server and defines the way in which the server must respond to those requests.

IDL   Interface Definition Language. A mechanism by which CORBA objects and their interfaces are defined for use through an ORB.

IIOP   Internet Inter-ORB Protocol. A TCP/IP application layer protocol that uses the Internet as an object request broker backbone, allowing client objects to interact with distributed objects on systems connected to the Internet.

internetwork   A network of networks.

interoperability   The ability of systems to communicate and interact with each other independently of the underlying systems. In particular, the ability of systems to work together despite being deployed on platforms running on different hardware or software operating systems and conncctcd to different network media.

intranet   A network of networks implemented within a single organization for members of that organization to use. In general, it includes HTTP and other Internet application servers to provide information to members of the organization. It may or may not be connected to the global Internet, although if it is, this connectivity is usually mediated through a firewall gateway.

IP   Internet Protocol. This protocol defines the way that data is transmitted between two hosts connected to the same internetwork, with neither host having any knowledge of the remote host or its network.

IPnG   Internet Protocol, Next Generation. A working name given to the effort to define the upgrade to IP made necessary by a shrinking address space and bloated routing tables as the global Internet's explosive growth continued into the 1990s.

IPv4   Internet Protocol, version 4. The version of IP current from the early 1980s well into the 1990s. It is characterized by each connected host having a unique 32-bit host address, as well as other less-obvious characteristics.

IPv6   Internet Protocol, version 6. The version of IP gaining approval starting around 1996 and being implemented commercially early in 1997. It is characterized by each connected host having a unique 128-bit host address, as well as many other improvements over the previous version of IP. Prior to being accepted by the IETF, the term IPnG was used to refer to whatever would ultimately become the next version of IP.

ISDN   Integrated Services Digital Network. A telecommunications service long heralded by many, first developed in the 1970s. Despite many technical and economic advantages, telephone company foot-dragging in deploying ISDN to businesses and consumers and unattractive pricing structures have hampered its growth in the market as of the late 1990s.

ISO   International Standards Organization.

Java   A network programming language designed for security and interoperability across platforms and specifically to enable the creation of applets and applications that can be distributed over the Internet and other TCP/IP internetworks. Java code is executed on every platform using a virtual machine. Java code runs as is on every platform that supports it without recompiling or operating system-specific versions.

JavaScript   An interpreted scripting language based on the Java network programming language.

Kerberos   A secure key distribution service developed at MIT. Kerberos uses symmetric encryption protocols and shared secrets to authenticate users over open networks and to allow hosts to securely exchange one-time-use keys for encrypting network sessions.

LDAP   Lightweight Directory Access Protocol. A protocol devised to allow basic access to X.500 directory structures.

MD5   Message Digest version 5. A cryptographic-quality digest function that takes data of any length as input and returns an apparently random string of fixed length as output.

MIB   Management Information Base. A distributed database of network parameters. The MIB is actually a framework within which each managed network device (that supports SNMP) stores the current values of various network parameters, like server status, amount of traffic since last boot, and so on.

middleware Software or systems that act as an intermediary level between end users and legacy or proprietary databases. Transaction processors, transaction monitors, and messaging software are all examples. They accept requests to be submitted to large databases or systems and forward them in an orderly fashion, keeping track of which have been processed and which have not.

network computer A computer or terminal that uses network resources, rather than local resources, for most of its functions. For example, a network computer might be a diskless terminal that downloads applications from a network application server and stores data on a network file server.

NFS Network File Service. A TCP/IP protocol devised by Sun Microsystems for fast and efficient file services using UDP.

NIS+ Sun Microsystem's Network Information Services+. A network directory service application.

NNTP Network News Transport Protocol. A TCP/IP application protocol that supports the exchange of news postings between news servers. News items are posted from individuals into public forums for discussion.

NSF National Science Foundation.

OLE Originally OLE stood for object linking and embedding, a Microsoft specification for interoperability across applications, but OLE has achieved status as a term in its own right and is no longer considered an acronym.

OMG Object Management Group. An industry consortium of organizations supporting object computing.

OOP   Object-oriented programming.

ORB   Object request broker. A mechanism by which different application objects can exchange requests and responses.

packet   A protocol data unit, often referring to an IP datagram.

PGP   Pretty Good Privacy. A program and implementation of the RSA (see RSA entry) public key encryption algorithm for use by individuals.

POP   1. Post Office Protocol: A protocol used for storing and retrieving e-mail from a server, which acts as a post office. 2. Point of Presence: The point at which a network services provider allows access to the network.

PPP   Point-to-Point Protocol. A protocol defining how data is transmitted between two hosts connected across a point-to-point link (for example, across a dial-up telephone link).

protocol data unit (PDU)   The unit in which a communications protocol deals with data. In other words, the container within which the protocol sticks data to be moved around. PDU is usually a matter of nomenclature only. Examples of PDUs include Ethernet frames, IP datagrams, TCP segments, and UDP datagrams.

public key cryptography   The use of asymmetric cryptographic algorithms to encrypt, decrypt, create digital signatures, or certify digital signatures. Public key cryptography relies on the characteristics of certain pairs of keys that allow data encrypted with one of the keys to be decrypted only by the other key.

RFC   Request for Comments. An Internet document used to present information about new and existing protocols. While many Internet standards are published in RFCs, not all RFCs represent Internet standards.

RIP   Routing Information Protocol. A routing protocol commonly used within TCP/IP internetworks.

router   A device that is connected to two or more physical networks and is capable of accepting datagrams sent out on one of those networks and forwarding them onto the appropriate network, moving them closer to their destination.

RPC   Remote Procedure Call. A mechanism for network programming that allows a host to call procedures that are resident on another host connected to the network, but in such a way that the procedures appear to be local to the calling host.

RSA   RSA refers to a public key encryption algorithm developed by researchers named Ron Rivest, Adi Shamir, and Len Adleman.

secret key cryptography   Cryptography based on symmetric algorithms in which a single key is used for both encryption and decryption.

SET   Secure Electronic Transaction. A specification for secure online credit card transactions created with the backing of Visa International and MasterCard International, as well as many other companies including IBM, Microsoft, Netscape, and CyberCash.

S-HTTP   Secure HTTP. A security protocol for the Hypertext Transport Protocol; it is relatively widely implemented on servers but has less support on Web browsers.

SMTP   Simple Mail Transport Protocol. The basic TCP/IP e-mail protocol, SMTP provides a structure for passing e-mail from a message transfer agent to a user agent.

SNMP   Simple Network Management Protocol. A protocol that defines a framework for transmitting network management information across TCP/IP internetworks.

SSL   Secure Socket Layer. A protocol created by Netscape and offered to the industry as an open standard. SSL operates below the application layer and just above the transport layer to enable applications to use secured channels for encrypted communication over open networks like the Internet.

TCP   Transmission Control Protocol. TCP provides a reliable virtual-circuit service between application layer processes, usually running on separate hosts (intrahost TCP links are possible, though not standard).

TCP/IP   Transmission Control Protocol/Internet Protocol. This acronym usually refers to the entire suite of TCP/IP protocols. TCP and IP represent the most important of them because IP is used by almost all internetwork traffic and TCP is used by most applications, particularly when there is need for a reliable virtual-circuit service.

Telnet   A TCP/IP terminal emulation program. Telnet clients accept keystrokes from the local hardware, convert them to a virtual terminal construct, and send them on to the remote host Telnet server. The server writes data to a virtual terminal screen, which is displayed by the client. The virtual terminal constructs allow client and server to interoperate despite hardware and software implementation differences. For example, a Telnet client can display an IBM 3270 mainframe session emulation on a Macintosh personal computer.

thin client   The client part of a client/server application that uses a standard client, with most or all of the program logic resident on the server. Thin client usually refers to a Web browser interface to an application served off an Internet or extranet Web server.

three-tier application   An application that uses middleware to mediate requests from clients and responses from servers. Applications are converted to three tiers to provide greater reliability and scalability; they can also more easily support multiple servers, distributed servers, and load balancing.

two-phase commit   A mechanism for completing transactions across unreliable networks that allows complete rollback of the transaction in the event of failure or rejection from either participant.

two-tier application   An application that uses direct transmission between clients and servers.

UDP   User Datagram Protocol. An unreliable datagram protocol used at the transport layer. UDP provides far better performance than TCP but with much lower reliability, particularly across large internetworks.

URI   Uniform resource identifier. The generic name for a terse, global network resource identifier. URLs and URNs are examples of URIs.

URL   Uniform resource locator. A global network resource identifier that includes a network resource type and just enough information to reach a specific referenced network resource across an internetwork.

URN   Uniform resource name. A global network resource identifier that is used to reference network resources more permanently than URLs. URNs can point to a resource whose location may change over time.

VAN   Value added network. Usually, a VAN is a private extranet that links trading partners using the same EDI service provider.

X.400   A global electronic mail addressing specification.

X.500   A global directory service specification.

X.509   A special-use directory service based on X.500 that specifies the format for a global directory of digital certificates.

Index

Note to the Reader: Throughout this index **boldfaced** page numbers indicate primary discussions of a topic. *Italicized* page numbers indicate illustrations.

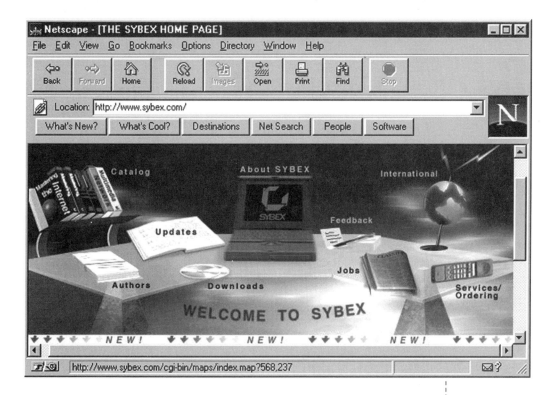